Educational Linguistics/TESOL/ICC
Graduate School of Education
University of Pennsylvania
3700 Walnut Street/Cl
Philadelphia, PA 19104

URBAN LANGUAGE SERIES

SOCIOLINGUISTIC ASPECTS OF

ASSIMILATION

PUERTO RICAN ENGLISH IN NEW YORK CITY

WALT WOLFRAM

CENTER FOR APPLIED LINGUISTICS : 1974

International Standard Book Number: 87281-034-8
Library of Congress Catalog Card Number: 73-89563

Printed in the United States of America

INTRODUCTION TO THE SERIES

The Urban Language Series is intended to make available the
results of recent sociolinguistic research concerned with the
position and role of language in a large metropolitan area.
The series includes descriptions of certain aspects of urban
language, particularly English, as well as theoretical considerations relevant to such descriptions. The series also includes studies dealing with fieldwork techniques, matters of
pedagogy and relationships of urban language study to other
disciplines. Where appropriate and feasible, accompanying
tape recordings will be made available. Specifically excluded
from consideration are aspects of English as a second language
or second language learning in general.

It is hoped that the Urban Language Series will prove useful to several different kinds of readers. For the linguist,
the series will provide data for the study of language performance and for the development of linguistic theory. Historically, linguists have formulated theory from individual
rather than group performance. They have had to generalize
about what constitutes "standard" or "non-standard" from intu-
itive judgments or from very limited data. This series is
designed to make available large portions of language data as
well as analyses in order to broaden the knowledge from which
linguistic generalizations may come.

For the sociologist the series will provide access to
the nature of social stratification by means of language. It

is the contention of some scholars that a person's use of
language is one of the most important cues to his social
status, age, race or sex.

For the educator, the series will offer among other
things a description of the very things which are most crucial to the classroom—the linguistic correlates which separate the accepted from the unaccepted.

Although the value of focussed attention on the special
problems of urban language has been recognized for some time,
relatively few substantial studies have been published. To
a certain degree, this series represents a pioneering venture
on the part of the Center for Applied Linguistics.

Roger W. Shuy
Center for Applied Linguistics

SOCIOLINGUISTIC ASPECTS OF ASSIMILATION

PREFACE

During the past decade, there has been a growing interest in the study of language in its social context. This interest has been stimulated by concerns on two different levels. On a theoretical level, it has become apparent to some that language, which is ultimately a social phenomenon, cannot be properly understood unless its social context is considered. From this perspective, it appears that many theoretical problems in linguistics cannot be solved unless we look at language variation in society. On a practical level, interest in linguistic diversity has been motivated by an increasing concern for the education of the economically impoverished. If we are to seriously undertake the education of socially subordinate groups in our society, we must start with an adequate descriptive base of social differences. Some of these differences are, of course, manifested in linguistic diversity. The need for an adequate descriptive understanding of language differences should be apparent to anyone who deals with language in education.

Both of these concerns have motivated the study reported here, although admittedly there is an emphasis on the theoretical. On this level, we want to examine the implications of a particular language situation to understand the nature of patterned variation. Ultimately, we want to see how this situation sheds light on fundamental issues in linguistics. On a practical level, we want to provide a descriptive base for

understanding the language assimilation patterns of the children
of immigrants, in this case the children of parents who have
migrated from Puerto Rico. Too many times, this type of situation has been dismissed with statements like "The children of
immigrants simply assimilate the English of the surrounding
English-speaking community". Although in some cases it is
difficult to dispute such a conclusion, this cavalier type of
over-simplification and generalization neglects the essential
dynamics of language contact and linguistic assimilation, the
HOW and WHY of which are of great interest.

The research that led to this book was carried out under
Office of Education Grant No. OEG-3-70-0033(508) to the Center
for Applied Linguistics in 1970-1971. The aims of this research grant were to determine the relative influence of Black
English and Puerto Rican Spanish on the speech of second
generation Puerto Rican teen-agers. Many individuals con-
tributed to the original research and the subsequent refinement
of the analysis. Dr. Roger W. Shuy initially encouraged me to
undertake the project, and he followed up the initial impetus
with continued support through each stage. I am indebted to
Marie Shiels Djouadi, Elaine Bowman, and Marcia F. Whiteman
who all served on the original research team. Parts of Chapter Two are the direct work of Ms. Djouadi, and she has read
and commented on every version of this manuscript. Ms. Whiteman
was responsible for some of the data extraction, and Ms. Bowman
demonstrated her diverse capabilities by undertaking tasks
ranging from secretary to fieldworker. Charles-James N. Bailey,
Ralph W. Fasold, and Ronald Butters read and commented extensively on the entire manuscript, offering many helpful sug-
gestions. I have further profited from discussions of this work
with Paul Anisman, Frank Anshen, Albert H. Marckwardt, William
Labov, William K. Riley, Rudolph C. Troike, and Ronald Williams.
Despite the many people who showed an interest in this work,

the inadequacies still remaining are of my own doing. Sherry
Goldbecker meticulously worked on the format and style, which
in my case is an undertaking of considerable magnitude. And
Freda Ahearn finished off the task with a careful typing of
the manuscript. Her high-quality typing has become legendary
at the Center for Applied Linguistics.

Obviously, this study would not have been possible without the informants. For establishing our contacts, we are
indebted to Youth Development Incorporated and its director,
Jim Vaus. Richard Crow, a YDI staff member at the time of the
fieldwork, served as a most valuable source in providing background data on informants. In all too many research projects,
everyone is acknowledged except the people who willingly provided the data for research. Our informants in this study
cannot be thanked sufficiently. Although they may have been
puzzled greatly by the seeming inanity of our probing, they
willingly tolerated the intrusion into their everyday world.
Although they are referred to only anonymously in this study,
our warm associations remain very specific.

Finally, I would like to acknowledge the contribution of
my parents, Carl and Johanna Wolfram. It was they who first
stimulated my interest in the linguistic assimilation of the
children of immigrants. But they did not do so through aca-
demic instruction or "window gazing"; they accomplished this
by allowing me the opportunity of growing up in this situation
as my real world. For providing this opportunity I would like
to dedicate this effort to them.

W.W.
Arlington, Va.
October 1973

CONTENTS

1 INTRODUCTION

1.1 <u>The study of Puerto Rican English</u>. Although language
variation among English dialects has always been of some linguistic interest, only in recent years has there been extended
descriptive concern for social dialects in American society.
The study of what we shall here call Puerto Rican English (PRE)
is an attempt to expand our descriptive knowledge of American
social dialects by applying recent sociolinguistic methods of
analysis. When we use the term PRE here, we are referring
specifically to the English spoken by second generation Puerto
Rican teen-age males living predominantly in East Harlem, New
York. Although this may appear to be a rather restricted sub-
set of what the varieties of PRE may include, it is expected
that much of the description will have wider application,
e.g. to a number of northeastern urban areas, than simply to
the specific situation we are describing here. And, of course,
many of the sociolinguistic principles brought forth may well
have universal application for the study of social dialects.

The study of PRE as another variety of English is essential for a number of reasons. To begin with, it is important
for both scientific and applied reasons to have accurate
descriptive accounts of a range of social dialects in the
United States. Important linguistic and sociolinguistic principles come to the surface from our knowledge of these various
social dialects. For example, the discovery of ordered linguistic and social constraints on inherently variable linguistic

forms is an essential contribution of recent sociolinguistic
studies which is confirmed and expanded in our study.

From an applied viewpoint, we need to know how the various
social dialects in the United States are structured if we are
going to base our educational strategies on sound descriptive
facts; shibboleths about speech and vagueness concerning language diversity cannot serve as a foundation for educational
decisions with respect to language. For example, in East
Harlem, where black and Puerto Rican school children may have
considerable interaction, we need to know to what extent, if
any, similar language materials can be used for these two
groups. Ma and Herasimchuk (1968) indicate that there appears
to be similarity among some of the linguistic characteristics
of blacks and Puerto Ricans in New York City, but their reference is only incidental, since it is outside the scope of their
study of bilingualism. Labov, et al. (1968), although including the nonstandard English of Puerto Rican speakers in
their title, focus only on those characteristics of speech
that are common to the black community.

As we shall see in this study, some features normally
associated in northern urban areas with Black English have
been taken over by second generation PRE speakers, regardless
of how extensive their contacts with blacks may be; other
characteristics show up only in the speech of those Puerto
Ricans who have extensive black contacts; and, of course, there
are features that might be derived historically from Spanish,
but that must be described synchronically as an integral part
of PRE.

We see, then, that the study reported here is an investigation of languages in contact. Some aspects of the structure
of PRE can be understood only through a knowledge of various
nonstandard dialects of English, while others involve an understanding of Puerto Rican Spanish. Separating the sources from

which specific linguistic characteristics of PRE may be derived is, in itself, an important sociolinguistic matter that
requires a thorough understanding of the dynamics of language
influence.

Although we can account for the occurrence of certain PRE
structures by closely investigating the structure of our language sources, this cannot be considered a study of bilingualism, for we are concerned here with only one of the languages spoken by our informants. Nor can it be considered a
study of language interference in the strict sense. In the
conventional sense, interference is a condition that is dependent on bilingualism (Weinreich 1953:11). But we are not concerned mainly with phenomena that are dependent on bilingualism;
rather, we are concerned with patterns that have become habitualized and established. Perhaps this can be best illustrated
by drawing an analogy with English varieties spoken by second
and third generation Germans in southeastern Pennsylvania.
Our knowledge of German may help us account for the occurrence
of some rather divergent dialect variations in southeastern
Pennsylvania. But these features are not dependent on the
bilingualism of second and third generation Germans; they are
features that must be described synchronically as an integral
part of the dialect. The distinction between interference
and established dialect variations is an important sociolinguistic matter which we shall turn to later in more detail.

Up to now, we have spoken of PRE as if it were some sort
of homogeneous entity, but this is, in itself, a matter of
considerable sociolinguistic interest. On one level, our informant group of lower-socioeconomic-class, second generation
Puerto Rican teen-age males from East Harlem could be considered homogeneous when compared, for example, with a group
of middle-class, white teen-age males from a New York suburb.
But on another level, there is heterogeneity in our group of

informants: Some informants, for example, show quite extensive
cóntacts with black peers, while others have virtually none;
some show cultural values that are quite indigenous to lower-
socioeconomic-class life-styles, while others express educational and occupational aspirations that indicate considerable motivation for eventually attaining middle-class life-
styles. The extent to which linguistic characteristics are
common to our PRE informants as a whole, to subgroups, or even
uniquely to individuals is a consideration that will be treated
specifically in our description of the linguistic variables
chosen for this study.

From a linguistic standpoint, we are interested in the
nature of language variation as it relates to languages in
contact. To begin with, we want to know how linguistic features from various potential sources are integrated into the
emerging language variety. In order to observe this, we will
investigate several representative variables to see what the
constraints on variability are, given the particular language
contact situation. In this regard, we follow earlier studies
of linguistic variation that incorporate constraints of variability into the formal representation of optional rules.
Some of the observed variation is, of course, accounted for
by independent linguistic features that favor or prohibit the
operation of a particular rule. Other types of influences on
variation can be accounted for only by looking at language in
the context of society: That is, the description of the sociocultural situation in Chapter Two is essential in understanding
the nature of certain types of influences on variation. Finally, we want to understand the general principles of linguistic
variation that emerge from this particular language situation.
In order to take on significance, data must be seen in some
sort of theoretical framework. Ultimately, knowledge is not
furthered by simply reporting data. It is the investigation

of data in terms of a particular theoretical framework that is
responsible for advancing our knowledge about language.

1.2 The selection of informants. The analysis reported here
is based on data regarding the speech of 29 Puerto Rican and
15 black teen-age males from East Harlem and the Bronx. Our
original contacts with these informants were made possible
through the cooperation of Youth Development Incorporated
(YDI), a nondenominational, club-like organization with head-
quarters in East Harlem at the time of our fieldwork during
August of 1969.

In addition to public recreational facilities, some
remedial educational instruction and nondenominational re-
ligious instruction were optionally offered at YDI's head-
quarters. During the summer months, YDI operated camp facilities at Lake Champion, New York, the site of the fieldwork
that serves as the basis for this analysis. At the time of
our fieldwork, there were approximately 150 males between the
ages of 13 and 18 present: Two-thirds were Puerto Rican and
one-third black; there were no non-Puerto Rican whites present
at that time.

The decision was made to start by interviewing several
informants who had considerable status among their peers in
order to facilitate other interviews. It was anticipated that
other individuals would recognize that the leaders had been
chosen initially, that being asked for an interview would then
have some status significance. It was further reasoned that
positive reports from informants initially would enhance our
chances of obtaining interviews with other informants. Although somewhat of a risk, this procedure proved to be generally quite successful in obtaining informants for interviews.
The association of the interviews with peer status was apparently understood by other members. In fact, several peer

associates of our original contacts asked if we might talk with them rather than waiting for us to request an interview.

Having established contacts with several of the peer leaders, we then selected informants on the basis of our acquaintance with them through informant contacts, references to other individuals from our initial interviews, recommendations from workers who knew the informants through more extensive, day-to-day interaction, or a combination of these. Informants were obviously not chosen at random; instead, they were selected in order to approximate the racial distribution of the teen-agers served by YDI.

1.3 The interview. The interview was divided into several main areas. First, there was a fairly extensive free conversation section. Our topics for this section were based largely on previous questionnaires adapted to our population of young teen-age males (see Labov 1966a; Labov et al. 1968; Shuy, Wolfram, and Riley 1967; Fasold 1972), while the topics actually discussed were largely determined by the interests of each informant. The general areas covered ranged from games and leisure to gang fights. As a part of the first section, certain questions about group social structure were asked to obtain sociological background information that would help us assess social interactions and roles.

During the second section, involving responses to certain sentence stimuli largely adopted and developed from Fasold (1972), we attempted to elicit specific constructions germane to our analysis of particular nonstandard linguistic features. Responses to some of these stimuli were crucial in arriving at descriptively adequate analyses of certain linguistic features.

Finally, the informants were asked to read several types of materials, including a prose passage, word lists, and minimal word pairs.

The different sections of the interview were always presented in the above sequence in order to move from the informal to the formal aspects of the interview. The interview
lasted approximately one hour. (The general outline of the
interview is given in Appendix A.)

Prior familiarity with the informants was considered
essential in minimizing the unnaturalness of the normal interview situation. Thus, certain interviewers participated in
scheduled and unscheduled camp activities before and during the
interviewing, permitting interviewers and informants to become
acquainted in a more natural situation and encouraging the
establishment of rapport between the two groups. For example,
the author spent considerable time playing "pick-up" basketball with a number of the informants. This type of activity
was evidently significant in establishing rapport, as indicated in several comments made by informants during the course
of the interviews:

> When I first saw you play basketball, I thought you
> was, you know, I thought you played for pro, I
> thought you was playing pro basketball cause I seen
> you, you know, shooting all them balls in and see
> how you can dribble and all, I thought you played
> pro basketball. (1:8)[1]

> You got a good shot, man, you know, you got that
> shot, man, one hand shot, you got it nice, see,
> you time the ball, chu, chu, chu. (31:1)

Interviews were generally conducted in a vacant room in
an unused building on the camp grounds. Interviewers introduced
informants to the interview by telling them that we wanted to
know about some of the things teen-agers from various parts of
the country were interested in. We did not necessarily dis-
guise our interest in language but were nonspecific in talking
about what aspects of language variety we might be concerned
with. Usually, this was sufficient introduction for the informants, since we had established some familiarity prior to

the interview, but any questions were answered by honest but nonspecific comments.

Since we were concerned only with the English of our informants, the interviews were conducted almost exclusively in English. Usually, Spanish was used only when referring to some verbal activity in English and its potential Puerto Rican Spanish analogue. For example, in the discussion of "sounding" (the verbal ritual of insulting a person's mother), an informant might comment on a potential analogue for this activity by giving a Spanish example. The use of Spanish in the interview was quite incidental and will not be considered here.

In general, the style of the interview tended to be relatively casual, more casual than the style that was elicited in random samples as reported in Shuy, Wolfram, and Riley (1967), but it was not necessarily in-group. It does not compare with the group style of Labov et al. (1968) for obvious reasons; it does, however, compare more favorably with Labov et al.'s (1968) single interviews than with Wolfram's (1969) and Fasold's (1972), which were conducted by interviewers who had no prior contact with the informants.

In addition, a second set of interviews was conducted in New York City in the spring of 1971. These interviews were limited to those 14 of the original 29 Puerto Rican informants who could be located through various formal and informal contacts. The purpose of the second interview was to obtain more information about the informants' use of Spanish and about peer contacts. No information for linguistic analysis was desired from the second interview, so the questioning was quite direct. (The questionnaire used in the second interview is given in Appendix B.)

NOTE

1. All quotes from informants are referenced by the informant's
    number and the page of the typescript on which the statement
    is found.

2 THE SOCIOCULTURAL SETTING

2.1 <u>Cultures in contact</u>. From the point of view of immigra-
tion phenomena, it would seem that New York is the most studied
city in the United States. For many generations, wave upon
immigrant wave has entered the city, adapting its ethnicity
to its environs until some sort of assimilation is achieved.
Yet, if the newest arrivals to the city are any indication,
few in-depth examinations beyond geographical studies of group
living patterns and statistical studies of employment patterns
have been made of cultural contacts between groups in the slow
process of assimilation. In particular, there is a paucity of
research on language contacts between groups in the city and
on the consequent phenomenon of language assimilation.

Studying dialect contacts involves dealing with groups
of people that are in some way different from each other.
This difference may be predominantly geographical, e.g. Mid-
western Chicago English versus Southern Atlanta English; it
can be socioeconomic where geography is a constant, e.g. New
York City upper-middle-class English versus New York City
working-class English; and it can be both geographical and
socioeconomic. Dialects that differ according to geography
can also differ according to socioeconomic groups within each
dialect. Each point of view is an abstraction based on a
collection of differing speech patterns that share a nameable
commonality. The distinction between the two groups whose
dialect contact we are studying, predominantly second generation

Puerto Ricans and blacks in New York City, is not primarily
geographical or socioeconomic, as in other sociolinguistic
investigations; instead, it is based on ethnic group membership.

The nomenclature "Puerto Rican" or "black" is an abstraction that is in many ways difficult to define in terms
of specific groups. That island-born Puerto Ricans and
southern-born blacks represent two different cultures in New
York City is obvious. But after a generation or more in the
same city, even in the same neighborhood, is it still possible
to speak of two different cultural groups and two different
dialects? Or has assimilation occurred in the second and
third generations? What is the Puerto Rican/black contact
situation in the neighborhood, in the schools, etc.? If
assimilation does indeed occur, in what direction does it go:
Puerto Rican to black or black to Puerto Rican? In other
words, what is the dominant culture and, therefore, the
dominant dialect?

In order to specify in what way the existence of two
different cultural groups and dialects can be presumed, the
cultural contact between Puerto Ricans and blacks will be
briefly outlined, concentrating on the place of Puerto Ricans
in the city and their relation to the blacks. While much of
this discussion focuses on the contact of these two groups
as they co-exist in Harlem the Puerto Rican culture in New
York City must also be studied on its own terms. What is the
relation of one generation to another: immigrants to second
generation, second to third, etc.? Are there some Puerto
Ricans who identify with the black culture more than others,
and if so, why?

This background material, gathered from anthropological
and sociological works, census material, and participant-
observer information provided by the fieldworkers, will then

provide a framework for the linguistic discussion that is the
principal focus of this study.

2.2 The residential background of informants. Of the 29 Puerto
Rican informants, 2 were born in Puerto Rico and migrated to New
York as infants; thus, for all practical purposes, they can be
treated as second generation informants, since they learned to
speak in the United States. There are also two informants who
are third generation Puerto Ricans. Of the 15 black informants,
5 have West Indian history: 2 with one parent from the West
Indies, 1 with both parents from the West Indies, and 2 with
both grandparents from the West Indies. The other black informants have parents or grandparents who migrated from the
southern United States.

     At the time of the fieldwork, all the informants were
residents of New York City, with 34 living in Manhattan and 10
in the Bronx. All but six informants have lived in New York
City all their lives, and of these six, only one has not lived
most of his life there.

     Padilla (1958) notes that when the Puerto Rican first comes
to the city, he either resides for a short time with relatives
or is aided by them in locating an apartment, usually in Spanish
Harlem or one of the other centers of Puerto Rican concentration. While the migrants change residence frequently (about
four moves per family, according to Lewis 1968:205), they
usually remain in the same borough, often in the same neighborhood. This pattern of mobility is illustrated by many of the
informants who indicate they have spent most of their lives in
the same general neighborhood. Most residence changes indicated by the informants have occurred within Harlem or between
the Bronx and Harlem.

     For example, Informant 26, a 17-year-old Puerto Rican,
has always lived within three blocks of his present location,

although he has moved several times. Examples of a change of
borough are found more occasionally: Informants 9 and 43 who
are brothers used to live with their family in the Bronx and
then moved to their present location in the projects at East
125th Street. There is only one example of a family's having
made significant moves in the present study: Informant 23 has
lived with his family in Manhattan, at two locations in Brooklyn
upstate in Buffalo, in Harlem, and now in the Bronx. A few informants state that they have lived in the same building all
their lives.

Perhaps the most revealing geographical grouping is provided in Table 1, which indicates the residence of each informant at the time of the original fieldwork.

2.3 Puerto Rican intragroup contact. In order to see to what
extent the Puerto Rican culture in New York City is homogeneous
or heterogeneous, it is important to examine the contact situation of Puerto Ricans with blacks and non-Puerto Ricans against
a background knowledge of the amount of contact existing between
residents of the island and residents of the city, and of the
relations existing between first, second, and third generation
Puerto Ricans.

There is a certain continuity between the island and the
city because not only is there constant migration, depending on
the United States economy, but also there is frequent visiting
between the two places. Handlin states that unlike previous
immigrants, both Puerto Ricans and blacks do not undergo the
decisive break experienced by the Europeans:

> The movement of individuals back and forth between
> the old home and the new never ceased, so that com-
> munications were close and the sense of connectedness
> was never broken. (Handlin 1965:109)

In addition, new migrants usually settle with or near relatives who have preceded them to the United States. In this way,

Table 1.   Residence of Puerto Rican and black informants.

Section*		Puerto Rican Informants	Total	Black Informants	Total
HARLEM					
1	110th to 116th St., 2nd to 5th Ave.	5, 14, 19, 20, 22, 26, 28, 29, 33, 44	10		
2	101st to 110th St., 2nd to 5th Ave.	27, 31, 35, 37	4	2, 3, 4, 6, 12, 13, 15, 17, 25, 41	10
3	116th to 125th St., east of Lenox Ave.	9, 10, 18, 32, 42, 43	6	8, 16	2
4	Central Harlem			1, 40	2
BRONX					
5	South of 159th St.	11, 21, 23, 36, 38, 39	6		
6	Crotona Park	7	1	24	1
7	Westchester Ave.	30, 34	2		

*Section numbers refer to the map in Figure 1.

the New York residents, that is, at least the residents of the Puerto Rican neighborhoods, are constantly in contact with the island and its language, even if they are second and third generation Puerto Ricans who have never been there.

As indicated above, many Puerto Ricans form enclaves. According to Lewis (1968:212-13), the fact that they are set apart as being identified with blacks, and are therefore subject to discrimination in jobs, school, and housing (see Section 2.5.3)

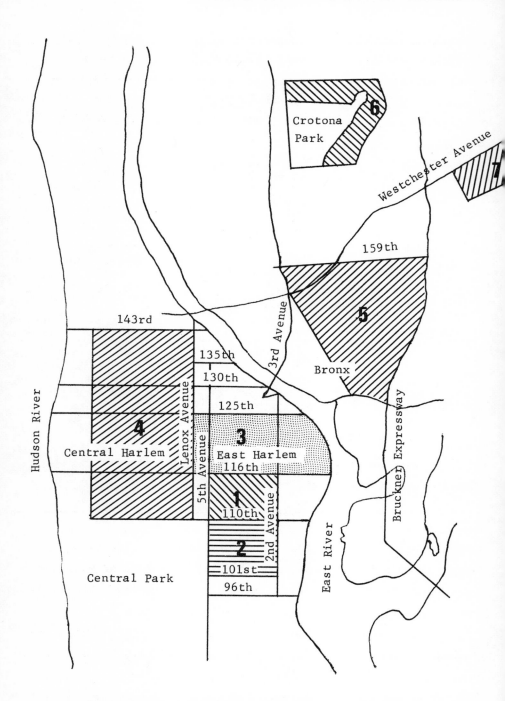

Figure 1.   Geographical location of informants.

has increased their feelings of inferiority. The total effect
has been to make them withdraw from the larger society and to
activate their sense of nationality and ethnic identity. Because of these factors, Mills, Senior, and Goldsen perceive
Puerto Rican culture, at least that of the first generation
residents in the core areas of the city, as being fairly homogeneous:

> ...on the whole there is a rather uniform educational
> achievement, standardized occupation in specific
> industries and in standardized areas of the city.
> These factors of institutional concentration which
> tend to make the migrants of Spanish Harlem and
> Morrisania homogeneous have more effect than certain
> other factors which tend to differentiate between them;
> and the overall result is a leveling of psychological
> and internal life. (Mills, Senior, and Goldsen 1950:169)

Although the above observation is generally true of first
generation immigrants, it is not clear that this uniformity and
this Puerto Rican orientation are present in the second generation and beyond. Nahirny and Fishman (1965:318 ff.) elabor-
ate the theory that second generation children of immigrants
often tend to throw off their ethnic heritage as a form of
rebellion for their being "different" from their American
counterparts. However, even while doing this, frequently some
form of ethnicity is retained in their very consciousness of
being children of immigrants. The children's acute sense of
marginality encourages them to become either more American
than the Americans themselves or more ardently ethnic than
their parents. At least for those who choose the first option,
any continuity with the ethnic heritage for the third generation is precluded. For this reason, Nahirny and Fishman (1965:
311) hold that "the ethnic heritage, including the ethnic mother
tongue, usually ceases to play any viable role in the life of
the third generation". Yet, at the same time, they see a reaction on the part of the third generation toward reidenti-
fication.

Glazer and Moynihan (1963:v) note a disinclination of the
third and fourth generations to "blend into a standard, uniform
national type". These authors see the loss of the immigrant
language and culture in the first and second generations as
making American cultural pluralism impossible; but at the same
time that these groups are stripped of direct ethnic influence,
they are still identifiable as a group even beyond the second
generation:

> Concretely, persons think of themselves as members of
> that group, with that name; most significantly, they
> are linked to other members of the group by new
> attributes that the original immigrants would never
> have recognized as identifying their group, but which
> nevertheless serve to make them off, by more than
> simply name and association, in the third generation
> and even beyond. (Glazer and Moynihan 1963:13)

While these observations are made more in reference to other
immigrant groups, they may be applicable to Puerto Ricans in
New York City as well.

Padilla (1958) notes that there is a higher status assigned
to those Puerto Ricans who are born and raised in New York than
to those born on the island. Most of those born in the United
States see themselves not so much as Puerto Ricans, for very
often they have never been, nor do they anticipate going, to the
island; rather, "They regard themselves as different from their
parents and the new migrants" (Padilla 1958:38).

In 1965, Handlin saw two alternatives for the future, depending on color consciousness in the general community:

> If color consciousness grows more intense, the Puerto
> Rican may be fragmented into three parts. The con-
> tinuing flow of new arrivals will struggle to main-
> tain themselves as Puerto Ricans. The colored Puerto
> Ricans already settled, and particularly those of the
> second and third generations for whom the difference
> of language fades in importance, will be pressed
> toward an identification with the more numerous Negroes.
> And the white majority of the second and third genera-
> tion Puerto Ricans who lose the consciousness of

> language will find an evergrowing incentive to drop
> their identification and to merge with some other
> surrounding ethnic community.... [If, on the other
> hand, there is a decline in color consciousness]
> white and colored Puerto Ricans in the awareness of
> their common identity could develop a coherent com-
> munity to which newcomers would be added and which
> would grow stronger through immigration. (Handlin
> 1965:59)

Given the rise of national awareness generated in black
nationalism and reflected in the Young Lords, the second alternative may indeed be becoming more attractive for many Puerto
Ricans in New York's core areas (see Hoffman 1968:39).

2.4 Puerto Rican and black contact.

2.4.1 Neighborhood contact. East Harlem is probably the most
important Puerto Rican area of New York City. Its geographical
boundaries are variously defined by Sexton (1965) and Lewis
(1968) as including roughly the area from the East River to
Central Park between 96th and 130th Streets, or more precisely
the area from 110th to 116th Street between 2nd and 5th Avenues
(see Figure 1). To its north and east lie predominantly black
neighborhoods, with the poorest section of Harlem, the Triangle,
immediately north of Spanish Harlem. Otherwise known as El
Barrio, Spanish Harlem is not homogeneously Spanish, as West
Indians, Irish, Russians, Hungarians, Italians, and blacks also
live there. Sexton (1965:109) characterizes it as being more
an economic than a racial ghetto, in contrast to Central Harlem.
Despite the fact that sections of Spanish Harlem seem to form
enclaves that perpetuate the Spanish language and customs,
geographical homogeneity is being replaced by integration, at
least on the periphery. Although there are ethnic concentra-
tions, no neighborhood seems to be completely homogeneous.

This lack of complete homogeneity is reflected in the
sample for the present study. Almost all of the Puerto Rican

informants indicate the presence of some blacks in their neighborhood. How many, however, seems to depend on the geographical
location, and, therefore, where the informant lives has a great
deal of influence on his black contacts, or if he is black, on
his Puerto Rican contacts.

At one end of the continuum, we have Puerto Ricans with
relatively restricted neighborhood contacts with blacks:

> Well, down in my neighborhood we got more Puerto
> Ricans than there is Negroes and Americans cause
> it's American people, there's only about two or
> three.... It's a lot of Negroes by the projects
> towards about two blocks from where I live, and
> down where I live at is, everybody there is just
> plain Puerto Rican. (11:10)

At the other end of the continuum are Puerto Ricans with predominantly black neighborhood contacts:

> My brothers, when we first moved in, the only
> friends we had were Negro, and they were like,
> they say, we acted all cool with them. They all
> acted cool with us. (14:7)

That blacks and Puerto Ricans live in the same neighborhood does not necessarily mean, however, that they share extensive contacts. According to Sexton (1965:13), in the old tenement housing these groups do not live in the same building but
in adjacent buildings or at opposite ends of the block. One
Puerto Rican resident in a predominantly Puerto Rican neighborhood in the Bronx states that his whole apartment building is
inhabited by Puerto Ricans, with the exception of one black
spouse of a Puerto Rican, although blacks do live on the opposite side of the street. Another resident of the same building
adds to the picture of the block:

> No, in my building, only Puerto Ricans live. ...in the
> city you know we're the only Spanish building in the
> whole block, in the block, you know, we live in. The
> rest are Negroes so we stick with them, you know. They
> make friends with you and you have a lot of friends.
> (36:7)

Despite the integrated nature of the block, the Puerto Ricans
living there name other Puerto Ricans as their best friends.

While much of this discussion deals with the culture contacts of Puerto Ricans and blacks living in Harlem, it is presumed that the situation is similar in those parts of the city
that are comparable in terms of socioeconomics or population
distribution, e.g. south Bronx or Brooklyn. The Puerto Ricans
studied by Lewis (1968:204) in New York City "formed little
islands within the city" where their language and many of their
customs were perpetuated. Most of their shopping was done in
Puerto Rican bodegas, and Spanish was the standard home language. However, many of these subjects were first generation
Puerto Ricans, some newly arrived, and length of time in New
York City seems to be one of the most important factors in
analyzing homogeneity of Puerto Rican contact. Padilla (1958:
26) notes three distinct groups of Puerto Ricans in New York
City: the recent migrants, the old migrants who have been in
New York for a relatively long period of time, and those Puerto
Ricans born and reared in New York City. The first group tends
to limit its contacts to other Puerto Ricans, preferably rela-
tives and people from the same hometown as well as other Puerto
Ricans in the same neighborhood, if not the immediate tenement
(Mills, Senior, and Goldsen 1950:99). As these migrants become
more acculturated, their way of life and their contacts change.
Puerto Ricans born and raised in New York City have more contacts with non-Puerto Ricans at school, at play, and at work
(Hoffman 1968:47), although they are rarely out of touch with
other Puerto Ricans. However, despite differences in the ways
of life and the cultural orientations of these groups, most
Puerto Ricans share a feeling of solidarity:

> There are ideals of behavior, standards of values,
> and rules for living that are considered appropriate
> to Hispanos, rather than to others, and there are
> forms of social control--sanctions and standards of

> approval and disapproval--that emerge from the body
> of ideals of behavior expected from Hispanos. In
> fact, many cultural diversities and behavioral ex-
> pectations cluster within subgroups of the larger
> Hispano groups, and each subgroup is geared to the
> others as if they were all parts of a system.... (Padilla 1958:48-49)

2.4.2 <u>School contact</u>. The question of school contact seems relatively straightforward. According to Glazer and Moynihan (1963:49), even in 1960 before permissive school zoning was fully established, over half of New York City's Puerto Rican and black children attended "integrated" schools. However, the authors note that this integration is "simply the ex-pression of the existence of the Negro ghetto" in the sense that the school population merely reflects the overall neigh-borhood population. "Integration" may here be taken to mean the existence of only a few minority group members.

Puerto Ricans are in the majority in the schools attended by most of the informants in the present study, although the schools are thoroughly integrated with blacks who typically comprise at least one-third of the school population. At school, if nowhere else, the Puerto Rican child is exposed to heterogeneity in culture and language. And traditionally, at school, if not at home, the Puerto Rican child begins his "intensive directed training in becoming American" (Padilla 1958:200).

2.5 <u>Solidarity and separation among Puerto Ricans and blacks</u>. In New York City, Puerto Ricans live as a minority surrounded by a larger minority, blacks. The second generation Puerto Rican, due to his increased exposure to blacks, is in a position to act on his perception of the relationship between the two communities in the establishment of his social relations. Al-though we might use a number of criteria for classifying Puerto Ricans with respect to their contact with blacks, it is quite clear that the most crucial variable is peer contact. Whom do they associate with in their friendship groups in the neighborhood? They may choose almost exclusively Puerto Rican peers, or they may choose to participate in a group that includes a significant proportion of blacks. In fact, in some cases, the peer group may be predominantly black.

Because of the importance of peer group structure for the investigation of cultural and linguistic assimilation, we have elicited specific information about the peer group structure from each Puerto Rican informant in this study. Each informant was asked to list his main friendship groups and to identify the race of each member of these groups. This information was then compared with observations by staff members who were familiar with the informants over an extended period and with our participant observations of social interactions during the fieldwork. Although there is obviously a continuum with respect to the extent of black contacts revealed by our informants, we have chosen to separate informants into two groups on the basis of our sociological information: those with extensive black contacts and those with restricted black contacts. Those with extensive black contacts indicate a mixture or a majority of blacks among their peers, while those with restricted contacts have few, if any, blacks in their immediate peer groups. The types of group structures, the initiation into peer groups, and the activities of the peer groups all give supportive information for our assessment.[1] Of the 29 Puerto Rican informants, 6 are considered to have extensive black contacts and 23 restricted black contacts on the basis of this information.

2.5.1 _Informants' perceptions_. A number of writers have noted that Puerto Ricans, particularly second generation Puerto Ricans, may establish close relationships with blacks (Padilla 1958:94). Some of our informants with extensive black contacts reflect

this good rapport, as indicated in the following dialogue between a fieldworker and an informant:

> FW: Are colored guys and Spanish guys in the same
>   gang ever?
>
> INF: Yeah. Plenty times.
>
> FW: Do they sometimes have the colored guy against
>   the Spanish?
>
> INF: No. Everybody believes in fun like that....
>   You grow up, you see a colored guy sitting
>   next to you. (27:13)

Puerto Ricans who have established extensive black contacts tend to minimize differences between the two groups.
For example:

> It's really hard to tell between a Puerto Rican and
> a Negro; it's really hard, you know. (18: second
> interview)

> You know, like before, it was a lot of race problem
> in East Harlem, like the community works together,
> you know, none of this bull-shit about now, you
> black, get away from me, you're white, you better
> go to hell or something like that. Ain't like that
> no more, you know. (5:7)

In reality, of course, there are considerably more differences than are admitted in the above comments. For example, a
member of the Puerto Rican community generally would have
little difficulty in distinguishing the blacks from the Puerto
Ricans. And we know that there are still many tensions that
exist between the black and Puerto Rican communities. However,
the actual situation is less important than the perception of
social relations by Puerto Ricans with extensive black contacts.

There is a commonality between the two groups in that they
are set apart by lines of demarcation: the blacks by a color
line and the Puerto Ricans by an ethnic line that is equally
real.

Although we can observe a certain commonality between
groups, the proximity of Puerto Rican and black also may be

the cause of intergroup tension. Sexton (1965:13) notes that
race and ethnicity underlie much of the open and hidden conflict in East Harlem. This tension can be seen in the statements of some informants from the present study:

> You see, we have half a building full of niggers,
> guys that really look for trouble. They all came
> down round about and couple of guys from our build-
> ing and we have round eight [sic] percent of the guys
> round here are Spanish. They surrounded the niggers
> on the outside.... I went straight down and hit
> couple of them on the head. Now I was at the bottom
> and when the Spanish finished with the niggers out
> there, they came in.... They don't fool around with
> the Spanish cause, what you call it, Spanish take
> their ass and make it inside out. (43:13-14)

> Like some of these Negro guys, I don't hang around,
> most of the guys that stick around there, they
> always, you know, look for trouble. (35:9)

Similar feelings of antipathy are expressed by a number
of our Puerto Rican informants. For example, when describing
various indigenous forms of behavior that would clearly be
considered antisocial in terms of mainstream values, they indicate that such actions are appropriate with respect to their
own peer group, while similar types of behavior by blacks are
cited pejoratively.

2.5.2 _Socioeconomic factors_. Generally speaking the Puerto
Ricans are on the lowest rung of the socioeconomic ladder in
New York City: They have less income as a group than either
white non-Puerto Ricans or nonwhites (Motley 1967:21; Kantrowitz and Rappenfort 1966:30). According to Sexton (1965:23),
at that time the jobless rate for blacks in Harlem was 50 percent above that for whites, and for Puerto Ricans it was 100
percent above the white norm. And the educational achievement
of a Puerto Rican adult, at least among the migrants, is an
average of 6.5 years lower than that of any other ethnic group
in the city (Lewis 1968:206).

According to most current indices for objectively measur-
ing socioeconomic class, the informants used in this study
would be classified as "working" or "lower-working" class. The
occupational roles of the heads of households are mainly restricted to operatives, service workers, and laborers. The
parents of only two Puerto Rican and two black informants are
reported to have occupations that might be classified as pro-
fessional or semi-professional.

Although we have not made evaluations of all the individual
residences of the informants, a survey of the general neighborhoods and an observation of a sample of the projects and tene-
ments in which the informants live indicate that they are quite
typical of working- or lower-working-class residences. Many of
the residences would clearly be classified as "slum dwellings".

The educational picture of the informants shows somewhat
more variation than do the occupations of the heads of household and the housing. Of the 23 informants who responded to
our questions about education, 4 (3 of them black) indicate
that their parents have had some college training. If these
statements can be relied upon, the level of education represented by the household heads seems to be much higher than what
we would expect of Harlem and south Bronx residents. It is
possible, however, that many of the informants may have over-
stated the educational levels of their parents.

The school records of the informants (some of which were
available to YDI's educational supervisor) generally indicate
that their educational achievement is far below the expected
norms for their age level. This is true of their reading levels
in particular, a fact that was well confirmed when they were
asked to read a small passage as part of the interview. Several
informants were unable to read even the word lists they were
given and would have to be considered functionally illiterate.
It is quite clear that the majority of our informants has been

alienated from the schools and that their values do not coin-
cide with the middle-class values placed on educational achievement. From the background information given to us by YDI workers, from interviews, and from personal observation, it appears
that many informants can be considered integral members of
indigenous peer groups, participating fully in the "street
culture". There are, however, several informants who must be
classified as cultural "lames", i.e. non-members in an indigenous peer group. The school performance of these informants
is considerably above that of the other informants, and their
value orientation toward education is consonant with the mainstream values placed on educational achievement.

The picture we have painted in the above paragraphs is
essentially one of ambivalence. On the one hand, Puerto Ricans
may share a feeling of solidarity with blacks because of the
minority status of both groups. But on the other hand, tensions may exist because, as we have seen, Puerto Ricans often
come below blacks in the "pecking order" of New York City[2],
and thus the two groups are in competition for higher status.
Puerto Ricans often indicate that they are aware of this competition (Lewis 1968:208), and in many instances, these ambivalent reactions to blacks are expressed by a single individual.

2.5.3 The effect of skin color. Although Puerto Ricans born
and raised in New York City have more contact with non-Puerto
Ricans than do those who have immigrated from the island, they
often consider themselves to be "both Spanish and American, as
two unintegrated aspects of themselves" (Padilla 1958:280).
The extent to which they perceive themselves as Spanish or
American depends on several factors. Among these are the
degree of acculturation of their parents, the family's socioeconomic status, and perhaps most significantly, at least outside the family[3], the color of their skin.

In Puerto Rico, discrimination is allegedly rooted more in social class than in color, although it also happens that the least socioeconomically advanced group contains most dark-skinned Puerto Ricans. Thus, Padilla (1958:73,75) explains racial considerations in Puerto Rico as being determined more by appearance than by ancestry, and race is thus reinterpretable depending on advance in income, education, etc. (see Hoffman 1968:37-39).

In terms of physical appearance, Latin Americans "assume the legitimacy of racial identities intermediate to those of white and Negro", while Americans dichotomize into a two-color system, according to Seda-Bonilla (1961:144). For convenience of our discussion of the effect of skin color, Puerto Ricans can be divided into three main categories: white, intermediate, and colored. Traditionally, the terms "white" and "colored" have been used to refer to lighter skinned and darker skinned Puerto Ricans respectively, but no popular classification of the intermediate group is designated. The term "black", which might seem preferable to colored, has a somewhat different cultural reference as it is typically used. In reality, skin color does not function apart from other types of physical characteristics such as hair texture and facial features.

While on the island mulattoes are considered white, and while a larger percentage of white than colored Puerto Ricans migrate to the United States, even these light-colored Puerto Ricans become the target of American discrimination. What the Negro American has long been aware of, i.e. that he is set apart from much of middle-class American society by his color, the Puerto Rican learns upon his arrival in the United States. Puerto Ricans are made extremely sensitive to color distinctions, and the effect "has been to strengthen the character of the identification of the Puerto Rican in the case of those who were colored and to weaken it in the case of those who were

white" (Handlin 1965:58-59). Consequently, those of intermediate color are left in a no-man's-land in terms of self-
identification in the United States.

Upwardly mobile white Puerto Ricans often seek identifi-
cation with the white American community as soon as possible
(Handlin 1965:58-59) and abandon the ghetto for Washington
Heights, areas of the Bronx and Queens (Glazer and Moynihan
1963:111), or areas farther away from the city. As they be-
come more assimilated, they move to nonethnic areas, severing
Puerto Rican contacts in an attempt to conceal their Puerto
Rican origin.

Seda-Bonilla (1961), in fact, reports that Puerto Ricans
living in a white neighborhood admit their Puerto Rican origin
hesitantly and only after three or four interviews. The same
author also mentions encounters with children in East Harlem
who refuse to be identified as Puerto Rican and who deny know-
ing Spanish. Two brothers (both of whom are quite light) in
the present sample are good examples of this attitude. Both
deny any knowledge of Spanish, saying they never use it, despite the fact that both their parents are island-born and that
they live in a predominantly Puerto Rican environment:

FW: Did you ever speak Spanish at home?

INF: Did I ever? No, ... not that I could remember.

FW: Do your parents speak Spanish?

INF: [after some pressing] Once in a while.

FW: [Do you speak Spanish] with your friends?

INF: Definitely. They speak Spanish to me you know.
      Go yeah, yeah, I don't know what they're saying.

FW: You don't understand Spanish?

INF: No.... No, I won't speak Spanish.

FW: What do you speak?

INF: I speak English....

FW: With older neighbors?

INF: What about it?... Oh, I can't speak Spanish.

FW: You can't say anything in Spanish?

INF: Well, yes, but.... (9: second interview)

In terms of assimilation, intermediate and colored Puerto
Ricans experience the same problems in different degrees. The
colored Puerto Ricans are often identified as black by the outside community and indeed, according to Seda-Bonilla (1961:147),
"find open acceptance in the American Negro society with cre-
dentials of the 'West Indian'". For those who remain in the
center of the city, particularly if they are dark and have
little possibility of relocating to another neighborhood, the
non-Puerto Rican culture to be assimilated to is the black
culture:

> ...he must "become like" the Negro in the metro-
> politan community. The world in which he is to
> function inconspicuously is the Negro world....
> He finds that he can hold only certain jobs, mix
> socially only with certain people. Almost always
> he must live in the Harlem ghetto, or in certain
> Negro sections of the Bronx. (Mills, Senior, and
> Goldsen 1950:133)

Rand notes the comment of a social worker on the Lower East
Side as indicative of this blackward assimilation:

> The Negroes were in New York first and had a head
> start, but now the Puerto Ricans are copying them.
> They are borrowing the Negroes' gang structure.
> Also their jive talk and bop language.... The
> Negroes are setting the pattern, but the Puerto
> Ricans are right in there contending with them.
> (Rand 1958:130-31)

Those colored Puerto Ricans who choose not to be identified with the Negro community must counteract the outside
community's appraisal of them as blacks. By emphasizing their
Puerto Rican origins they attempt to enhance the distance between themselves and blacks. This emphasis on their Spanish-
ness may be linguistic as well as cultural, so that use of the
Spanish language and customs is reinforced. Within the Puerto
Rican community, therefore,

> ...a reaction against what is regarded as a social
> disadvantage has been transformed into a source of
> family and neighborhood group solidarity which, in
> turn, serves as a source of emotional strength, re-
> inforcement, and support for the individual.
> (Padilla 1958:36)

Nonetheless, although they are considered Puerto Ricans (as
against blacks) in the Puerto Rican community, they report
being treated as the "lowest" within the family, and researchers
have found that Puerto Rican drug addicts are usually the dark-
est members of the family (Sexton 1965:10).

The intermediate Puerto Ricans face more ambiguity, since
they are not immediately categorized by outsiders as black and
thus have more of an option in choosing their identity. They
may choose to be conspicuous as members of a foreign-language-
speaking group rather than to be identified with blacks. Those
who do accept membership in the American Negro community become
completely acculturated to the black society to the point of
speaking like blacks, according to Seda-Bonilla (1961:147).
This acculturation is reflected in the present study in the
speech of those Puerto Ricans with extensive black contacts.
They have then only one battle to fight, that of discrimination
against blacks, rather than having the double problem of identifying themselves as Puerto Rican and as being distinct from the
Negro.

Rand (1958:13) seems to indicate that the Puerto Rican
population in Harlem consists of those who are the darker, less
European-looking in the New York City population, since they
"are the ones who find it hardest to leave the ghettos and be
assimilated". No doubt the majority of the Puerto Rican informants in the present study would be classified as intermediate or colored. Although we might hypothesize that the
darker informants are more likely to have extensive black contacts than are their intermediate counterparts, our sample does
not bear this out. However, this is probably due to the limited

sample, and we would expect a larger sample to reveal such a
pattern.

What emerges so far is a sketch of the Puerto Rican population of New York City confronted with assimilation alternatives. Coming from a "foreign" culture, speaking a "foreign"
language, the Puerto Rican is confronted with racial discrimination reportedly unknown on the island. However, unlike the
black whose isolation from white society is more nearly complete, the Puerto Rican has more possibilities for assimilation
with the white culture (Broom and Glenn 1965:36).

If he is light and can learn the language, he and his
children can become submerged in mainstream America, leaving
the black-assimilating and Puerto Rican-oriented groups behind
in the center city. But the dark-skinned Puerto Rican faces
a conflict in terms of acculturation that is in many respects
greater than the black's, for he has the double onus of being
both "foreign" and black-like. He is threatened with the discrimination meted out to American blacks, and his mobility is
thus restricted, frequently marooning him in the ghettos of
Harlem, the Bronx, Brooklyn, etc. (Burma 1954:161); Seda-
Bonilla 1961:146-47). He can either try to escape discrimination by emphasizing his membership in the Hispano culture or
identify with the blacks and become accepted in some form of
American culture.

2.5.4 <u>The use of Spanish</u>[4] The fact that blacks and Puerto
Ricans are forced together geographically and socioeconomically
in New York City tends to inhibit ethnic isolation on the part
of Puerto Ricans. Not only do both groups share the same
physical neighborhood, but they also are exposed to the same
media, attend school together, and very often work together.

At the same time, Puerto Ricans are never very far from
other Puerto Ricans, so that is is possible to maintain a

Puerto Rican-English ambiance. Part of this ambiance is encouraged by the use of Spanish. Fishman (1968a) analyzes interactions between and within groups in terms of domains. According to Hoffman (1968:26 ff.), "Domains are similar to the
sociologist's 'institutions', but are understood in terms of
behavior, as well as in terms of structure"; the five domains
he suggest for language analysis are home, neighborhood, education, officialdom, and religion. The general rule enunciated
by Hoffman is helpful:

> The more one functions within the Puerto Rican value
> system, the more he would be compelled to speak the
> language variants required by that system. As a
> person moves farther away from an exclusively Puerto
> Rican value orientation his freedom of language
> choice increases, subject only to the constraints
> imposed by new value orientations. (Hoffman 1968:41)

Relying on the preceding discussion, it seems safe to
generalize that Puerto Ricans in Harlem and other centers of
concentration in the city use both English and Spanish; there
is no completely monolingual Spanish domain, at least for first
and second generation speakers. A Spanish domain is most
closely approximated in the home, particularly (1) if the parents speak little English or are fairly new arrivals in the
city, or (2) if there is frequent contact with new arrivals
from the island. Children of preschool age apparently learn
English from their siblings and companions on the street rather
than from their parents, and many youngsters who are fluent in
English speak Spanish to their parents and older relatives.
In the neighborhood both English and Spanish are used, depending on the age and the Puerto Rican orientation of the speaker.
The very integration of the neighborhood, its stores, schools,
etc., does not encourage Spanish monolingualism.

Hoffman notes that Spanish often unites youngsters "in a
common, intimate, emotional bond even while many of them spoke
better English than Spanish" (1968:67). Spanish is associated

with intimacy and solidarity, hypothesize Greenfield and Fishman (1968:433; see also Padilla 1958:96-97; and Lewis 1968:
207), and it is used with friends and family. This is borne
out in the present study: Some informants may use Spanish
among Puerto Ricans, but they do not use it when non-Spanish-
speaking people are around, unless they want to tease or anger
the non-Spanish-speaking.

    Typical of a certain group of Puerto Rican informants are
those who speak Spanish in the home, but not on the street:

    FW: Do you speak Spanish to the kids in the groups?

    INF: No, we don't speak Spanish to each other...
          only in the house.... When I go outside I
          talk English only. (34:9-10)

    FW: Do any of them [the guys you hang with]
          speak Spanish?

    INF: Ah, we all speak Spanish.... We usually
          speak English. We just probably speak
          Spanish to our parents.... They speak
          English and Spanish but around the house
          they usually speak Spanish.... It's normal.
          I mean, nothing wrong with it, just like
          speaking English. (37:8)

Other informants, however, answer their parents in English,
even when the parents address them in Spanish:

    FW: Do you speak to your parents in Spanish?

    INF: Huh. They ask, they call, they ask questions
          to me in Spanish but I answer in English....

    FW: Do they want you to learn Spanish?

    INF: I already know, but I'm learning how to read
          and write in Spanish. He teaching me. (33:6)

And for a few informants, despite their Puerto Rican origins,
English is spoken at home:

              ...and my mother knows a lot of English. I
              speak English in the house and my father, too.
              (36:7)

    Part of this reluctance to use Spanish, perhaps even at

home, is from the fear of being classified as a "jibaro", a "hick". The following account illustrates this fear and the possibility of overcoming it if the speaker is highly valued enough by his peers:

> ...if I stay out till 11, my mother comes and gets me and then my friends say, couple of friends over there, they say, ah, 'Man, this guy's always speaking Spanish with his mother you know. Boy, he's a hick and a half', you know, and then they start to hate me and I have to get, you know, I say, 'Look, if you don't like the way I speak Spanish, don't stay with me', cause the guys over there, then, they, you know, as soon as they leave me they leave everything, you know. Like if they leave, if they leave to go someplace I bring 'em, need everything from me. (10:10)

The official domain and the work domain are most often English-speaking. The educational domain also includes a predominance of English. English is the language of instruction and, after the first school years, the language of the youngsters at school, even when the school is predominantly Puerto Rican. The ability to speak English is valued. Puerto Ricans born and raised in New York City who speak English sometimes resent being addressed in Spanish and will, on occasion, pretend not to understand when addressed in Spanish. For them,

> ...the knowledge of Spanish conveys no particular sense of accomplishment, nor is it something to boast about. Like non-Puerto Ricans, they regard the constant use of Spanish, as well as any other form of behavior that distinguishes Puerto Ricans from Americans, as detrimental to Puerto Ricans in New York. (Padilla 1958:100)

Are there, however, forces that reinforce the use of Spanish? To some extent, there are people who prefer to maintain their Spanish. As discussed previously, one group consists of intermediates who seek to differentiate themselves from blacks by emphasizing their Hispano origins and language. There also seem to be some immigrant families that simply see

being Puerto Rican as a positive value, whether or not they
desire to eventually return to the island (Lewis 1968:200-01).

This pride associated with being Spanish and speaking
Spanish is seen with one of the present informants:

FW: Do you speak it [Spanish]?

INF: I speak Spanish. I AM Spanish.

FW: Huh?

INF: I am Spanish. (27:9)

Some parents are proud of their Puerto Rican origins and
demand that their children speak Spanish:

FW: Do you answer [your parents] in Spanish?

INF: Well, I have to. My father asks me a question
      in Spanish. He won't take it in English. I
      have to answer him in Spanish cause he says, ah,
      ah, 'I'm not an Italian and I'm not a Negro, but
      I'm a Puerto Rican and have to speak to me in
      my language....' [He says] 'I was born in
      Puerto Rico and.... I'm gonna raise you like
      Puerto Ricans'. So if we speak...English in
      front of him...it's like cursing right in front
      of him. (10:9)

To promote the maintenance of their Puerto Ricanness, some
parents with this orientation discourage their children from
being on the street unless in the company of the family, otherwise demanding that the children spend their off-school hours
in the home. These are also the children who are seen alone
on the street and who go to school alone, according to Padilla
(1958:15). Some of these children remain "upstairs" all during
their childhood, while others, as soon as they have learned the
ropes, manage to gain acceptance in some sort of youth organization, with or without their parents' approval (Padilla
1958:229).

While it is difficult in one or two interviews to determine the informants' knowledge and use of Spanish, particularly
when the interview is conducted in English context, it is
nevertheless clear that all of the Puerto Ricans in our study

have had more or less extensive contact with Spanish, either
in their childhood or from childhood to the present. For a
general picture of the use of Spanish by the Puerto Rican informants, four categories of Spanish contact are useful:

      I: Knows Spanish and speaks Spanish to family
           and non-family

     II: Knows Spanish and speaks Spanish to family

    III: Knows Spanish but does not speak it

    IV: Claims not to know Spanish.

Information culled from one or two interviews with 28 of
the present 29 Puerto Rican informants,[5] shows that 16 know
Spanish and speak it to family and non-family, including
neighbors and peers. The frequency with which Spanish is used
with peers varies from often to occasionally. Seven informants
know Spanish and speak it with one or more members of the
family, but claim to speak it rarely outside the family.
Three know Spanish but do not speak it at present with any
frequency. Two informants deny ability to speak Spanish.

For most of the informants, Spanish is used most frequently in the family with the mother or grandmother, while
English is used more often with the father and siblings.
While the use of Spanish with family members follows a fairly
uniform pattern, Spanish usage outside the family depends on
many variables such as situation, age, participants, topic,
and so forth. The description of the interaction of these
variables, however, is outside the scope of this study, since
our primary focus is on the English used by our informants.

Fishman has suggested that the bilingual situation in
New York City is diglossic, with functional reinforcement of
English and Spanish in differing domains. The maintenance of
both languages, seen from this point of view, is hypothesized
for a long time to come:

      The 'doom' of Spanish in New York is not about to
      come to pass and perhaps we now have a bilingual

> group in the City which will simply not go away
> the way the other language groups did. (Fishman
> 1971:71)

On the other hand, Cooper and Greenfield hypothesize that
the Puerto Ricans

> ...seem to be headed in the same direction as
> previous immigrant groups in the United States,
> as they appear to be undergoing displacement of
> the 'mother' tongue by English in all domains of
> life.... (Cooper and Greenfield 1968:496)

Since the "choice of a language may in its turn serve as
a subtle behavioral index to the direction of acculturation
and to the vagaries of social adjustment" (Herman 1961:162),
it would seem that the New York City situation would enforce
the hypothesis of assimilation: That is, English is used more
often by more of the younger people in more situations. Further, it will be shown to include features of assimilation to
the dominant dialect surrounding them, i.e. the black dialect.
It is expected, however, that a certain differentiation between blacks and Puerto Ricans will be maintained (Glazer and
Moynihan 1963:313). The ethnic components are no longer mold-
ing together as they did in the nineteenth and early twentieth
centuries, according to Handlin (1965). Rather, what is seen
is a solidification of ethnic groups, and it is the task of
present research to examine "the extent to which a differentiation of interest and orientation is taking place within the
ethnic groups themselves and social antecedents to this process" (Doob 1970:532).

2.5.5 The use of Black English. The extent to which Black
English is adopted by Puerto Rican teen-agers is East Harlem
will be discussed in detail in the following chapters. In a
wider sociocultural context, however, we may anticipate our
discussion of actual linguistic assimilation by looking at
some aspects of the general perception of the language situation

on the part of the Puerto Rican groups. How do Puerto Ricans
view and react to the linguistic assimilation that is taking
place in a broader cultural framework?

To begin with, we have observed that Puerto Ricans with
extensive black contacts tend to minimize differences that
exist between the two groups. We may thus get informants in
this group who deny that the ways in which blacks and Puerto
Ricans speak English are different. For some of these informants, there is, of course, a great deal of objective similarity between the varieties of English used by the two groups.
But informants who would still perceptually be identified as
Puerto Rican may also tend to minimize these differences. The
tendency to minimize speech differences that we observe on the
part of Puerto Ricans is thus consistent with their perception
of the social relations of these groups in a wider context,
as noted above.

An interesting assessment of the unity of blacks and Puerto
Ricans by members of these groups has been observed in relation
to the use of Spanish in peer group situations. Several informants cited the fact that blacks learn to speak Spanish:

> FW: The Negro guys speak Spanish? Do you speak
>   Spanish with one another?
>
> INF: You know, like sometime I say, 'Tu madre es
>   puta', that means 'Your mother's a whore',
>   and the guy says, 'Tu abuela', you know,
>   'Your grandmother', and jive, and they say,
>   'Vamos a comer', 'Let's go eat', stuff like
>   that, yea, and they know how to say like,
>   somebody be talking, like two parents be
>   talking, they say, 'Estos niños son tecatos',
>   you know, like 'These kids are junkies', and
>   they go around and they say, 'Hey, man, your
>   mother's over there saying we're junkies, I
>   heard her', something like that. (5:11)

In reality, we find that Spanish usage among blacks in
these peer groups is generally restricted to a few phrases or
lexical items. One of our black informants gives an illustration

of this phenomenon when he is talking about a Puerto Rican who
is a member of a predominantly black peer group:

> We say like, 'Eh mira', you know, we talk in
> Spanish and ask him for a cigarette, 'Dame
> cigarillo', and he say, 'I don't have none',
> and he say, 'Look here, man', he make his
> speech, like if we have a party or something
> and that guy say, 'Look at that Spanish guy
> over there', he walk over to him, he say, he
> make his little speech, he say, 'Listen now,
> listen to me real good. I may be Spanyola on
> the outside, but inside I have a Negro heart,
> you know'. Everybody look at him and say, you
> know, they start clapping, they say, 'Reuben,
> say some more', and he be telling all that and
> then you know, most the time they say, 'What's
> happening', you know, he consider hisself a
> nigger, I wouldn't blame him. (1:17)

It is obvious from other comments by Puerto Ricans and
from our observations of social interactions that the claim
concerning the acquisition of Spanish by blacks is quite
exaggerated. The learning of a few fixed phrases is quite
different from acquiring language competence in Puerto Rican
Spanish.

Statements by Puerto Rican informants also tend to con-
tradict their observations that blacks speak Spanish. In
other contexts, Puerto Ricans mention that Spanish is generally avoided around black peers. The reasons for this avoid-
ance are stated succinctly by one Puerto Rican with extensive
black peers: He observes that the reason he does not use
Spanish with his peers is "So the guy could know that I'm boss,
I don't want to hide nothing". For Puerto Ricans to use Spanish with black peers is socially inappropriate since it may be
associated with ineptness in cultural adaptation. As illustrated in the previous quote, Puerto Ricans with predominantly
black peers have to prove that they belong. The use of Spanish
with another Puerto Rican in the peer group would thus be
counterproductive to this purpose. Furthermore, the use of

Spanish may be disruptive to a social group for if a black peer does not understand it, he may view it suspiciously. Puerto Ricans who use Spanish around black peers may be suspected of criticizing or attempting to conceal information from their black peers.

If Spanish is not likely to be used around black peers, we may ask why some of the Puerto Ricans make special mention of the fact that blacks speak Spanish. Part of the reason may be related to the tendency of Puerto Ricans with extensive black contacts to minimize differences between the two groups. But we may also hypothesize that there is a desire on the part of these informants to interpret assimilation as reciprocal: That is, not only are Puerto Ricans assimilating aspects of the surrounding black culture, but also blacks are assimilating aspects of Puerto Rican culture.

In reality, this cultural assimilation is largely one-way: It is the Puerto Ricans who are copying the blacks. Black teen-agers do not pick up aspects of Puerto Rican English that might identify them as being Puerto Rican, such as occasional syllable-timing, the tendency not to reduce vowels in unstressed syllables, and so forth; nor do they pick up any real conversational ability in Puerto Rican Spanish. When more integrative aspects of linguistic competence are considered, the few phrases or lexical items learned by some blacks in East Harlem must be considered tokens, indicating a relatively superficial level of borrowing. But these small tokens apparently are interpreted quite symbolically by some Puerto Ricans who desire to see the assimilation process working both ways.

Now let us turn to the Puerto Ricans with restricted black contacts. Unlike the Puerto Ricans with extensive black peer group contacts, they show no tendency to minimize the speech differences between the groups. Therefore, we find informants in this category perceiving blacks and Puerto Ricans as talking quite differently. The following reactions are quite typical:

FW: Is there a difference between the way Puerto Ricans and blacks talk?

INF: Say, like a white person, he will say, 'You try to be cool'. Now a black person will say, 'You all try to be cool'. So there's an accent right there. (39:second interview)

FW: Is there any difference between the way Puerto Ricans and blacks talk?

INF: Yes, there is a big difference. ...Spanish, he'll say, 'Slap me five', but the Negro will come up and say, 'Put some skin on my hand', you know, and he'll use 'man', and he'll say, 'Come on, man, let's go and do our little thing'.

FW: Puerto Ricans don't say that, right?

INF: They say it, but it's different, way different by the way Negroes say it. (43:second interview)

FW: Do you think that black and Puerto Ricans sound any different when they talk?

INF: Yeah, I think the Negro stretches the word.

FW: Give me an example of him stretching the word.

INF: Like when they say 'man', I would say, 'Hey, man, cut it out'. Listening to a Negro, they don't speak like that. They say 'maaan', and it starts moving, you know. They emphasize on the word more. (11:second interview)

This perception of speech differences is consistent with their perception of differences between blacks and Puerto Ricans in East Harlem on a broader cultural level. Despite the fact that the social positions of Puerto Ricans and blacks are quite similar in the wider context of American society, we have already mentioned that there may be considerable intergroup tension. In such a context, it is quite predictable that differences in speech should be brought out to parallel the perception of other social differences.

At this point, we may anticipate our discussion of linguistic assimilation in the following chapters by noting that
despite their perception of speech differences, Puerto Ricans
with restricted black contacts do show some influence in certain aspects of their speech. We will see, for example, that
there is some phonological influence, regardless of the extent
of contact. If we had included vocabulary in our study, we
would also see that there are a number of indigenous black
terms that have been borrowed into the lexicon of both groups
of Puerto Ricans. But these similarities are perceived as
insignificant when compared with the amount of assimilation
revealed by Puerto Ricans with extensive black contacts. In
fact, there is evidence that some Puerto Ricans are not con-
scious of the extent to which black speech may have influenced
their own speech. This is vividly illustrated in one incident
that occurred following an interview. The informant, never
having heard his voice on a tape recorder, asked to play back
part of the interview. After listening to his voice for a
minute, he worriedly exclaimed to the interviewer, "Man, I
sound just like a nigger". The assimilation of Black English
may be viewed negatively by Puerto Ricans in this group, despite the fact that they have assimilated aspects of Black
English in their own speech.

> FW: Do a lotta Spanish kids sound like black
> kids?
>
> INF: Sometimes....
>
> FW: How about you? Do you think you ever sound
> like a black when you talk?
>
> INF: I don't know. Do I?
>
> FW: I want your opinion. Do you think you'd
> like to?
>
> INF: No.
>
> FW: Why not?

INF: I want to talk like I always talk. I don't
      care if I can talk English, at least I can
      talk.

FW: Do you think that when a Spanish guy talks
      like a black guy that makes him sound cool?

INF: Corny.

FW: Does it make him sound tough?

INF: Not tough but corny.

FW: You know some guys who talk that way?

INF: Yeah.... I think they're trying to show off,
      like, if they got a colored friend, they want
      to show off in front of him.[6]

The integral adoption of Black English by Puerto Ricans
with extensive black contacts may be viewed as an attempt to
be something that a Puerto Rican naturally is not, and therefore may be considered pretentious. And even though Puerto
Ricans with restricted black contacts may be further removed
from traditional Puerto Rican culture than their parents,
they may view it as a symbol of the rejection of the Puerto
Rican community of which they are still a part.

Any negative reactions toward the assimilation of Black
English on the part of the teen-agers with restricted black
contacts are clearly reinforced in the home. If parents perceive certain aspects of their children's English to be influenced by black speech, they may react quite negatively. We
have already seen that many parents speak to their children
in Spanish and require that their children answer them in
Spanish. If it is considered inappropriate for children to
answer parents in English at all, then the use of a dialect
of English that is discernibly influenced by Black English
will elicit an even stronger reaction from the parents. One
informant explained that a friend who talked like a black was
smacked by his father who said, "You can talk English, but
normal English". There is considerable evidence that the

parents view their children's acquisition of Black English features as quite insulting.

The reactions of Puerto Ricans with restricted black contacts toward the assimilation of Black English can be characterized as basically ambivalent. On the one hand, they are quite aware of the differences that exist between the two groups in a number of areas of culture, and they tend to perceive these differences in speech as in other areas. On the other hand, they are faced with the reality of the social situation in which it is very difficult to avoid some influence from the black community that surrounds them. By perceiving the amount of influence on their own speech as insignificant, they do not have to deal with this limited assimilation while reacting negatively toward the amount of assimilation that takes place among their counterparts with extensive black contacts.

2.6 Summary. Although we have not given a comprehensive ethnographic description in the preceding sections, our brief account of selected aspects of the Puerto Rican community in New York City presents a wider sociocultural framework into which our present linguistic study can be placed. When compared with other reports of East Harlem and with our own background information, it appears that our small sample of Puerto Rican informants represents a fairly "typical" group of second generation teen-age males from the area. We see a range of black contact in the neighborhood and the schools that is well documented in other studies. The conflicting strains of solidarity and separation between Puerto Ricans and blacks present a fairly representative picture of the social dynamics between the two groups. We further observe residency patterns that characterize lower-socioeconomic-class Puerto Ricans in terms of both location and mobility. The concentration of

Puerto Ricans with dark skin also appears to be representative of the area when compared with other segments of the Puerto Rican population in New York City, because of the various assimilation alternatives based on skin color. And from our informants' reports we find that the use of Spanish shows the distribution that we would expect of second generation Puerto Ricans. We conclude, then, that we are describing linguistic characteristics for a group of Puerto Ricans who, in most respects, typify the second generation teen-ager.

NOTES

1. See Wolfram (1971:252-376) for details concerning some of the activities of the various groups of Puerto Rican informants.

2. Despite the objective facts concerning educational and economic status, most Puerto Ricans do not consider the personal prejudice against them to be nearly as intense as it is against blacks. Thus, one informant, after describing a discriminatory incident toward himself as a Puerto Rican in a Bronx park, was asked whether the same would have happened had there been blacks present:

> INF: Oh, man, if Negroes go in, I think they'll shoot them.
>
> FW: Are you better off than Negroes in this respect?
>
> INF: Yeah. They're treated much worse. (34:10)

The institutional discrimination against Puerto Ricans may match or exceed that against blacks in American society, but the feelings of personal prejudice are not perceived to be as intense.

3. The contrast between family acceptance and societal acceptance is well documented in Thomas (1967).

4. More specific information on Spanish-English usage can be found in Fishman et al. (1968). With respect to the

informants in this study, more detail is given concerning their use of Spanish in Shiels (1972).

5. Informant 31 must be omitted from the present discussion since no information on his use of Spanish was available.

6. This quote is excerpted from a supplemental series of interviews on PRE by Paul Anisman. I am grateful to him for bringing it to my attention.

3 LINGUISTIC VARIABILITY

Perhaps the most significant contribution of sociolinguistic
studies in the last few years has been the discovery that
various social dialects in the United States are differentiated from each other not only by discrete sets of features
but also by variations in the frequencies with which certain
features or rules occur. Studies of social dialects in the
United States in the mid and late 1960's clearly indicate that
differentiation of dialects cannot be indicated by simple
categorical statements; instead, dialects are, more typically,
quantitatively distinguished. Furthermore, many instances of
fluctuation in the usage of socially diagnostic linguistic
features have been found to be the result of "inherent variability" rather than dialect borrowing or mixture. Labov's
study of the social stratification of English in New York City
(1966a); Shuy, Wolfram, and Riley's sociolinguistic study in
Detroit (1968); Labov et al.'s treatment of Black English in
New York City (1968); Wolfram's investigation of sociolinguistic differences in the Detroit black population (1969); and
Fasold's account of black working-class speech in Washington,
D.C. (1972), all indicate the essential variable parameter in
the study of social dialects in the United States.

3.1 The linguistic variable. The study of linguistic variables rather than only categorical constants adds a new di-
mention to the examination of speech differences, namely, the

quantitative measurement of variable speech forms. Earlier
studies (Fischer 1958; Labov 1966a; Wolfram 1969) indicate that
as quantitative methods are utilized, correlations between linguistic and social patterns emerge. These treatments are done
largely within the framework of what Labov called the "linguistic
variable". The linguistic variable, itself an abstraction, is
realized in actual speech behavior by variants, that is, individual members of a class of variants constituting the variable.
Labov noted:

> Whereas the linguistic variant is a particular
> item--a morph or a phone--the variable is a
> class of variants which are ordered along a con-
> tinuous dimension and whose position is determined
> by an independent linguistic or extra-linguistic
> variable. (Labov 1966b:15)

The formulation of the linguistic variable has been established in sociolinguistic descriptions as the unit that serves
as a basis for correlating linguistic variation with extra-
linguistic factors. Variants or categories of variants are
distinguished with reference to their potential correlation
with social factors. For example, Wolfram (1969:83) divides
the morpheme-medial and -final θ̱ variable into four categories
of variants:

Category	Phonetic Realizations	Examples	
θ	[θ] [tθ]	[tʰuθ] ~ [tʰutθ]	'tooth'
		[nəθɪŋ]	'nothing'
f	[f]	[tʰuf]	'tooth'
		[nəfɪn]	'nothing'
t	[t˥] [ʔ] [ṱ]	[nət˥n̩] ~ [nəʔn̩]	'nothing'
		[wɪṱɪm]	'with 'em'
∅		[wɪ#mi]	'with me'
		[nəɪn]	'nothing'

The particular value of a given linguistic variable is viewed
as a function of its correlation with extra-linguistic variables

and with independent linguistic variables. For example, in the
study referred to above, the value of each linguistic variable
is viewed as a function of its correlation with socioeconomic
class, racial isolation, age, sex, and contextual style.

The quantitative measurement of linguistic variables necessarily involves counting variants. Although this may appear,
at first glance, to be a simple procedure, sometimes even the
simplest type of counting raises a number of subtle problems.
In fact, Labov et al. have gone so far as to note that "the
final decision as to what to count is actually the final solution to the problem at hand" (Labov et al. 1968:14). In the
first place, it is necessary to delimit the number of variants
that can be identified reliably and to select relevant categories of variants for tabulation. For example, in the above
categorization, it is noted that [θ] and [tθ] are members of
one category, and that [t⁷], [ʔ], and [t̯] are members of
another. In some cases, the classification of variants is
based on a decision as to which distinctions are socially
relevant for tabulation. Thus, we have decided that the distinctions between [t⁷], [ʔ], and [t̯] are not socially important
in the delimitation of the morpheme-medial and -final th
variable.

It is also important to identify the total population of
utterances in which an item may "potentially" vary. For example, in Labov's (1969) discussion of copula absence, he
notes that there are certain types of syntactic constructions,
e.g. clause-final position, in which copula contraction of the
type He's ugly or You're nice is not permissible in standard
or nonstandard dialects; instead, a full form of the copula
must be present, e.g. I know he is. In other environments,
standard English may use the contracted form of the copula
while some nonstandard dialects may fluctuate between the contracted form and copula absence, e.g. He's ugly~He ugly. To

get an accurate account of variation, it is necessary to separate these various types of environments, eliminating those
contexts in which copula presence is categorical.

Further, it is necessary to identify and classify relevant
linguistic environments (phonological, grammatical, and seman-
tic) that may affect the variation of items. In this procedure,
environments in which distinctions between variants are neutra-
lized for phonetic reasons, must be excluded. Thus, in the
tabulation of word-final consonant clusters, it may be necessary
to exclude clusters that are immediately followed by a homor-
ganic stop, e.g. test day, since it is sometimes impossible to
determine whether the final consonant of the cluster is present
or absent. The importance of identifying relevant linguistic
environments for quantitative measurement cannot be overesti-
mated.

Once the procedures of quantifying are set forth, relative
frequencies of the variant categories are then calculated as
they correlate with various social classifications. Thus, we
observe the following distribution of variants for the th variable in terms of four social classes of black population, as
delimited in Wolfram (1969:84):

Table 2. Comparison of variants for potential θ in morpheme-
medial and morpheme-final positions for Detroit blacks.

	%θ	%f	%t	%∅
Upper-middle class	87.9	5.5	6.1	0.6
Lower-middle class	82.6	11.0	5.8	0.6
Upper-working class	40.8	37.9	19.5	1.8
Lower-working class	28.7	44.7	20.0	6.6

In Table 2, we see that the relative frequencies of the four
variant types correlate with social class in the Detroit black

community. The variant θ is used significantly more frequently
by the middle-class groups than by the working-class groups,
which use the other three variants more frequently than do the
middle-class groups. In this way, we show that the th variable correlates with social class in the Detroit black community.

At this point, it is essential to note that the variants
of a variable are determined primarily on the basis of sociological (or sociolinguistic, if you will) rather than linguistic categorizations. Thus, we differentiate four variants for
the morpheme-medial and -final th variable because we hypothesize that this categorization might reveal relevant contrasts
for different social groups of speakers. With respect to the
linguistic system, the variants of a linguistic variable might
be part of one or more structural units. These variants, or
even the subvariants of a variable, might be derived from linguistic rules quite unrelated to each other. The question that
this raises is: what relevance does the linguistic variable
have to the linguistic rules of a given language or dialect?
As originally formulated by Labov (1966b), the linguistic variable was a convenient fiction, having no real theoretical linguistic validity. However, this is not to say that it was use-
less as a heuristic tool, for it had value in determining the
correlation between linguistic and sociological data. As we
shall see, it still may be quite useful as a fictional construct
for getting at sociolinguistic data. But this methodological
usefulness must be clearly distinguished from its theoretical
validity for linguistic systems.

3.2 Variable rules. Traditionally, language grammars did not
concern themselves with the notion of variability beyond indicating that some rules were posited as obligatory and others
as optional. The fact that a particular optional rule might

apply more frequently in one context (linguistic or social)
was considered irrelevant in the formulation of rules for any
given language or dialect. If a grammarian observed that the
degree of fluctuation varied more in certain contexts than in
others (and Labov (1971) has collected a number of examples to
demonstrate that this type of observation was made), it was
dismissed as incidental information: That is, it had no relation to actual rule formulation. Degree of optionality was
simply not considered within the province of linguistic description of language competence. Detailed studies of variability, however, have indicated that there is a systematic
regularity to much of this variation. In part, this regularity can be attributed to extra-linguistic factors such as
socioeconomic class, style, age, sex, and so forth. But it
has also been demonstrated (particularly in Labov et al.
(1968) and Wolfram (1969) that variability can be correlated
with independent linguistic variables such as phonological or
syntactical environment. The effect of linguistic constraints
on variability is quite striking in its regularity. For example, take the case of word-final consonant clusters in which
the final member of the cluster is a stop and both members have
the same voicing specification. In a number of varieties of
English, the final stop member of the cluster can be deleted.
According to the rule, desk may be pronounced as [dɛs] and
hand as [hæn]. This deletion rule may operate not only on
monomorphemic clusters, i.e. clusters in which both members
are part of the same morpheme, but also on bimorphemic clusters,
i.e. clusters in which the members are part of two different
morphemes. This means that words such as messed or fanned may
be pronounced as [mɛs] and [fæn] respectively. But the extent
of deletion is not equal for the two types of items. For all
groups for which this variable has been studied, it is observed that deletion is more frequent in monomorphemic clusters

than it is in bimorphemic ones. In addition to this constraint,
it has also been noted that the cluster is deleted more frequently when it is followed by a word beginning with a consonant than when it is followed by a vowel or a pause. The
relative effect of these two environments can be seen in
Table 3, taken from Wolfram's (1969) data and arranged by
Fasold (1970). The frequencies are tabulated for four different social groups of blacks in Detroit. The single hatch (#)
indicates an internal word boundary; the double hatch (##)
indicates an external word boundary.

Table 3.   Comparison of simplified consonant clusters in the
           speech of Detroit blacks.

	%C__##C	%C#__##C	%C__##V	%C#__##V
Upper-middle class	.79	.49	.28	.07
Lower-middle class	.87	.62	.43	.13
Upper-working class	.94	.73	.65	.24
Lower-working class	.97	.76	.72	.34

In Table 3, it is readily noted that the same rank order
obtains for all four social classes of blacks in Detroit: That
is, the most frequent context for consonant cluster simplification is when the cluster is followed by a consonant and is
part of a monomorphemic cluster; the next most frequent when
it is followed by a consonant and is part of a bimorphemic
cluster; the next most frequent when it is followed by a vowel
(or a pause) and is part of a monomorphemic cluster; and the
least frequent when it is followed by a vowel (or a pause) and
is part of a bimorphemic cluster. When we examine the two
types of constraints, we notice that they can be ordered according to the principles of geometric ordering. Thus, we have the

following array for consonant cluster simplification:

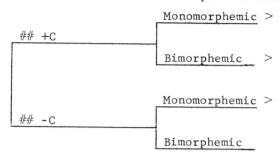

Studies of variable linguistic behavior according to the various constraints have indicated several important observations. First, we note that this type of ordering is quite regular for various social groups. For example, although the actual frequencies in Table 3 differ from social group to social group, the rank orders of the constraints are quite parallel. The types of constraints indicated above have been verified in a number of settings. For example, Labov et al. (1968), Wolfram (1969), Legum et al. (1971), and Fasold (1972) all reveal that both the following environment and the presence or absence of a grammatical marker in the cluster are important constraints on optionality. Frequencies differ from study to study and, in some cases, the ordering of constraints may be different, but the relative effect of these environments is quite regular.

The impressive regularity of these types of constraints on variability is responsible for Labov's (1969) original postulation that optional rules in grammars should be modified in such a way as to allow for the specification of constraints on optionality. Thus, for example, an optional rule may include some kind of specification to indicate the regular and ordered effect of environment on variability. In Labov's original formulation, he uses Greek prescripts to indicate this ordering:[1]

$$X \rightarrow (Y) \; / \; \alpha Z \longrightarrow \beta \sim W$$

In the above formulation, there are two constraints on the optionality of the rule that produces Y from X. The first constraint is the preceding Z and the second, the following W. If Z is +, the rule is favored; if it is -, it is inhibited. For W, the ~ indicates that the absence of the feature favors the application of the rule and that its presence inhibits it. According to the principle of geometric ordering, the following rank of constraints on optionality obtains:

$$+Z \ -W \ >$$
$$+Z \ +W \ >$$
$$-Z \ -W \ >$$
$$-Z \ +W$$

The actual frequency of rule application seems to be only incidental to the ordering and is, in essence, a heuristic device for the establishment of the ordering. The frequency level appear to be a part of performance, but the ordering of constraints is a part of competence that needs to be accounted for in a descriptive grammar. Optional rules that incorporate these features have become known as "variable rules". Whereas the linguistic variable we discussed earlier had no real linguistic significance in terms of the formal representations of a grammar, the variable rule is posited as a formal aspect of linguistic theory to be accounted for in language grammars. Its acceptance on a theoretical level seems to be based on several premises, which we will discuss below.

3.2.1 <u>Inherent variability</u>. The establishment of variable rules is, first of all, based on the assumption of "inherent variability". By inherent variability, we are referring to the fluctuation of variants that cannot be dismissed as dialect borrowing or switching within codes of a speaker's repertoire: That is, the fluctuation is part of a unitary system. One could, of course, theoretically dismiss the notion of inherent

variability by assuming that all instances of variation are
simply matters of "code switching". From this perspective, if
a variant typically associated with language variety X is observed in a person's speech in which features of language
variety Y are predominant, it is assumed to be an instance of
code switching. The fluctuating variants are assigned to different systems or subsystems within a speaker's linguistic
repertoire, and he is seen to be shifting from one code to the
other.

We should mention here that switching is typically associated with a SET of features rather than with isolated variants, and that switching usually takes place in response to
some stylistic, situational, interlocutor, topic, or other
functional shift. On a linguistic level, we would expect some
change in the linguistic environment to account for the distribution of variants. What we are faced with, however, is the
observation that variation takes place while the extra-linguistic
and linguistic context remains quite constant. Variation in a
constant extra-linguistic and linguistic context is difficult to
dismiss. But even within the most constant of contexts, it can
still be claimed that our failure to uncover further conditioning detail to account for shift is only a function of our finite
powers of observation. Hence, it may be claimed that the provision of more sociopsychological or linguistic detail would
allow us to account for "apparent" fluctuation in terms of a
purely categorical framework. Although it may be a heuris-
tically useful procedure to admit inherent variability only
after an exhaustive attempt to account for fluctuating variants
in categorical terms, our best powers of observation still
leave us with inexplicable fluctuation. Ultimately, of course,
it is impossible to prove that inherent variability does exist,
since we are always subject to our finite observations. Unable
to prove the claim logically, we must resort to the fact that

the existing data on fluctuation do not support the categorical
explanation. Hence, we assume inherent variability.

If we assume that fluctuation between forms is not simply
a matter of code switching between coexistent systems, we are
faced with the question of how one can differentiate what may
be considered "dialect mixture" or "dialect borrowing", i.e.
variant forms that are importations from other dialects, from
inherent variability. The distinction between dialect mixture
(assuming that this notion is also accepted) and inherent variability may be of particular importance for the investigator
of languages in contact, whether on an interlanguage or intra-
language level. Students of interlanguage contact situations
may maintain, for example, that it is possible for a speaker
of L_1 to borrow a form from L_2 without integrating it completely
into the system of L_2. Isn't it, for example, quite possible
for a speaker of English to borrow a term from German following
the morpheme structure sequence rules of German even if they
"violate" the English morpheme structure rules? By the same
token, investigators of nonstandard language varieties have
been confronted with this issue because of the effect that a
superordinate variety may have on a subordinate one. Are not
some of the fluctuating items used by speakers of the subordinate variety sometimes borrowed from the superordinate one?
In some cases, heuristic procedures for differentiating dialect
mixture from inherent variability have even been set up[2]. Thus,
for example, some linguists, e.g. Labov et al. (1968:164-67,
Wolfram (1969:45-47, and Fasold (1972:131), analyzing the sporadic use of -$\underline{Z}$ third person singular present tense forms, have
cited the evidence of structural hypercorrection, frequency
levels, and sociological context to show the difference between
fluctuating forms that are "borrowed" and those that are
"inherent". As attractive as these analyses may appear to be
in terms of language contact situations, this distinction is

dependent on the observation of both sociological and linguistic phenomena[3]. There appears to be no purely linguistic basis
for such a differentiation, as unsatisfying as that may seem
to students of language contact.

   At this point, one may anticipate the discussion of linguistic constraints on variability and ask if sensitivity to
linguistic environment may be used as a linguistic basis for
distinguishing inherent variability from dialect mixture:
That is, do fluctuating items that are inherently variable show
a structured sensitivity to surrounding linguistic environment
that is not matched for fluctuating items resulting from dialect
mixture? Although it may be tempting to set up such a criterion,
it should be cautioned that such a position may not be justified
when examined in closer detail. For example, suppose that L_1
does not have any word-final consonant cluster but L_2 does. A
speaker of L_1 uses a word from L_2 that ends in a consonant
cluster. In some instances, it is observed that the cluster
is intact, and in some instances, it is reduced in order to
conform to the morpheme structure rules of L_1; this is a very
natural expectation in terms of linguistic change of any type.
One can predict that the cluster would have a tendency to be
reduced more frequently when followed by a vowel than when
followed by a consonant for natural phonetic, i.e. universal
reasons. Similarly, we can expect the stress patterns to affect the incidence of the variants and to be ordered hierarchically with the following vocalic/nonvocalic environment.
On the basis of some exploratory evidence, this is what appears
to happen with fluctuating items, whether they are labeled
"inherently variable", "borrowed", or "interference". Thus,
our attempts to distinguish these notions purely on a formal
linguistic basis turn out to be somewhat futile. This does
not, however, mean that it is necessarily futile to attempt to
distinguish these various concepts at all. A realistic view

of the dynamics of language contact would appear to admit such
distinctions. But in differentiation, it is essential to
understand that the defining characteristics take us beyond
linguistic structure per se, involving language in the context
of society.

We take the position, then, that inherent variability is
theoretically and empirically justifiable, and that it can be
distinguished from dialect borrowing and code switching. To
distinguish between inherent variability and dialect mixture
from a synchronic viewpoint does not necessarily mean that
current inherent variability is not originally introduced
through dialect borrowing. In fact, historically, it appears
that much of what we label inherent variability from our synchronic perspective is the result of dialect mixture. Regardless of its historical origin, a synchronic description has to
deal with the fact that the fluctuation of items is an intrinsic part of the language system.

3.2.2 Replicable regularity. Another premise that lies at the
foundation of the theory of variable rules is what we might call
"replicable regularity". The step beyond traditional optional
rules in a grammar is premised on the systematic patterning of
variation. This regularity is demonstrated in the isolation
of various linguistic and extra-linguistic contexts that favor
or inhibit the operation of a particular optional rule. The
constraints on variability are further shown to be ordered with
respect to each other, so that a regular hierarchy of constraints
can be formalized for a given rule. Although frequency tabulations serve as a basis for determining relationships, most pro-
ponents of variable rules relegate the actual figures to the
status of a heuristic procedure. The significant relationships
are matters of more or less.

In our previous discussions, we have already alluded to

the fact that types of linguistic and nonlinguistic effects on variability are observed to be quite regular for a given individual and a given homogeneous speech community: That is, if we take speakers A and B from language variety X, we will find that the effect and the relative order of the constraints are quite regular in their speech. For example, if we break down one of the groups listed in Table 3 according to individual speakers, we would expect the same ordering of linguistic constraints on variability to hold from speaker to speaker. This is done in Table 4 for the upper-working-class population of Table 3. The frequencies for the four environments distinguished in Table 3 are given for each of the 12 informants who make up this category.

In Table 4, we see the same general pattern of ordering on an individual level that is observed when we calculate the percentages for the group as a whole. There are only two exceptions to this pattern, and we can predict that they would follow the same pattern if we had more examples in the various categories. For most speakers, we are impressed with how few examples are actually needed in order for the general pattern to emerge.

We would also expect that if we take two different samples of speech for each informant, we could duplicate the same pattern that emerges in Table 4. This type of regularity seems to have been established on individual speakers and different homogeneous groups of speakers.

At this point, one may question how stable these patterns are over an extended time period. Some theorists, e.g. Bailey (1973b) and Bickerton (1971), have posited that all variability such as the above is simply an indication of language change in progress: That is, languages essentially move from the categorical use of form X to form Y, and during this progression, there is an interim stage during which X and Y fluctuate.

Table 4. Comparison of simplified consonant clusters in the speech of upper-working-class blacks in Detroit.

Informant	C ___ ##C		C# ___ ##C		C ___ ##V		C# ___ ##V	
	%	(No. Del./Total)	%	(No. Del./Total)	%	(No. Del./Total)	%	(No. Del./Total)
1	.75	(6/8)	.67	(6/9)	.58	(7/12)	.17	(1/6)
2	1.00	(7/7)	.71	(5/7)	.62	(8/13)	.33	(1/3)
3	1.00	(12/12)	.64	(7/11)	.63	(5/8)	.25	(1/4)
4	1.00	(9/9)	.75	(3/4)	.73	(8/11)	1.00	(1/1)
5	1.00	(8/8)	1.00	(9/9)	.83	(10/12)	.33	(2/6)
6	1.00	(6/6)	.67	(6/9)	.64	(9/14)	.17	(1/6)
7	1.00	(8/8)	.67	(8/12)	.67	(8/12)	.00	(0/3)
8	1.00	(8/8)	.55	(6/11)	.58	(7/12)	.50	(2/4)
9	.85	(11/13)	.80	(4/5)	.57	(4/7)	.33	(1/3)
10	1.00	(10/10)	.92	(11/12)	.80	(8/10)	.00	(0/2)
11	.75	(6/8)	.71	(10/14)	.50	(6/12)	.00	(0/1)
12	.90	(9/10)	.77	(10/13)	.70	(7/10)	.00	(0/2)

In the initial stages of language change, X may be variable
with Y in certain types of environments, e.g. E_1, while remaining categorical in others, e.g. $E_2...E_n$. In a next stage,
X and Y may fluctuate in all environments. During this stage,
environments in which there was earlier fluctuation (E_1) will
have a greater incidence of X than environments in which the
variable stage occurred later (E_2). In another stage, E_1 may
indicate the categorical realization of Y, while E_2 still
fluctuates between X and Y. The final result is the categorical realization of Y in all environments. If this is true,
and in most instances it appears to be so, the relationships
of more and less imply earlier and later changes[4].

Even if one operates under the theoretical assumption that
all variability is an indication of language change in progress, this does not negate the validity of variable rule
formulation. The fact that optional rules, in the traditional
use of the term, may be indicative of changes from one categorical form to another does not mean that they can be dismissed from a descriptively adequate account of an individual's
grammar. By the same token, we can claim that variable rules
are needed to account for the degree of optionality that we
postulate as a part of language competence.

Furthermore, it appears that the language change described
above may, in some cases, become stagnant ("stagnant rules"):
That is, variability may remain constant for many generations.
In this sense, variability may reveal a stability matching
that of many categorical rules. In these cases, to say that
variability is only an indication of language change in progress appears to be a generalization of no more significance
than the sort that we make about language in general--that
language is always changing.

Although we may see the time dimension typically applied
in more or less relationships, the essential fact that we

must account for is the regularity of these relationships.
We maintain that this regularity represents the speaker's
language competence. When we use the term competence, we are
referring to the fact that this knowledge of variability is
part of the speaker's capability in terms of how he uses his
language. What we are saying, then, is that the speaker knows
that some rules are variable and what factors favor such rules.
In addition, he has knowledge of the hierarchical order of
these constraints. The actual frequency level of application
is a manifestation of his knowledge, i.e. performance, but it
is not actually a part of his capability.

3.2.3 <u>Language specificity</u>. By themselves, the premises discussed above do not justify the incorporation of constraints
on variability into the grammar of a specific language variety.
In order for us to justify our formalization of variable rules
in the grammar of PRE, for example, we need to demonstrate
that there are aspects of variable constraints that are unique
to this speech community. If we found that constraints could
be predicted on the basis of a universal theory of optional
rule constraints, there would be no need to represent them in
a specific language. Instead, they could simply be postulated
as part of a general language metatheory. This is the position
that Kiparsky is endorsing when he says:

> ...if something is universally predictable, it is
> not learned and can be taken out of the grammar,
> i.e., it can be made to follow from some general
> principle about language with a capital <u>L</u>. What I
> am conjecturing is that Labov's data can be taken
> out of the grammar of English, the grammar of
> German, Spanish, etc., and derived from a theory
> about optional rules in general. (Kiparsky 1971:
> 645)

Linguists taking this position maintain that, although variable
rules may provide important insights for a theory of optional

rules in general, it is unnecessarily redundant to include this sort of information for a specific language variety.

There are two aspects to the question of constraint universality. The first may be referred to as "effect predictability" and the second as "order predictability". When we use the term effect predictability, we are referring to the fact that a particular type of environment will always have a particular effect on variability. For example, we may predict that the effect of a following consonant on a consonant cluster will always be to effect reduction, as opposed to the effect of a following vowel or pause. It appears quite plausible to suggest that some of these effect may be universally predictable. For example, syllable structure and distinctiveness of category, which relate to a general theory of markedness in language, may produce such predictability. Such predictability is, of course, based on the assumptions that it is possible to precisely isolate those factors that do affect variability, and that these isolable factors do conform to general principles of naturalness in language. In actuality, some of the constraining factors that have been isolated in studies of variability do not appear to be sufficiently precise, but this may be attributed to incomplete analyses rather than to a violation of this general principle.[5] Moreover, it is assumed that a chance selection of independent linguistic features will not show the same clear-cut pattern of effect predictability as do those conforming to general conditions of naturalness.

The second aspect of constraint universality, order predictability, refers to the specific hierarchical ordering of constraints. For such ordering to be part of our general theory of optional rules, we must be able to predict not only the effect of the constraint but also how it is ordered with respect to other constraints. For example, we would have to

posit as universals such statements as: The effect of a following consonant/nonconsonant on deletion will always be greater
than that of stress/unstress. It is quite possible to maintain
that effect predictability derives from some universal principle
of our metatheory of language, but that order predictability is
language-specific. This is, of course, an empirical question
that can be answered on the basis of a number of studies of
variability, and a question to which we will return after we
have actually described some aspects of variable speech behavior in PRE.

To sum up our theoretical orientation, the study of PRE is
approached from the viewpoint that variability is an integral
part of a speaker's competence in his language. In order to
account for a speaker's capability in his language, a grammar
must be able to include linguistic factors that favor or inhibit the operation of rules. It must also indicate how these
factors are ordered with respect to each other. For this study,
the frequency of application (either actual or probabilistic)
is not considered as a part of his capability. In the account
that follows, we will look at several aspects of the PRE phonological and grammatical systems. Rather than study many features superficially, we have chosen to look at a small inventory of features in greater detail. In this way, it is hoped
that more general principles of sociolinguistic theory will
emerge. Where appropriate, the independent linguistic constraints on variability that we have discussed in this chapter
are formalized as a part of our representation of PRE. It is
assumed that the reader is familiar with the type of quantifi-
cation techniques typified in Labov (1966a) or Wolfram (1969),
and with the formal representation of variable constraints
suggested by Labov et al. (1968), Labov (1969), and Fasold
(1970, 1972).

NOTES

1. This use of Greek prescripts is not to be confused with the
    use of matching Greek prescripts for paired feature speci-
    fications in generative phonology.

2. In some instances (Loflin 1970, Fickett 1971), it appears
    that the operating principle for determining dialect mixture
    is that any obligatory rule in standard English that would
    have to be considered optional in Black English is dis-
    missed as dialect mixture. Obviously, such a simplistic
    approach cannot help but result in a very distorted picture
    of even the most ideal construct of Black English.

3. DeCamp (1972:87) correctly points out that hypercorrection
    is a concept that is dependent on both sociological and
    linguistic facts.

4. Although more and less variable relationships imply earlier
    and later changes, there are apparently some exceptions to
    this. For a discussion of such exceptions and their impli-
    cations for variable rules, see Fasold (1973).

5. Bickerton (1971) has indicated that it is possible to pick
    out a quite "unlikely" independent linguistic variable and
    demonstrate that it can be ordered in the geometric hier-
    archy of constraints in a regular pattern. We would not,
    however, expect this situation to be typical. My own
    attempts to isolate different types of variable constraints
    certainly do not support the observation that this situ-
    ation is typical. The fact that some constraints may turn
    out to be invalid on the basis of further investigation
    does not necessarily reflect any inherent theoretical
    weakness. At best, it points to a problem of heuristics.

Having presented the sociocultural setting of Puerto Ricans in East Harlem and the linguistic perspective from which we will examine this sociolinguistic situation, we can now turn our attention to some actual speech data. In the following three chapters, we will examine several selected linguistic aspects of the speech of second generation Puerto Ricans. From these descriptive analyses, we will derive general principles that relate to a number of aspects of current sociolinguistics.

Probably the most widely recognized phonological indicators of social status in American English are the interdental fricatives d̠ and θ̠, both of which are represented orthographically by th. Although both the voiceless and the voiced interdentals provide for the study of linguistic variability in PRE, we will restrict discussion here to the voiceless fricative θ̠, represented in words such as think, nothing, and mouth. We are dealing here with a phonological feature that, in one way, is common to many nonstandard varieties of English in the United States. But, in another way, this sociolinguistic variable has realizations that in northern urban contexts are generally considered to be unique to Black English speakers. In order to view the different dimensions of this variable and the way in which it patterns, it is necessary to discuss it in terms of the different positional occurrences of potential θ̠, its standard English correlative.

4.1 Morpheme-initial θ. Labov (1966a), in his study of the
social stratification of English in New York City, demonstrates
that one of the stable sociolinguistic variables for the New
York community as a whole is morpheme-initial θ. The types of
variants that can be identified tend to be common to several
different nonstandard types of American English. The common
phonetic realizations identified in this study include:

       [θ]   an interdental fricative

       [tθ]   an interdental affricate

       [t]   an unaspirated (generally lenis dental) stop

       [t^h]   an aspirated stop

In addition to the variants listed above, we have also
transcribed several instances in which neither an interdental
fricative nor a stop is realized. Instead, we find either s
or ∅, i.e. no phonetic realization. It is important to note,
however, that all of these examples follow a word ending in a
sibilant, as in:

   (1)   a.   [wəz ɛŋkIn] 'was thinking' (27:9)

           b.   [nɛks sɛŋ]   'next thing'   (21:12)

We can anticipate our discussion of progressive assimilation in morpheme-final θ by noting that when morpheme-initial
θ follows a sibilant, it may be assimilated to the sibilant.
In the discussion of the cases of progressive assimilation in
Section 4.2.2, it will be observed that all the examples occur
within external word boundaries. The few examples that we have
here (accounting for less than 10 percent of all potential
instances of θ following s) would seem to indicate that this
assimilation process may, on occasion, be extended across
external word boundaries.

    Of the variants listed above, the nonstigmatized variant
is θ, but it appears that the affricate is also used to a considerable extent in standard English. Labov et al. (1968:92)
consider the affricate to have an "intermediate value" with

respect to social stigmatization. In this study, however, we
will consider θ and tθ to be submembers of the same variant and
will not distinguish between them in our tabulations. This
decision is due primarily to our unreliability in transcribing
the difference between socially significant affrication and the
slight stop onset [^{t}θ] that is almost inevitable before interdental fricatives in certain environments, e.g. following a
pause, following a consonant.

The socially stigmatized variants in American English are
the stops, both the unaspirated lenis dental stop and the
aspirated stop.[1] It is important to note that the phonetic
quality of this stop is generally [-tense], distinguishing it
from the other voiceless stops that are not derived from underlying //θ//. Labov et al. (1968) have formalized both the affrication and the stop realizations of underlying interdental
fricatives variably by the following low-level phonological
rule:

$$\begin{bmatrix} +cons \\ -voc \\ +diff \\ -grave \\ -strid \end{bmatrix} \rightarrow ([\text{-cont}] \ ([\text{+abr off}])) \ / \ \# \ [\alpha \ \overline{voiced}]^2$$

This rule converts the non-strident apical fricatives /θ/
and /ð/ to affricates [-cont], with one input variable,
and as a second option with another input variable, to
the corresponding lenis [-tense] stops. The feature
[+ abrupt offset] seems appropriate here, since we are
dealing with mellow affricates which are not continuants,
but do not have the abrupt offset characteristic of stops.
It is the addition of this feature that converts an affricate into a stop, which is defined by an abrupt onset
and offset. (Labov et al. 1968:99)

One will note that in this formalization of the affricate
aspect of the rule by Labov and his associates, the feature
[-continuant] is considered to be a sufficient specification for
the derivation of the affricated interdental. Since none of the
distinctive feature specifications is adequate to produce this

output, the burden is placed on the nondistinctive specifications for the interdentals, i.e. [abrupt offset]. Only the
redundant feature specifications can prohibit a stop from being the output. This, of course, presumes that the redundant
features are present at this point in the phonological rules.[3]

The second aspect of the rule, as has already been noted,
involves the addition of the feature [abrupt offset]. Labov
et al. (1968), however, do not describe what they consider to
be the exact status of this feature in the phonological description. On the one hand, it may be considered generally to
be a nondistinctive feature that becomes distinctive in a
specific situation in order to derive the proper phonetic output for the stop realization of this rule. On the other hand,
it may be considered to be a distinctive feature that must be
incorporated into the distinctive feature matrix of some nonstandard dialects. In essence, this means that a new systematic phoneme that contrasts with other types of alveolar
stops is being introduced into the lexical representations.
The former alternative, i.e. to allow a nondistinctive feature
to become distinctive, appears to be preferable to the latter
because of the low-level rule involved and the prevailing redundancy of the feature [abrupt offset] for other types of
contrasts in English phonology.

4.1.1 Variant frequency. Having described the variants and
how they have been incorporated into the description of the
nonstandard dialects in which they are found, we can now look
at the actual frequency of the variants. To begin with, we
will look at the incidence of the two main categories:
(1) the interdental fricative or affricate; (2) the stop,
either the aspirated or the unaspirated lenis dental variant.
The frequency of the stop variants (both [t^h] and [t] being
considered as submembers of the same variant) is given in the

following table, comparing the Puerto Rican and black informants.   Examples are taken exclusively from the spontaneous conversation section of the interview, but not more than 25
examples are taken from any one informant.

Table 5.   Comparison of t realization for potential θ in
           morpheme-initial position for Puerto Rican and
           black informants.

	No. t/Total	% t
Puerto Rican	156/542	28.8
Black	49/222	22.1

Table 5 indicates that the incidence of t is higher for
the Puerto Rican group as a whole than for the black group.
A further breakdown of the t variants in terms of the aspirated
and unaspirated realizations reveals that the relative incidence of the unaspirated variant is higher for the Puerto
Ricans than for the blacks: 63 percent of all t occurrences
are unaspirated for the Puerto Rican group, as opposed to 49
percent for the black group.   This seems to be due to a general
pattern of PRE that reflects to some extent the Spanish unaspirated stop realization in initial position.

In Table 5, we looked at the Puerto Rican group as a
whole, but it is also possible to look at the range of t incidence for individuals within the group.

Figure 2 indicates that there is considerable individual
variance in the frequency of t occurrence, ranging from over
50 percent to less than 10 percent.   For other socially stigmatized variants, we might hypothesize that the relatively high
occurrence of the stigmatized variant would correlate with those
informants who have extensive contact with blacks.   But an investigation of the speakers who show the highest incidence of
t does not show this to be the case.

% of t

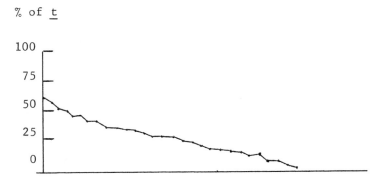

Figure 2.   Rank frequency curve of t realization for
             potential θ in morpheme-initial position
             for Puerto Rican informants.

4.1.2 Constraints on frequency. Two types of environmental

constraints on the incidence of t were examined. First, it

was hypothesized that a preceding consonant, as opposed to a

preceding vowel, might increase the incidence of t.   In

Table 6, the figures are given for both the Puerto Rican and

the black informant groups in these two environments.

Table 6.   Comparison of t realization for potential θ in
            morpheme-initial position or vowel for Puerto Rican
            and black informants.

	C##___	V##___
Puerto Rican		
No. t/Total	66/228	88/298
% t	28.9	29.5
Black		
No. t/Total	18/88	33/121
% t	20.5	27.3

We see that our hypothesis concerning the preceding consonant

is not confirmed in Table 6, at least not for the Puerto

Ricans: That is, no variable constraint based on the preceding segment is apparent.

The second type of environment was delimited on the basis of the nature of the following segment. In English, the morpheme structure sequence rules allow only one consonant to occur following θ, namely, r; otherwise, only vowels can occur. In Table 7, we have divided the following context on the basis of the distinction between r and a vowel. Only those cases of r in which there is actual surface realization of r are tabulated. If the phonetic realization indicates postconsonantal r absence, it is tabulated as if it were followed by a vowel rather than by r.

Table 7. Comparison of t realization for potential θ in morpheme-initial position based on the following segment for Puerto Rican and black informants.

	___r	___V
Puerto Rican		
No. t/Total	59/168	97/374
% t	35.1	25.9
Black		
No. t/Total	14/48	35/174
% t	29.2	20.1

Table 7 indicates that there may be a variable constraint on the incidence of t dependent on whether it is followed by r or by a vowel. However, the relative difference based on the distinction of following environments does not appear to be as clear-cut as some of the other types of linguistic constraints isolated in the discussion. The application of the Chi square test of statistical significance for the two environments among the Puerto Rican informants indicates that this distinction

is significant at the .05 level of confidence. Most clear-cut
constraints on variability show a higher confidence level.
Nonetheless, it appears that a descriptively adequate account
of variation in the interdental fricatives will incorporate
this constraint.

We may then incorporate this constraint, along with Labov's
previously stated variable constraint based on voicing, into
our description of PRE. We conclude that Labov's voicing constraint is the first order constraint and that the following r
is the second order constraint, since an examination of ḏ → d
for several informants indicates that the incidence of ḏ for
potential ḏ is consistently higher than that of t for potential
θ, whether the following segment is a vowel or r: That is,
ḏ → d > θr → tr > θV → tV. The constraint of the following r
applies only to underlying //θ// since the morpheme structure
sequence rules prohibit r following underlying //ḏ//. The distinctive feature specifications from Chomsky and Halle (1968)
will be adopted in our restatement here (and with other rules),
rather than retaining the distinctive features from earlier
versions of generative phonology[4].

(2) $\begin{bmatrix} +cons \\ -voc \\ +cor \\ +ant \\ -strid \end{bmatrix}$ → ([-cont] ([+sim rel])) / ## [A $\overline{vd}$] [B cons]

In the formalization given in (2), capital Greek letters are
used for variable constraints instead of the small Greek letters
used by Labov (1969) or the integers suggested by Fasold (1970).
This avoids the ambiguous usage of Greek letters pointed out by
Fasold (1970:557), while maintaining the notion of variability
conventionally implied by the Greek letters[5].

In the specification of the following constraint on t, it
should be noted that it is sufficient to state the environment
as consonantal, since the morpheme structure sequence rules

automatically eliminate the occurrence of any consonant other
than r. It is also interesting to note two facts about the
phonetic realizations of t and r in this sequence: First, the
overwhelming majority (90 percent) of t realizations preceding
r is unaspirated. Second, the predominant phonetic realization
of r in this environment is a flap; thus, the usual phonetic
realization is:

    (3) a. [třu] 'through' (7:4)

          b. [tři] 'three' (10:2)

The overwhelming incidence here of the unaspirated variant
seems to be due to the flap realization of r, since we do not
generally get examples of an aspirated variant when the flap
occurs, as in (4).

    (4) *[t^{h}řu]   'through'

The aspirated variant tends to occur almost exclusively with
nonflap realizations of r, as in (5).

    (5) [t^{h}rowIn] 'throwing' (26:4)

    It seems most reasonable to attribute the overwhelming
use of the unaspirated stop and flap to its identity with the
common Spanish phonological sequence [tř], as in [třes] or
[třagar]. Other nonstandard varieties of English may sometimes use the same [tř] sequence, but one would not expect it
to occur with the same relative frequency. (The limited examples from our black informants indicate that it occurs in
less than 50 percent of all tr clusters derived from //θ// .)

4.2 Morpheme-final θ. The variants that can be isolated for
morpheme-final potential θ show considerable divergence from
the variants discussed in our previous section on morpheme-
initial θ. This difference is manifested in both the phonetic
realizations and the frequency ratios of the several variants.

    In Table 8, the distribution of variants in morpheme-final
position is given, excluding the item with which will be

discussed in Section 4.2.5. The figures, given for the Puerto
Rican informants as a group, represent examples taken only
from the spontaneous conversation section of the interview.

Table 8.   Distribution of variants for potential θ in morpheme-
            final position for Puerto Rican informants.

Variant	Phonetic Realization	No.	% of Total
θ	[θ] [tθ]	56	38.1
f	[f]	64	43.5
t	[t˥] [ʔ] [ť]	4	2.7
∅	No phonetic realization, assimilated fricative [f] [s] [š]	18	12.2
s	[s] [z] when not followed by a sibilant	5	3.4
Total		147	

As is indicated, the most common variant is f, but the
incidences of both θ and f rank considerably above the other
variants, accounting for over 80 percent of all cases. Because
of the various phonological processes needed to account for the
variants, each variant will be discussed individually.

4.2.1 The incidence of s. Of the variants that we have delimited above, one that is quite predictable from Puerto Rican
Spanish is s. A Puerto Rican Spanish speaker learning English
will often use s as a correspondent for standard English θ, so
that tooth and both may be realized as [tus] and [bos] respectively. It would thus appear that those few instances of s that
cannot be attributed to the assimilation of θ to a following
fricative (see Section 4.2.2) can be explained as a type of
"vestigial interference". We have deliberately used the term
vestigial interference to refer to the relative infrequency of

interference phenomena that may be expected to occur with some
degree of regularity at some stages in the acquisition of
another language.

In the case of Puerto Rican Spanish speakers learning
English, final θ may commonly be realized as s because of the
failure to keep the two rule systems disjunctive. But speakers
who have merged systems with respect to this phonological rule
may be expected to use s considerably more frequently than the
3.4 percent that is actually observed in our corpus. Presumably
as a speaker acquires genuine competence over the rules of two
languages disjunctively, the incidence of s for θ will be reduced accordingly. At the point that it becomes infrequent
enough statistically to fall into the range of chance occurrence, i.e. it occurs in less than 5 percent of all potential
places in which it might legitimately occur, we may say that,
for all practical purposes, the speaker has a disjunctive competence[6].

However, when occasional lapses indicate incomplete disjunction, it seems appropriate to speak of vestigial interference. Ultimately, of course, the definition of such a
concept is a statistical one, relying on the validity of our
cutoff point as an indication of rule disjunction between two
languages or dialects. What is essential to note here is that
our second generation Puerto Rican informants have not as a
group established the incidence of s as a correspondent for
standard English θ in morpheme-final position. In a statistical idealization of our group, it seems reasonable to dismiss it, since only a small minority of informants uses it at
all.

With respect to those informants who show some incidence
of s, however, we may raise the question of how habitualized
it is in their speech. If we find that there is a substantial
frequency of s occurrence for these informants, we may want to

postulate that there is one variety of PRE in which s has been
incorporated as an integral part of the dialect. But when we
look at the four informants who account for the few examples
of s, we find that they use it in only 13.5 percent of all
potential cases. The relative infrequency of its usage by
only a small minority of the Puerto Rican informants would
thus appear to justify our categorization of the s variant as
a matter of vestigial interference. But this does not necessarily mean that no rule should be posited for those speakers
who do use it. An adequate representation of this minority
variety of PRE would have to account for the occurrence of s
as long as it is realized at a frequency level that cannot be
dismissed as incidental.

4.2.2 The incidence of ∅. Unlike the s variant, which we
dismissed as outside of the rules that we will need to account
for our data in some reasonable way, ∅ is realized at a frequency level (12.2 percent) that cannot be dismissed quite as
readily. In all but one instance, ∅ occurs when followed by a
consonant across either an internal or an external word boundary. Thus, it would appear that its incidence, at least when
it is followed by a consonant, must be accounted for in the
phonological rules we must posit to describe this dialect
adequately.

     We will not be concerned here with the single rare in-
stance of ∅ (less than 5 percent) for potential θ followed by
a nonconsonantal environment. Instead, we will concentrate
our attention on those instances in which θ is followed by a
consonant, in order to determine what it is about the nature
of consonants that may cause the surface realization of //θ//
to be ∅.

     In order to understand the increased incidence of ∅
realization before words that begin with a consonant, it is

necessary to look more closely at the nature of assimilation in
both standard English and various nonstandard dialects of English. In casual style, //θ// may assimilate to the following
consonant if it is a voiceless fricative:

(6)   a.   [kʰip yɝ maº šət][7]   'Keep your mouth shut'

       b.   [hi hæz ə maº fɝ ɛvri   'He has a mouth for every

           əkʰeIž̵ɨn]   occasion'

       c.   [hIz tʰi sim yɛlə]   'His teeth seem yellow'

Although we have not done a rigorous frequency tabulation,
it is quite clear that the assimilation process is more common
before the sibilants [s] and [š] than it is before the labio-
dental fricative [f]. Phonetically this might be expected because of the tongue's involvement with [s] and [š] and its non-
involvement with [f]. We will return to this apparent variable
constraint later in our discussion.

In the above examples, only voiceless fricatives are given
as the relevant context for effecting assimilation. Voiced
fricatives do <u>not</u> effect such assimilation:

(7)   a.   *[kʰip yɝ maº zIpt]   'Keep your mouth zipped'

       b.   *[kʰip yɝ maº vɛri   'Keep your mouth very

           stIl]   still'

       c.   *[hi hæz ə maº dæt   'He has a mouth that moves

           muvz ɔl də tʰaem]   all the time'

       d.   *[ši hæz ə maº ža ža   'She has a mouth Zsa Zsa

           gəbɔr wʊd ɛnvi]   Gabor would envy'

Given the fact that the assimilation does not operate when
the following fricative is voiced, the rule just for θ would
have to be written as:[8]

$$(8) \quad \theta \rightarrow \left(\begin{bmatrix} \alpha\text{strid} \\ \beta\text{cor} \\ \gamma\text{ant} \end{bmatrix} \right) \ / \ \underline{\qquad} \ \#\!\!\# \ \begin{bmatrix} -\text{voc} \\ +\text{cont} \\ -\text{vd} \\ \alpha\text{strid} \\ \beta\text{cor} \\ \gamma\text{ant} \end{bmatrix}$$

Although θ̱ cannot be assimilated before a voiced fricative,
as illustrated in (7), there is a voiceless assimilation rule
that may apply to voiced fricatives following a voiceless
fricative to make them voiceless. And if this rule applies,
changing the underlying voiced fricatives to their voiceless
counterparts, θ̱ is then subject to the fricative assimilation
rule. Thus, sentences like the following seem to be quite
acceptable in an allegro style of· standard English:

(9) a. [kʰip yɝ maᵒ sIpt]   'Keep your mouth zipped'

     b. [hi hæz ə maᵒ θæt goᵁz   'He has a mouth that
          ɔl ɖə tʰaᵉm]   goes all the time'

     c. [kʰip yɝ maᵒ fɛri stIl]   'Keep your mouth very
                                     still'

The acceptability of sentences like (9) can be best explained in terms of a sequence of two rules: one that assimilates following voiced fricatives to voicelessness when following voiceless fricatives, and Rule (8), discussed above.
The voiceless assimilation rule covering fricatives may be
written as:

$$(10) \quad \begin{bmatrix} \text{-voc} \\ \text{+cont} \\ \alpha\text{ant} \\ \beta\text{cor} \\ \gamma\text{strid} \end{bmatrix} \rightarrow ([\text{-voice}]) \ / \ \begin{bmatrix} \text{-voc} \\ \text{+cont} \\ \text{-vd} \\ \alpha\text{ant} \\ \beta\text{cor} \\ \gamma\text{strid} \end{bmatrix} \ \#\# \ \underline{\qquad}$$

Presumably, the rule for standard English voiceless assimilation
would have to be more general, e.g. to account for assimilation
of noncontinuant voiceless consonants, but for our purposes
here, we will be satisfied with the less general version.

In addition to the regressive assimilation, i.e. the assimilated sound precedes the conditioning sound, which we have
discussed above with reference to //θ// in standard English, it
is important to note one type of progressive assimilation,
namely, when //θ// follows the sibilant s̱. Thus, the assimilation

of //θ// in an item like <u>sixth</u> must be accounted for by the preceding <u>s</u>:

(11) a. [sIKs $t^h a^e m$]   'sixth time'

      b. [sIKs æpəl]   'sixth apple'

This assimilation must be considered as peculiar to sibilants,
since a preceding <u>f</u> assimilates to the <u>θ</u> in standard English,
rather than the assimilating <u>θ</u> to <u>f</u>, so that we have:

(12) a. [fIθ $t^h a^e m]^\vartheta$ 'fifth time'

      b. [fIθ æpəl]   'fifth apple'

Therefore, we must posit a rule in standard English to
account for (11) but not (12):

$$(13)\quad \theta \to ([+strid]) \quad / \begin{bmatrix} -voc \\ +strid \\ +cor \end{bmatrix} \; \# \; \underline{\hspace{2cm}}$$

In addition to the frequent application of this progressive
sibilant assimilation rule within word boundaries, we have
noted in (1) that it occasionally operates across external
word boundaries.

Up to this point, it has been implicit that sentences
such as (6) are the result of two processes: First, there is
an assimilation process that operates to make <u>θ</u> identical to
certain fricatives in certain types of environments; then,
there is a rule that deletes one of the members in a geminate
consonant cluster. Thus, in order to get at the actual surface
realization of the sentences in (6), there is a gemination reduction rule that operates on the output of Rule (8). Assuming
that this rule is needed elsewhere in the grammar, it might be
given informally as:

(14) C → ∅ / ___ an identical C

In the ordered sequence of rules, this must obviously follow
Rule (8).

What are the reasons, then, for suggesting that the phonetic realizations in (6) are products of assimilation and

subsequent deletion of geminate consonants? In justification
of our interpretation here, there are several specific observations concerning the data and some general principles of language processes that can be cited. In the first place, there
are instances in which some phonetic basis for considering
these as the result of assimilation may occur. In some instances, there may be the vestige of a phonetically lengthened
fricative. Thus, the sibilant in sixth can sometimes be perceived to be lengthened:

(15) a. [sIKs: $t^h a^e m$]   'sixth time'

b. [sIKs: æpəl]   'sixth apple'

This phonetic lengthening fluctuates with the nonlengthened
realizations given previously in (11). Thus, Rule (14) is not
obligatory. Also, in the case of assimilation across external
word boundaries, there are instances in which a perceived onset
of the word occurs during the duration of the fricative, so
that a careful phonetic transcription of items like mouth shut
and ninth street might be:

(16) a. [ma^{o}š 'šət]   'mouth shut'

b. [nə^{e}ns 'strit]^{10} 'ninth street'

Although this type of phonetic vestige is admittedly present
in only a small minority of cases of allegro style, an assimilation process seems to be the most reasonable way of handling
this phenomenon.

In further defense of our interpretation of θ absence as
assimilation followed by deletion rather than simply as deletion,
we can note the natural differences between assimilation and
deletion as language processes. Assimilation tends to be
restricted in terms of specific environments in which it can
take place. When we look at the above case, we see that the
∅ realization for θ is almost exclusively restricted to following fricatives. Because of the natural class relationship of
θ to other fricatives, we may expect this to be assimilation

within a natural class. But when we look at deletion as a
process, we typically find the relevant environments for deletion to be more general. For example, in studies of word-final
consonant cluster reduction, e.g. tes' case for test case, we
find that deletion is affected to some extent by any obstruent,
nasal or lateral, and to some extent by other sounds as well.
This is not to say that the delineation of different types of
consonantal environments will not show some effect on the variability of reduction, for this is certainly the case in many
instances. One does note, however, that the differences in
consonantal effect tend to be gradient rather than sharp.
Thus, if we look at consonant cluster reduction before words
beginning with consonants (Wolfram 1969:62), we note that while
all consonants effect reduction to some extent, certain consonants may effect it more than others. This seems to be the
way in which deletion processes generally operate.

Assimilation and subsequent deletion as language processes
tend to show the mutually exclusive type of distribution that
we have observed here. Therefore, even if our claim that there
are sequences like (15) and (16) were to be disputed on empirical grounds, we would still be inclined to suggest that the
interpretation given above is a natural solution in terms of
how we can expect languages to operate.

Finally, phonetic sequences such as θs or sθ appear to
involve a transition that may be difficult to maintain for
physiological reasons, thus resulting in a tendency toward
assimilation. Although this, in itself, may not be the type
of formal evidence on which we can base our entire solution,
it does tend to reinforce our interpretation as the correct
solution to the $\emptyset$ realization of θ for standard English.

With our above discussion concerning the nature of //θ//
assimilation in standard English in mind, we can now return
to the cases of $\emptyset$ realization that we have encountered with

our Puerto Rican informants. Is this exactly the same type of
phenomenon as that which we observe in standard English, or is
it different? To begin with, we note that over 70 percent of
all occurrences of potential θ before the fricatives f̲, s̲, and
š̲ are absent; when just sibilants are considered, it is over
90 percent. When we compare these figures with the figures
for nonfricative consonants (including obstruents and sonor-
ants), we find the contrast quite apparent: The realization
of ∅ before nonfricative consonants is less than 5 percent.
This plainly indicates that the assimilation process that we
have observed for standard English is very much operative for
this variety of English as well.

The limited instances of ∅ before nonfricative consonants
are given below:

(17) a. [ne^{I}mI wəz]   'Namath was'   (14:2)

      b. [č^{h}ru də]   'truth the'   (23:3)

      c. [č^{h}ru ma^e]   'truth my'   (23:6)

      d. [ma^o wəz]   'mouth was'   (27:12)

      e. [ma^o yɨ no^U]   'mouth you
                                       know'   (34:7)

      f. [bo^U hæv]   'both have'   (38:3)

      g. [ne^{I}mI wəz]   'Namath was'   (39:2)

No clear-cut conditioning for ∅ realization is apparent
in the above list. These examples seem to be relatively rare
cases of the deletion of θ before nonfricative consonants,
rather than cases of an extended assimilation process in PRE.
With the possible exception of following labials, where 4 of
17 cases of potential θ are absent, the rarity of ∅ before
nonfricative consonants does not appear to be an integral part
of the phonological processes of the variety(s) of English
spoken by our Puerto Rican informants. Even in the case of
following labials, however, the paucity of examples does not
allow us to make a strong case for a regular phonological
process that deletes or assimilates underlying //θ// before w̲.

Our conclusion, then, is that the nonstandard variety(s)
of English spoken by our Puerto Rican informants simply shares
the assimilation rule for final θ that exists for standard and
other nonstandard varieties of English. The few examples of
∅ before nonfricative consonants do not figure prominently in
our interpretation, since rare cases of deletion may be matters
of performance rather than competence. In standard English,
the assimilation rule operates on a segment when it is followed
by a fricative or preceded by a sibilant. The same type of
constraint appears to operate for this nonstandard dialect in
that assimilation occurs with considerably greater frequency
when the following morpheme begins with a sibilant, as opposed
to a labio-dental fricative.

If we conclude that the frequency difference between
labio-dental fricatives and sibilants is to be incorporated
into our variable rule, we are faced with an interesting problem concerning the conventions for stating variable rules.
Instead of the statement of the rule as in (8), we will need
to state the environment disjunctively, specifying f as

$$
\begin{bmatrix} -\text{strid} \\ -\text{cor} \\ +\text{ant} \end{bmatrix} \text{ and } \underline{s} \text{ and } \underline{\check{s}} \text{ as } \begin{bmatrix} +\text{strid} \\ +\text{cor} \\ \alpha\text{ant} \end{bmatrix} \text{ if we are to build}
$$

the variability factor into the rule. Because we must specify
the environment for the rule as at least partially disjunctive,
we can no longer retain our matching + or - values indicated
by the Greek prescripts in Rule (8). Traditionally, the Greek
prescripts are used to indicate some matching variable co-
efficient somewhere in the rule. Now, if we are to retain the
generality of the assimilation rule for fricatives, while incorporating our variable constraint for the frequency difference between labio-dentals and sibilants, we can do so only by
establishing a slightly different convention for the use of
the Greek prescripts under certain conditions. The convention

change that we suggest here in order to retain the rule output
as originally postulated may be stated as follows:

> If a rule has an environment E with disjunctive sub-
> parts E_1 and E_2, where E_1 and E_2 contain opposite
> signs for the same feature $\underline{X}$ (say, $+\underline{X}$ in E_1 and $-\underline{X}$
> in E_2) and the rule specifies that feature $\underline{X}$ in the
> segment undergoing change assimilates to the value
> of $\underline{X}$ in E_1 if E_1 is present and to the value of $\underline{X}$
> in E_2 if E_2 is present, then feature $\underline{X}$ in the seg-
> ment to the immediate right of the arrow will be
> marked with a Greek letter prescript (say, $\alpha\underline{X}$)
> which is to be interpreted as having the value of
> $\underline{X}$ in E_1 ($+\underline{X}$) if E_1 is present and the value of $\underline{X}$
> in E_2 ($-\underline{X}$) if E_2 is present.[11]

Adopting this convention change will allow us to state the
rule, with the variable constraint for labio-dentals and sibilants, as:

$$(18) \quad \theta \rightarrow \left(\begin{bmatrix} \alpha ant \\ \beta cor \\ \gamma strid \end{bmatrix} \right) / \underline{\hspace{2cm}} \#\# \begin{bmatrix} -voc \\ +cont \\ -vd \\ \left\{ \begin{matrix} A \begin{bmatrix} \alpha ant \\ +cor \\ +strid \end{bmatrix} \\ \begin{bmatrix} +ant \\ -cor \\ -strid \end{bmatrix} \end{matrix} \right\} \end{bmatrix}$$

In the above convention, the capital Greek letter $\underline{A}$ indicates
that $\underline{s}$ and $\underline{\check{s}}$ can be expected to undergo the assimilation process more regularly than $\underline{f}$. It is noted here that the constraint refers to the entire feature matrix rather than simply
to one feature. In Labov et al.'s (1968) original formulation,
it was used only with reference to single features. However,
inasmuch as it is necessary to distinguish certain logically

related units by more than one feature, this seems to be an
inevitable extension of variable marking.

Before concluding our discussion of ∅ surface realizations,
it is necessary to point out that the assimilation process we
have been discussing must operate on underlying //θ// for those
speakers who have the θ → f rule (see Section 4.2.3) in certain
environments. To put it another way, it must be applied before
underlying //θ// has been changed to f. This conclusion is based
on the fact that this variety, like standard English, does not
permit assimilation of f to sibilants. Thus, examples like
*[læ so] 'laugh so' and *[ɔ so] 'off so' are not found in our
corpus, just as they are not typically found in standard English. An examination of the speech of 10 informants indicates
that there are no examples of assimilation or loss of underlying //f// before sibilants. In order to disallow the assimilation of underlying //f// before sibilants while permitting the
assimilation of underlying //θ//, we must apply the assimilation
rule to //θ// before it is changed to f. A generative phonological rule can operate only on the output of all previous
rules, so that once θ becomes f, all subsequent rules must
operate on all f's, regardless of their derivational history.

4.2.3 <u>The incidence of f</u>. Having accounted for the ∅ surface
realizations for potential θ, let us now turn our attention to
the incidence of f realization. Of the socially stigmatized
variants, f occurs by far the most frequently. In looking at
the source for this variant, we must first rule out the matter
of language interference from Spanish. As we have seen earlier,
for Spanish speakers the expected interference variant for
standard English θ is generally s. But this variant is seen
to occur very infrequently. In accounting for f, therefore,
it is reasonable to turn to the structure of Black English,
in which it is the most common correspondent for standard English θ in morpheme-final position. The following table compares

the incidence of the variants for the Puerto Rican and the
black informants:

Table 9. Comparison of variants for potential θ in morpheme-
final position for Puerto Rican and black informants.

Variant	Puerto Rican		Black	
	No.	% of Total	No.	% of Total
θ	56	38.1	8	16.3
f	64	43.5	36	73.5
t	4	2.7	2	4.1
∅	18	12.2	3	6.1
s	5	3.4	-	-
Total	147		49	

The above table clearly indicates the increased incidence of the
θ variant when the Puerto Rican group as a whole is compared
with the black group.

   We can, however, look more closely at the type of distribution that is found for a number of the Puerto Rican informants.
In the following rank frequency curve, the relative incidence of
f for θ is shown for the 12 Puerto Rican informants who have at
least 5 examples of potential θ in their interview (excluding
the item with).

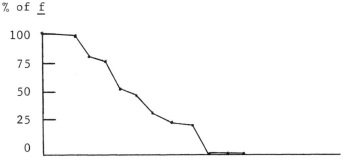

Figure 3. Rank frequency curve of f realization for poten-
           tial θ in morpheme-final position for Puerto
           Rican informants.

Figure 3 indicates a complete range of f frequency among
our Puerto Rican informants. At the upper end of the scale are
two informants who show the categorical presence of f in morpheme-final position, while at the lower end are three informants who reveal the categorical presence of θ. Because of
this distribution, it is instructive to look briefly at the
informants who reveal categoricality at either end.

The two informants who show the categorical use of f in
morpheme-final position have extensive contacts with blacks.
Consideration of the ethnic identity of their peers and our
observations of their social contacts all testify to this.
On the other hand, the three informants who reveal the categorical presence of θ do not show this type of social interaction. In fact, two of the informants (who are brothers)
relate in their interviews that they have little peer contact
with blacks. The third informant has a minority of black
peers, but he cannot be considered to have the extensive types
of contacts that are characteristic of the two informants who
reveal the categoricality of f. Thus, looking at the linguistic distribution and the social characteristics of informants
who represent the two ends of the linguistic continuum, we are
led to hypothesize that the frequency of f is a function of
the extent of black contacts because of the integral role of
f in Black English. This hypothesis can be tested by comparing 10 black informants (BL), those Puerto Rican informants
who have extensive black contacts (PR/BL), and those Puerto
Ricans who have limited black contacts (PR).

The distribution of f realization in Table 10 is quite
straightforward, and our hypothesis is confirmed. The Puerto
Ricans with extensive black contacts match (in fact, they exceed, but not to any significant degree) the extent of f
realization found among the black informants, while the Puerto
Ricans with limited black contacts reveal significantly less f
realization than either of the other groups.

Table 10. Comparison of f̲ realization for potential θ̲ in
           morpheme-final position for BL, PR/BL, and
           PR informants.

Informants (No.)	No. f	No. θ	% f
BL (10)	36	8	81.8
PR/BL (6)	20	3	87.0
PR (23)	53	44	54.6

At this point, we must turn to the descriptive account of
f̲ as a correspondent of standard English θ̲ in morpheme-final
position for those Puerto Rican speakers who reveal this variant.
Previous discussion of morpheme-final [f] as a correspondent of
standard English [θ] (for Black English) have concluded that
some cases of [f] must be derived from underlying //θ// on the
basis that only [f] derived from underlying //θ// can alternate
with [t] in its surface realization. Fasold notes:

> ...we see that there is indeed a contrast between
> the [f] which matches Standard English [θ], and
> the [f] which matches Standard English [f]. In
> certain situations, words with word-final [f] in
> Black English are pronounced with a [t]. Consider
> the two sentences:
>
> > Get off my bike!
> > Come back with my bike!
>
> One possible Black English pronunciation of these
> sentences is:
>
> > [gɪt ɔf ma bayk]
> > [kəm bæk wɪf ma bayk]
>
> In rapid speech, the [f] in 'with' can be pro-
> nounced as [t], but not the [f] in 'off':
>
> > *[gɪt ɔt ma bayk]
> > [kəm bæk wɪt ma bayk]
>
> It is necessary, then, before the phonological
> rules apply, to designate which kind of [f] is
> which. Given the system of English phonology,
> it can be shown fairly convincingly that the

> appropriate segment to represent the underlying
> final consonant of 'with' is)θ(, even if it is
> never so pronounced. (Fasold 1969b:78-79)

Wolfram supports the same position for the identical formal

reasons, when he says:

> What is clear, then, is that it is necessary to
> postulate two underlying sources for the surface
> realization of [f] in Black English; one of
> these can be alternately realized as [t] in
> certain environments, while the other cannot.
> (Wolfram 1970:9)

Although the alternation of [f] with [t] is part of the

formal evidence for the postulation of underlying //θ// in some

lexical items, that postulation is still restricted to those

examples in which this type of alternation actually occurs.

For those forms not revealing this alternation, and these are

in the majority, it has been suggested that the generative

phonological rule should be written in such a way that only

the features shared by f and θ are specified. This can be

stated by the following rule:

$$(19) \quad \begin{bmatrix} -voc \\ +cont \\ +ant \\ -strid \\ -vd \end{bmatrix}^{12} \rightarrow ([-cor]) \, / \, \underline{\qquad} \#\#$$

Fasold concludes that:

> The answer to the specification problem is to
> specify...the fricatives in words in which t
> is observed in allegro speech as θ, and to
> partially specify the fricatives in morpheme-
> final position in all other words. (Fasold
> 1967:4-5)

Although the evidence from t and f alternation is correct,

this type of alternation is actually observed in a restricted

number of items, e.g. the unstressed preposition with, θ follow-

ing a nasal, etc. This leaves the majority of items as un-

specified with respect to underlying //f// or //θ// if we look at

formal motivation. (Other reasons for considering them all as θ have been given, but these do not hold the same weight as the formal motivation we are talking about here.)

When we look at it more closely, we find that there is another type of alternation that extends the motivation for the full specification of θ in morpheme-final position. This alternation is related to the assimilation of θ when the following segment begins with a sibilant. We have observed that when a morpheme-final θ is followed by a morpheme or a word beginning with a fricative, particularly a sibilant, the θ may assimilate, as in the sentences in (6). Now, when the underlying form is //f//, the assimilation process does not apply, so that we get:

(20) a. [kʰip ræ°f šət əp]   'Keep Ralph shut up'

b. [tʰɝn ɔf sɛsəmi   'Turn off Sesame Street'
strit]

The following alternations appear to be unacceptable for both standard and nonstandard dialect speakers:

(21) a. *[kʰip ræ° šət əp]   'Keep Ralph shut up'

b. *[tʰɝn ɔ sɛsəmi   'Turn off Sesame Street'
strit]

When we look at our speakers who use morpheme-final [f] as a correspondent for standard English [θ], we still find that they undergo the assimilation process that operates only when //θ// is the underlying form. Since we can construct the sort of environment in which //θ// undergoes assimilation for practically any word-final instance of underlying //θ//, there is no reason to believe that any rule input should remain partially unspecified in this position. We thus conclude that Fasold's (1967) decision to leave some instances of morpheme-final [f] as the realization of a segment that is not fully specified as θ cannot be justified. The rule must have as its input fully specified //θ// instead of the partial specification given in Rule (19).

Up until now, we have discussed the incidence of f and θ

in morpheme-final position as if the only constraint on the
incidence of f is nonlinguistic, i.e. a function of peer contact with blacks. But our investigation of a number of phonological variables has indicated that for practically all instances of f, there is some independent linguistic constraint
on variability. One of the very common constraints indicated
by previous studies is whether the following morpheme (either
within or across external word boundaries) begins with a vowel
or a nonvowel, i.e. a consonant or a pause. We may investigate the possible influence of this constraint in the following
table:

Table 11.   Comparison of f realization for potential θ in
            vocalic and nonvocalic environments for Puerto
            Rican and black informants.

	V				-V			
	f	%f	θ	%θ	f	%f	θ	%θ
Puerto Rican	14	58.3	10	41.7	50	52.1	46	47.9
Black	16	88.9	2	11.1	20	76.9	6	23.1

Although there is a slight increase of θ for both groups when
the following environment is nonvocalic, the variable does not
show the clear-cut conditioning on variability that other variables have had on the basis of this distinction: That is, no
statistical significance can be demonstrated on the basis of
the difference between these environments.

     One environment that previous studies have indicated is
significant for the variability of f and θ realizations is the
distinction between morpheme-medial and morpheme-final positions
Wolfram's study (1969:89) reveals that f is used approximately
twice as frequently in morpheme-final position as it is in
morpheme-medial position. The following table reveals the difference between f realizations in morpheme-medial and -final
positions, again including the black informants for comparison:[1]

Table 12.   Comparison of f realization for potential θ in
             morpheme-medial and morpheme-final positions for
             Puerto Rican and black informants.

	Morpheme-Medial	Morpheme-Final
Puerto Rican		
No. of f/Total	12/50	64/110
% f	24.0	58.2
Black		
No. f/Total	3/15	36/44
% f	20.0	81.8

The difference between the two environments is quite evident,
the morpheme-final position clearly favoring the incidence of
f.

This sort of obvious constraint on variability can then
be incorporated into Rule (19) which we posited earlier for
θ → f. This rule can now be reformalized as:

(22)   θ → (f) / ___A#

In this way, we can account for the observed variability that
we find in our corpus.

4.2.4 The incidence of t. Apart from the incidence of t in
with and nothing, which we will consider in more detail below,
the occurrence of t for potential θ in morpheme-medial and
-final positions is infrequent. Because of its low frequency,
i.e. less than 3 percent when all morpheme-medial and -final
occurrences of potential θ are considered, we may ask if this
is, in fact, a legitimate variant that must be described as an
integral part of the dialect. Wolfram's (1969:87) study of the
θ variable for black speakers in Detroit revealed that t tends
to be conditioned by its contiguity to a nasal segment, in both
morpheme-medial and -final positions. Thus, in words like

arithmetic and month, underlying //θ// can be realized as t.

The actual occurrence of these types of environments is restricted in our spontaneous conversation section of the interview, so that our data from this style are inconclusive. However, in order to compensate for the paucity of examples with potential θ contiguous to a nasal in this style, the items month and arithmetic were given as a part of the word list reading section of the interview. Although this represents a different style, it is instructive to look at the distribution of variants for these two items in the reading lists.

Table 13. Distribution of variants for potential θ contiguous to a nasal for Puerto Rican and black informants.

Variant	Puerto Rican	Black
θ	26	11
f	4	6
t	13	5
Ø	1	-

The incident of t as a legitimate variant is clearly indicated in Table 13. For the Puerto Rican group, even in a very formal style, t is realized in over 29 percent of all cases. This observation clearly attests to the validity of a rule that might be represented as:

(23) θ → (t) /[+nas][14]

Now, it is important to note here that we are positing a rule that accounts for a relatively infrequent variant when the overall incidence of t is considered. In our discussion of the s variant, which occurred at approximately the same frequency level as t in our overall tabulation, we conclude that it is not an integral part of the dialect we are describing. The difference between the infrequency of s and that of t lies in the

fact that the overall infrequency of t is simply a function of
the failure to isolate environments that would raise its incidence to a level of accountability, i.e. it must be included
in our formal description of a native speaker's competence.
But in the case of s, the delimitation of natural types of
environmental differences that might raise its incidence to
the level of accountability did not appreciably increase its
incidence. Low overall frequency, in itself, is not a valid
reason for dismissing certain types of potential variants that
may have to be described as an integral part of a given dialect.

While we have seen that the delimitation of a contiguous
nasal may effect a rule such as $\theta \rightarrow t$, we still have not accounted for several examples of t for potential θ. Do we need
to extend our rule to account for two examples of teeth and
mouth as [t^{h}it] and [ma^{o}t] respectively? A close look at the
natural types of environments that might account for this
realization does not show an appreciable increase in its incidence: It is still realized in less than 5 percent of all
potential occurrences[15] It is, therefore, our cautious conclusion that the t variant for these items is not an integral
part of the dialect, i.e. it might be a performance error of
some type or vestigial interference since Spanish speakers may
also use t for θ. Based on this conclusion, it need not be
accounted for by the rules of the dialect, although there is a
clear-cut need for the $\theta \rightarrow t$ rule contiguous to nasals. This
may appear to be an arbitrary statistical decision, but we
must mention that the distinction between competence and performance can only be determined statistically in some cases
in which the actual speech of a spontaneous conversation provides our primary data.

Having established the effect of nasals on t realization
on the basis of our previous discussion, we can now turn to
the incidence of t in the item nothing. Of the variants that

have been observed for this item (t̲, ∅̲, θ̲, and f̲), t̲ is the
most frequent, occurring in 47 percent of all cases (40 of 85)
for the Puerto Rican informants and in 64 percent of all cases
(29 of 45) for the black informants. Although nothing does
not have an immediately contiguous nasal in the underlying
representation that will need to be posited, i.e. //nəθIŋ//,
it is observed that there is a noncontiguous nasal in the
following syllable. And when we look at the phonetic realization of this item, we observe that the actual phonetic environment is a contiguous syllabic nasal. Thus, the most
frequent phonetic form for t̲ (or the phonetic alternate [ʔ]
or [t˺]) is:

    (24) a. [nət˺ṇ]

          b. [nəʔṇ]

We do not get:

          c. *[nətən]

          d. *[nəʔən]

    The fact that (24a) and (24b) are, for the clear majority
of informants, the only types of the form that occur makes it
reasonable to suggest that for most speakers, Rule (23), which
changes θ̲ → t̲, actually operates after the nasal has been
placed immediately contiguous to underlying //θ//. This means
that the vowel centralization rule (Rule 25), which changes
I̲ → ə̲, and the subsequent rule for schwa deletion (Rule 26) in
this sort of environment must precede Rule (23): That is,
I̲ → ə̲ and ə̲ → ∅̲ must come before θ̲ → t̲. Eliminating details
irrelevant for our discussion here, the rules for vowel centralization and schwa deletion might be approximated as:

$$(25)\quad \begin{bmatrix} -stress \\ -tense \\ V \end{bmatrix} \rightarrow ə$$

$$(26)\quad ə \rightarrow (∅) \; / \begin{bmatrix} +cons \\ -nas \end{bmatrix} \begin{bmatrix} \underline{\qquad} \\ -stress \end{bmatrix} [+nas]^{16}$$

For some reference to the sorts of environmental constraints that will have to be built into a more accurate statement of this rule, see Bailey (1969a).[17] I have here simply
followed William K. Riley's observation (personal communication) that syllabication for nasals can occur following practically all consonants in casual style, although there is considerable variability in the syllabication depending on the
type of consonant.

4.2.5 _The case of with_. Finally, we must discuss the incidence of variants for the item _with_, since the realization of
some of the variants in this item appears to operate differently from those in our previous account. The following table
compares the incidence of variants for _with_ for the Puerto
Rican and the black groups of informants:

Table 14. Distribution of variants for potential θ in _with_
           for Puerto Rican and black informants.

Variant	Puerto Rican		Black	
	No.	% of Total	No.	% of Total
t	150	59.5	62	63.9
∅	64	25.4	17	17.5
θ[18]	24	9.5	6	6.2
f	14	5.6	12	12.4
Total	252		97	

The above table indicates that all the main variants that we
delimited at the beginning of our discussion for medial and
final potential θ are realized by both groups. The general
incidence, furthermore, indicates that t and ∅ are the most
frequently occurring variants.

     Before discussing the conditions for the incidence of t
and ∅ in this item, it should be noted that there is an

additional subvariant of t which we have not discussed previously, namely, [č]. This is observed in contexts such as:

    (27) a.   [wɪč yə]   'with you' (9:8)

          b.   [wɪč yə]   'with you' (10:10)

The realization [č] can be accounted for by a palatalization
rule when t occurs preceding a word (generally unstressed)
beginning with y, and is not necessarily restricted to the
item with. We thus get:

    (28) a.   [bɔč yɝ šuz]   'bought your shoes'

          b.   [bɪč yɝ hænd]   'bit your hand'

    The palatalization rule, which operates for both voiced
alveolar stops, e.g. [dɪǰ yə] 'did you', and voiceless alveolar
stops, e.g. (28), may be given as:

$$(29) \quad \begin{bmatrix} -\text{voc} \\ -\text{cont} \\ -\text{nas} \\ +\text{cor} \end{bmatrix} \rightarrow ([-\text{ant}]) \; / \; \underline{\quad} \; \# \# \begin{bmatrix} -\text{voc} \\ -\text{cons} \\ -\text{back} \end{bmatrix}$$

This rule, which also applies to standard English, accounts
for the examples of the subvariant [č]. The affricate [č] is
rightly considered as a subvariant of t because the input of
the palatalization rule is necessarily an alveolar stop and
not a fricative, i.e. *[maᵒč yə] 'mouth you'.

4.2.5.1 Accounting for the incidence of t. In our previous
discussions of t for potential θ in morpheme-medial and -final
positions, we have seen that the incidence of t is mainly conditioned by its contiguity to a nasal. But for with, no such
environmental statement can be made. It occurs preceding a
vowel or any of the nonnasal consonants, in addition to its
occurrence when the following word begins with a nasal. How,
then, do we account for the incidence of t in with? Several
alternatives can be considered here. As a first alternative,
we may look for some sort of phonological conditioning for the
occurrence of t. Wolfram (1969:87) has suggested that one

possible phonological explanation for the occurrence of $\underline{t}$ in
$\underline{with}$ may be the fact that, as a preposition, it tends to occur
in unstressed types of environments. For example, it is generally $\underline{not}$ assigned either 1 or 2 stress in the application of
stress ranking, as in:

(30) a. with my new bike

b. with a red cross

However, the majority of examples of potential $\underline{\theta}$ that have been
discussed previously would have to be assigned a stress ranking
of 1 or 2, as in:

(31) a. a nice too<u>th</u> brush

b. in a phone boo<u>th</u>

At first glance, then, it would appear that stress might
be the relevant conditioning environment for the $\underline{t}$ realization,
and that the rule might be written as:

$$(32) \quad \theta \rightarrow (t)/ \begin{bmatrix} -stress \\ V \end{bmatrix} \underline{\quad\quad} \#\#$$

But before we conclude that this is the clear-cut solution
in accounting for $\underline{t}$ with $\underline{with}$, we must see if there are any contexts in which $\underline{with}$ might be assigned a surface stress ranking
of 1 or 2. We notice that in several contexts, $\underline{with}$ can occur
with a stress ranking of at least 2 and possibly 1. Generally,
these contexts are due to the emphasis on $\underline{with}$ or to the occurrence of $\underline{with}$ in clause-final position by ellipsis or rearrange-
ment of syntactical units. Thus, we can get:

(33) You coming with us?

This distribution for our informants is given in Table 15.

Even with the limited number of examples in Table 15, we
can see that the data do not confirm the observational adequacy
of Rule (32): $\underline{t}$ still occurs in approximately one-third of the
cases. On the other hand, however, when we compare Table 15

Table 15. Distribution of variants for potential θ when <u>with</u>
           is stressed for Puerto Rican and black informants.

Variant	Puerto Rican	Black
<u>t</u>	4	3
<u>f</u>	6	3
<u>θ</u>	2	2

with Table 16 below, we do see what appears to be a constraint
on the variability of <u>t</u>, the change from θ to <u>t</u> operating more
frequently when <u>with</u> is unstressed than when it is stressed.
But a careful examination of the phonological conditioning
environments does not turn up an exclusive environment for the
operation of θ → <u>t</u> for <u>with</u>.

If our failure to discover a consistent phonological environment for the realization of <u>t</u> in <u>with</u> is an accurate
assessment of the data, what are our alternate solutions?
On the one hand, we might suggest that it is necessary to
posit two underlying lexical representations for the item
<u>with</u>:   one that would be given with underlying //t// and one
with underlying //θ//. Although we would need a rule such as
θ → <u>t</u> as a part of the dialect we are describing, it would be
necessary to specify the two underlying representations for
<u>with</u> because we cannot discover any consistent phonological
environment in which this rule can apply to a single underlying representation of this item. Presumably, this is the
type of solution one might suggest for speakers who variably
realize an item such as <u>either</u> as [aᵉdɚ] and [idɚ]. We might
have to postulate a rule that changes a high front vowel into
a diphthong or vice versa, i.e. <u>i</u> → <u>aᵉ</u> or <u>aᵉ</u> → <u>i</u>, to handle
other phonological processes; however, we probably would not
be able to isolate an exclusive phonological environment for
this change that would allow us to incorporate it into a

previously established phonological rule. Thus, we might conclude that we must posit dual underlying representations to
account adequately for the speaker's competence in his use of
the alternate forms. Admittedly, however, such a conclusion
is not intuitively satisfactory and might be adopted only as a
last resort. Perhaps a more important reason for viewing this
solution skeptically is the variability of t and f or θ, depending on the stress assignment on with. We would not generally expect phonological conditioning of this type on the
variability of items that are, in essence, entered in the lexicon as different units. The choice of lexical items would be
expected to vary much more according to extra-linguistic factors, such as participants, style, setting, etc. For example,
[idə] might be expected more frequently in informal styles and
[a^edə] more frequently in formal styles, but we would not expect their alternation to vary according to phonological environment if they were authentic lexical differences.

    The alternate solution to dual lexical representations is
to represent with with a single underlying representation,
which would presumably be //wIθ//, and then allow the application
of the θ → t rule to be item-specific with respect to with.
In other words, one environment for the application of θ → t
is the lexical item with. In this way we can still build in
the constraint on variability depending on stress so that the
change of θ → t for this item can be represented as:

$$(34) \quad \theta \rightarrow (t) \ / \ \#\# \begin{bmatrix} wI \ \underline{\hspace{2em}} \\ A \ \text{-stress} \end{bmatrix} \ \#\#$$

This rule, then, can be coalesced with Rule (23) by describing
the environmental sets disjunctively, so that we now have the
following for Rule (23):

$$(35) \quad \theta \rightarrow (t) \ / \quad \left\{ \begin{array}{c} [\text{+nas}] \\ \#\# \begin{bmatrix} wI \ \underline{\hspace{2em}} \\ A \ \text{-stress} \end{bmatrix} \#\# \end{array} \right\}^{[19]}$$

Admittedly, the conclusion that $\underline{\theta} \to \underline{t}$ can be conditioned lexically is not a completely satisfying solution. But until we have further phonological data that might lend consistency to a statement dependent exclusively on phonological environment, we must settle for a less intuitively satisfying solution to account for the descriptive facts.

4.2.5.2 <u>Accounting for the incidence of $\emptyset$</u>. In order to consider the distribution of the $\emptyset$ variant for <u>with</u>, it is first necessary to observe the distribution of all variants according to whether the following environment is consonantal or nonconsonantal. The distribution of variants for the Puerto Rican and black informants is illustrated in the following figure and table:

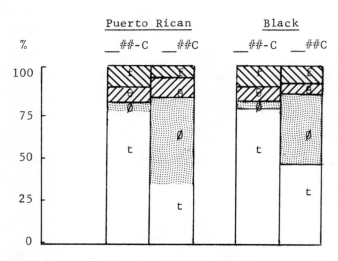

Figure 4.   Distribution of variants for potential $\underline{\theta}$ in <u>with</u> in nonconsonantal and consonantal environments for Puerto Rican and black informants.

Table 16. Distribution of variants for potential θ in <u>with</u> in nonconsonantal and consonantal environments for Puerto Rican and black informants.

Variant	Puerto Rican				Black			
	＃＃-C		＃＃C		＃＃-C		＃＃C	
	No.	%	No.	%	No.	%	No.	%
t	114	78.1	36	34.0	43	76.8	19	46.3
∅	3	2.1	61	57.5	1	1.8	16	39.0
θ	18	12.3	6	5.7	4	7.1	2	4.9
f	11	7.5	3	2.8	8	14.3	4	9.8
Total	146		106		56		41	

Several observations can be made on the basis of the above data. To begin with, we observe that the following consonantal environment is almost exclusively responsible for the incidence of ∅. When followed by a vowel or a pause, some segment is generally present. It is also important to note that the main difference is found in the incidence of t; t is the variant that is reduced in an inverse proportion to the greater frequency of ∅ before consonants: that is, the sum of t and ∅ is approximately the same for the two environments.

If the incidence of ∅ in <u>with</u> is compared with the incidence of ∅ for other types of morpheme-final potential θ for other types of morpheme-final potential θ, we find that its frequency with <u>with</u> is much greater: 57.5 percent for <u>with</u> followed by a consonant; 15.3 percent for other morpheme-final items followed by a consonant. To understand the significance of this difference, it is necessary to recall that ∅ realization for items other than <u>with</u> is largely due to the assimilation process described in Rule (18). This assimilation process, it was noted, is largely restricted to certain types of fricatives. But when we look at the incidence of ∅ for <u>with</u>, we

note that it does not show these same types of restrictions.
It is observed before practically any consonant, as attested
to in the following examples:

(36) a. [wɪ maᵉ]   'with my'   (14:5)

      b. [wɪ kʰɛli]   'with Kelly'   (11:5)

      c. [wɪ hɪm]   'with him'   (14:6)

      d. [wɪ stɪkbɔl]   'with stickball' (5:2)

      e. [wɪ gɝlz]   'with girls'   (44:6)

      f. [wɪ beᶦsbɔl]   'with baseball' (44:1)

It is obvious, then, that ∅ realization for with cannot
be accounted for simply by the application of our assimilation
rule. Rather, it appears to be a deletion of t after it has
been derived from underlying //θ//.[20] We will see in Chapter 5
that the deletion of final t and d is a rule that will be needed
anyhow, so we can simply apply the rule now to account for ∅ in
with as well as in other items. Obviously, this alveolar stop
deletion rule must be ordered after Rule (35), which changes θ
to t in with. It also appears that this deletion rule should
be ordered after the palatalization rule (Rule (29)), so that
it cannot operate on items that will end in [č]. If we allow
the palatalization rule to be ordered before this deletion
rule, we can account for the fact that y is the only nonvocalic
segment before which we have no examples of deletion: out of
11 potential examples before y, none shows ∅ realization. We
see that the change from t to č before y makes certain examples
of with ineligible for the t deletion rule.

A final point that can be made concerning ∅ realization
relates to the comparison of ∅ for the Puerto Rican and the
black informants. The Puerto Rican informants, as a group,
tend to show more ∅ realization than do the black informants.
Anticipating our discussion of final t and d deletion in the
following chapter, we may note that this fits the general pattern for final t deletion, which is considerably more frequent
in Puerto Rican English than it is in Black English.

4.3 <u>Summary of rules</u>. Following is a list of the rules that
we have formulated as necessary in order to account for the
various realizations of underlying $/\!/\theta/\!/$, renumbered as (37) and
placed in the proper order insofar as is known. (Each rules
original numbering is indicated in parentheses after its title.)
Some of the rules do not relate directly to the derivations from
underlying $/\!/\theta/\!/$, but they are included here because they account
for certain processes necessary to understand the rules per-
taining directly to $\underline{\theta}$. In most cases the reasons for particular
orderings have been discussed in the preceding sections; in a
few cases, however, there are no formal motivations for select-
ing the ordering of the rules that have emerged on the basis
of our discussion, so that the order may be arbitrary.

(37) a. Voiceless
          assimilation
          (10)

$$\begin{bmatrix} -voc \\ +cont \\ \alpha ant \\ \beta cor \\ \gamma strid \end{bmatrix} \rightarrow ([-voice])/ \begin{bmatrix} -voc \\ +cont \\ -vd \\ \alpha ant \\ \beta cor \\ \gamma strid \end{bmatrix} \#\#\_\_$$

      b. Regressive
          fricative
          assimilation
          (18)

$$\theta \rightarrow \left(\begin{bmatrix} \alpha ant \\ \beta cor \\ \gamma strid \end{bmatrix} \right)/\_\_\#\# \begin{bmatrix} -voc \\ +cont \\ -vd \\ \left\{ \begin{matrix} A \begin{bmatrix} \alpha ant \\ +cor \\ +strid \end{bmatrix} \\ \begin{bmatrix} +ant \\ -cor \\ -strid \end{bmatrix} \end{matrix} \right\} \end{bmatrix}$$

      c. Progressive
          sibilant
          assimilation
          (13)

$$\theta \rightarrow ([+strid])/ \begin{bmatrix} -voc \\ +strid \\ +cor \end{bmatrix} \# \_\_$$

      d. Vowel
          reduction
          (25)

$$\begin{bmatrix} -stress \\ -tense \\ V \end{bmatrix} \rightarrow \partial$$

      e. Schwa
          deletion
          (26)

$$\partial \rightarrow (\emptyset) / \begin{bmatrix} +cons \\ -nas \end{bmatrix} \begin{bmatrix} \_\_\_\_\_ \\ -stress \end{bmatrix} [+nas]$$

f. Morpheme-
    final stop
    (35)

$$\theta \rightarrow (t) \; / \; \left\{ \begin{array}{c} [+nas] \\ \#\# \begin{bmatrix} wI\_\_ \\ A \; -stress \end{bmatrix} \#\# \end{array} \right\}$$

g. Morpheme-
    initial
    stop
    (2)

$$\begin{bmatrix} +cons \\ -voc \\ +cor \\ +ant \\ -strid \end{bmatrix} \rightarrow ([-cont] \; ([+sim \; rel])) / \\ \#\#[A \; \overline{vd}] \; [B \; cons]$$

h. Palatali-
    zation
    (29)

$$\begin{bmatrix} -voc \\ -cont \\ -nas \\ +cor \end{bmatrix} \rightarrow ([-ant])/ \; \_\_ \; \#\# \begin{bmatrix} -voc \\ -cons \\ -back \end{bmatrix}$$

i. Alveolar
    stop
    deletion*

$$\begin{bmatrix} -voc \\ -cont \\ -nas \\ +cor \\ +ant \end{bmatrix} \rightarrow (\emptyset) \; / \; \_\_ \; \#\#$$

j. Labio-dental
    fricative
    (22)

$$\theta \rightarrow (f) \; / \; \_\_A\#$$

k. Geminate con-
    sonant re-
    duction
    (14)

$$C \rightarrow \emptyset \; / \; \_\_ \; an \; identical \; C$$

*   In this summary, (i) is simply an approximation of
     Rule (39), which will be discussed in detail in
     Chapter 5.

Now, it is noted that some of the rules in the above set
are common to both standard English and various nonstandard
dialects, while others are peculiar to nonstandard dialects
such as PRE. For example, the assimilation rules (a, b, and
c) are common to nonstandard and standard dialects of English,
but the stop realizations and labio-dental fricative realizations for underlying //θ// (f, g, and j) are unique to certain
nonstandard varieties. In this sense, this variable seems to
be quite like other nonstandard variables that show both shared
and unique aspects when compared with standard English.

It should further be noted that some independent linguistic
constraints on variability have been incorporated for rules re-
lating directly to the derivation of phonetic realizations from
underlying //θ//. Although we have isolated some constraints
that are to be incorporated in an adequate descriptive account,
it should be observed that this variable does not reveal an
extensive ordering of constraints. In fact, only one variable
rule shows as many as two hierarchical orders. This cannot be
attributed to our lack of detail in searching for valid linguistic constraints; rather, it appears to be an indication
that there is a limited amount of hierarchical ordering in the
constraints on variability. Unlike other variables that may
reveal a fairly extensive natural hierarchy of constraints,
e.g. final consonant clusters, this variable shows only a
limited hierarchy.

NOTES

1. There is some question as to the feature of t that is actu-
    ally stigmatized. According to Bailey (personal communi-
    cation), it is the place, not the manner of articulation,
    that is the stigmatized aspect. Thus, according to Bailey,
    a gingival stop would be stigmatized, but a dental stop
    would not be.

2. Labov et al. (1968) have built the feature of voicing into
    this rule as a variable constraint that raises the relative
    frequency of rule application. But they do not state
    whether this variable constraint is to be applied if only
    the first part of the rule (in actuality, the first of two
    rules) is chosen. According to the empirical data pre-
    sented by the authors, however, it is clear that this con-
    straint can only operate when both options of the rule have
    been chosen. They observe:

        ...we find that Negro speakers use a great many
        affricates for (th), (th-2), but that the pre-
        vailing form for (dh) is the stop, (dh-3).
        (Labov et al. 1968:96)

Without explicitly establishing the convention that a variable constraint can apply only to the last option in a coalesced rule output involving two or more optional outputs, an adequate account of variability can be achieved only by keeping the rules separate.

3. Labov et al. (1968) do not say where or how the nondistinctive features have been previously introduced. Generally, they have been placed in very low-level phonological rules, but Stanley (1967:394) has suggested that there is good reason to include these nondistinctive predictions in the morpheme structure sequence rules.

4. See Wheeler (1971) for some of the theoretical shortcomings of this convention.

5. This convention change was suggested by William K. Riley in personal communication.

6. When we say that s falls into the range of "chance occurrence", we are referring to a statistical rather than a structural fact. Performance errors may occur randomly in terms of their frequency, but they are structured in terms of the types of "slips" that may occur.

7. The transcriptions here and elsewhere are meant to be only broadly phonetic. Finer phonetic detail is not typically included.

8. In actuality, the same type of assimilation operates for the voiced counterpart of θ̱ in casual speech, so that we have sentences like:

[yu bri zɛst fɝ laᵉf] 'You breathe zest for life'

[yu bri vɛri hɛvəli] 'You breathe very heavily'

[šiz ə smu žaža gəbor taᵉp] 'She's a smooth Zsa Zsa Gabor type'

These appear to be quite acceptable in an allegro style of standard English. This means that the rule would specify those features common to ḏ and θ̱.

9. Apparently there are some standard English speakers for whom the appropriate assimilation here is [fIf]. For these speakers, the progressive assimilation rule is stated more generally.

10. It is interesting to note that for (16b) there is a vocalic

shift that is conditioned on the basis of the existence
of a voiceless segment following the n in ninth. When
there is a voiceless consonant forming a cluster with n,
there is a centralizing tendency in the vowel nucleus,
but when there is no voiceless consonant, it does not
centralize. Thus, we get:

[nə^en stɔri]   'ninth story'

but [na^en stɔriz]   'nine stories'

This phenomenon indicates that the assimilation and deletion rules must follow the rule for centralization.

11.   Although the convention we are suggesting here is initi-
      ated in order to incorporate a variable constraint, the
      same convention might allow certain types of rule col-
      lapsing presently prohibited in a more traditional inter-
      pretation of generative phonology, i.e. a theory that does
      not formally admit the incorporation of variable constraints.

12.   This feature specification assumes that both [θ] and [f]
      are [-strid], but this is a matter that is still not re-
      solved. Chomsky and Halle (1968:177) consider [f] to be
      [+strid], but their description of stridency, i.e. "a
      rougher surface, a faster rate of flow, and an angle of
      incidence closer to ninety degrees will all contribute to
      greater stridency", seems to unite rather than distinguish
      [θ] and [f]. At any rate, this is not crucial to our dis-
      cussion, since we could simply state the rule as:

$$
\begin{bmatrix} -voc \\ +cont \\ +ant \\ -vd \end{bmatrix} \rightarrow \left(\begin{bmatrix} -cor \\ +strid \end{bmatrix} \right) / \underline{\qquad} \#\#
$$

      if we decide that [f] is [+strid]. Wheeler (1971:100) has
      recently suggested that the feature [strident] can be dis-
      pensed with altogether, its functions having been taken
      over by [distributed] and [delayed release].

13.   Bailey (personal communication) notes that the incidence
      of f for θ is actually related to syllabication rather
      than to morpheme position. For example, he notes that
      ether could have f but ethereal could not. If this is
      true, and it appears to be a reasonable hypothesis, then
      the designations morpheme-medial and -final are approxi-
      mative of a more strictly phonologically conditioned
      phenomenon.

14.   Following the suggestion made by Bach (1966), the absence

of the ___ to indicate placement in terms of environment
is an abbreviation for an "either after or before" relationship. Thus, /[+nasal] is an abbreviation for:

$$\left\{ \begin{array}{l} \text{[+nasal]} \underline{} \\ \underline{} \text{ [+nasal]} \end{array} \right\}$$

If a rule changing a preceding nasal segment to a
nasal vowel has taken place, i.e. V[+nasal] → Ṽ, the frequency of rule application is greatly reduced. For an
elaboration of nasal consonant deletion in English, see
Bailey (1973a). It is doubtful if Bailey's interpretation would allow for a surface nasal consonant to ever
occur in month, but my data would indicate that it can.
Bailey also suggests that the t in nothing may be interpreted as a generalization of a rule that changes underlying voiced fricatives to stops before syllabic nasals,
e.g. seven and eleven.

15. Some instances of t may be due to the type of vestigial
     interference that we suggested to account for the oc-
     casional occurrence of s, since t may also be an inter-
     ference variant for morpheme-final θ among Spanish speak-
     ers learning English.

16. The application of the rule is, of course, more general,
     extending to at least r and l in addition to the nasals.
     Within the feature specifications for English set up by
     Chomsky and Halle (1968:176-77), it would appear that the
     inclusion of r and l in this type of rule would have to
     be handled by setting up the environments disjunctively.
     But if one introduced the feature [syllabic], which Bailey
     and Milner (Chomsky and Halle 1968:354) see as a necessary
     feature specification, the rule could be stated in a much
     more general fashion. For example, assuming that l, r,
     and the nasals have been given the feature [+syllabic]
     under special circumstances such as those we are talking
     about here, the rule might be stated more generally as:

$$\theta \rightarrow (\theta) \: / \: \begin{bmatrix} +\text{cons} \\ -\text{syll} \end{bmatrix} \begin{bmatrix} \underline{} \\ -\text{stress} \end{bmatrix} \text{[+syll]}$$

     This sort of evidence appears to be strong support for
     the introduction of the feature [+syllabic].

17. Bailey's (1969a) interpretation is that syllabic nasals
     are permitted only after homorganic syllable-final ob-
     struents.

18. We must note, of course, that in some varieties, we get
     [wɪd] instead of [wɪθ]. In terms of the variants, this

would simply be included as the standard variant θ. To
account for this variant, the input for the rule changes
would have to be generalized to include //đ// and //θ//. We
will only deal with //θ//, with the understanding that for
some varieties, the rule will have to be altered slightly,
e.g. <u>d</u> for //đ//.

19. Technically speaking, Rule (35) should not include <u>with</u>
since this exception is to be noted in the lexicon: that
is, the lexical entry for <u>with</u> will simply specify that
Rule (35) applies to it in the appropriate environment.

20. The assimilation rule may, of course, still operate on
instances of <u>with</u> in which θ is not changed to <u>t</u>. If the
assimilation rule is ordered before θ → <u>t</u>, then it will
account for instances of ∅ before fricatives, the <u>t</u>
deletion rule accounting for other examples of ∅. If,
on the other hand, θ → <u>t</u> is ordered before assimilation,
the assimilation process operates only on those instances
of underlying //θ// that have not undergone the θ → <u>t</u> change.
The former order is chosen here, although our data furnish
no overwhelming argument for doing so.

The th variable discussed in the preceding chapter is one of the most socially diagnostic variables operating in American society. In initial position, it is part of a variable that apparently cuts across all regional and ethnic varieties of English in its social significance. In some positions, we see that the interference variant from Spanish-influenced English and the English variant of the surrounding black community are in competition: Black English calls for [f] (varying with the standard English variant [θ]) and Spanish-influenced English calls for [s]. It is obvious that the Black English realization is favored for all speakers, even those with restricted black contacts. Those with more direct black contacts, of course, are influenced to a significantly greater extent than are those with restricted contacts.

Now, we turn our attention to a variable, namely, syllable-final d and t, that operates in a somewhat different way. In syllable-final position, when preceded by a vowel or constricted r, underlying //d// or //t// may be realized in PRE in several different forms. For underlying //d//, t and ∅ are the main non-d realizations; for //t//, ∅ is the main non-t realization. Previous studies of social dialects have indicated that this variable is not restricted to our population; rather, it has broader significance than the group we are studying here. It has been noted in studies of Spanish-influenced English and Black English.

One of the characteristic features of Puerto Rican Spanish
is the deletion of d in syllable-final position. Thus, in
words like verdad 'truth' and ciudad 'city', the final d may
be deleted, giving [bɛřdá] and [siudá] respectively. Because
of this phonological pattern in Puerto Rican Spanish, this
process might be predictable in Spanish-influenced English for
this community. Ma and Herasimchuk (1968) have tabulated this
variable in the speech of a Puerto Rican community in Jersey
City and have found that d and t deletion is characteristic to
some extent. Their brief discussion cannot, however, be compared with our analysis here for several reasons. In the first
place, they do not make any environmental distinctions in tabu-
lating variability. As will be seen, an accurate assessment
of variability for this feature is dependent on the distinction
of several different environments. Their failure to distinguish environments such as the effect of a following consonant
or vowel allows them to come to the conclusion that "PRE
speakers most usually give some phonetic marker for final /t/
or /d/" (Ma and Herasimchuk 1968:740). We will see that this
statement does not necessarily hold when various environmental
constraints are examined.

Ma and Herasimchuk have also combined variants of these
variables in such a way that it is impossible to get a valid
picture of how the various phonetic realizations operate with
respect to underlying //t// or //d//. For example, they consider
the glottal stop [?] as a variant for either t or d, but do
not separate the two potential underlying sources from each
other. This procedure can be quite misleading, since in the
case of underlying //t//, glottal stop may be a standard variant,
while in the case of underlying //d//, it is quite clearly a
nonstandard variant. To consider glottals derived from either
//t// or //d// as one variant does not allow for an accurate social
differentiation. Glottal realizations may operate quite differently for these two underlying sources.

Furthermore, one may question the perceptual reliability
of their categories of variants. They have set up three variants for t and d: (1) [t] or unreleased [t˺]; (2) glottal
stop [ʔ]; (3) no phonetic realization at all. Previous studies
have established that we can expect reliability in perceiving
impressionistically the differences among t, d, and ∅, but
the perception of the difference between glottal stop and unreleased [t˺] cannot be expected to show such a high degree of
reliability. To separate glottal stop and unreleased [t˺]
into two different variants would appear to reduce the reliability of perception considerably.

Labov et al. (1968), Wolfram (1969), and Fasold (1972)
have all looked at the phonological processes that operate on
d deletion in Black English. Labov et al. (1968) have considered postvocalic d and t deletion to be a part of the same
rule that deletes d and t following consonants. No detailed
frequency study, however, is made of the deletion of postvocalic d. Wolfram (1969) has restricted his study to cases
of postvocalic d that do not have any grammatical function,
e.g. bad but not showed. His analysis has isolated several
types of constraints on the variability of d, including following vowel or nonvowel and stress. Fasold (1972) deals
exclusively with d as a grammatical marker and finds that
some of the same general constraints isolated by Wolfram for
nongrammatical d are operating on d when it is a grammatical
marker. The various constraints isolated by Wolfram and
Fasold will be examined in some detail later, and the rules
needed to handle these variable constraints will be discussed
in that context.

5.1 The variants. As suggested above, we can identify three
relevant variants for underlying //d// and two for underlying

//t//. The variants for d and the various submembers of those variants are given below:

Variant	Phonetic Realization	Examples	
d	[d]^1 [d̪]	[hʊ:d]	'hood'
		[hʊ:d̪ ɔn]	'hood on'
t	[t˥] [ʔ] [ʔt˥]	[hʊ:t˥] ~ [hʊ:ʔ] ~	
		[hʊ:ʔt˥]	'hood'
Ø		[hʊ: bæk]	'hood back'

This differentiation of variants essentially follows that of Wolfram (1969:95).

It should be noted that the tabulation of d includes both d that is a morphophonemic representation of the grammatical suffix -ed, i.e. following vowels as in prayed, and d that is part of the stem of a word. The grammatical function of d includes its usage as a past tense marker, e.g. He cried for a long time; as a derived adjective, e.g. He's a colored kid; and as a participle, e.g. He was tried for murder.

The variants for t are as follows:

Variant	Phonetic Realization	Examples	
t	[t] [t˥] [ʔ]	[hæt ˥] ~ [hæʔ]	'hat'
Ø	Ø; lengthened following consonant	[hæ]	'hat'

Unlike d, t can only be used as part of a word stem following a vowel; for t there is no underlying analogue to the grammatical function of postvocalic d.

The tabulations of d and t were made for each informant by counting the first 20 potential occurrences of inflectional d followed by a nonvowel and the first 15 followed by a vowel. The same procedure was carried out for the noninflectional function of d and t. In addition to the variants for d identified above, we also have an occasional instance of [d] for d intervocalically. This phonetic realization is obviously a matter of Puerto Rican Spanish influence because of the

fricativization of voiced stops postvocalically in Spanish.
This phonetic realization is not indicated here in any of our
tabulations of d for two reasons. First, initial tabulation
indicates that its incidence is so low that it clearly fits
into the category of vestigial interference as we have defined
the concept previously. Furthermore, there is considerable
difficulty in consistently perceiving the difference between
lenis [d̦] and fricativized [đ] when transcribing from a tape
recorder, thus prohibiting a reliable tabulation of [đ].

5.2 The incidence of ∅ for underlying //d//. Previous studies
of the ∅ realization for d indicate that there are several
different types of environments that may affect the realization of ∅. Some of these are general types of environments
that have been seen to affect variability for a number of
features; others appear to be more specific in their application.

One of the most commonly noted influences on variability
is the presence or absence of a vowel following a segment.
Studies of variability in Black English by Wolfram (1969) and
Fasold (1972) have revealed that this is one of the major constraints on d deletion. Both have indicated that a vocalic
environment inhibits the incidence of ∅. In Table 17, we present the figures for d deletion based on whether the following
segment is vocalic or nonvocalic. The nonvocalic environment
includes both a following consonant of some type and a pause.
For the sake of this table, we will combine the d and t variants for d under the category of presence, so that we only have
a binary classification into presence and absence. Figures are
given for the 29 Puerto Rican informants, based on the extracted
examples we described above.

Table 17. Frequency of ∅ realization for potential d in
           vocalic and nonvocalic environments for Puerto
           Rican informants.

	___## V	___## -V
No. del./Total	70/340	427/737
% del.	20.6	57.9

The difference between ∅ realizations for the two environments
is quite clear-cut: a following nonvowel favors the operation
of d deletion. This constraint is the same as that identified
by both Wolfram (1969:99) and Fasold (1972:41) for the deletion of d in Black English.

Another factor that previous studies have shown to affect
the variability is stress. The general principle that has been
observed is that occurrence in an unstressed syllable favors
the deletion of segments, whereas occurrence in a stressed syllable inhibits deletion. This has been observed for a number
of different variables and has specifically been described for
d deletion by both Wolfram (1969) and Fasold (1972). The
relative frequency of d deletion in stressed and unstressed
syllables can be observed in Table 18. Since we have already
noted the importance of a following vocalic or nonvocalic environment, it is appropriate to consider the effect of stress
in terms of these environments. There are two main types of
environments that we have classified as unstressed in our
tabulations: (1) d that occurs in an unstressed syllable of
a polysyllabic word, such as treated, stupid, or record;
(2) that occurs in an unstressed modal. The latter is illustrated in sentences such as I don't think he should gó and
John would gó if he weren't so tired. Stressed environment
refers to any instance of potential d that occurs in a stressed
syllable of a word such as betrayed, head, or showed.

Table 18.   Effect of stress on the frequency of ∅ realization
for potential d for Puerto Rican informants.

	___##V		___##-V	
	Stressed	Unstressed	Stressed	Unstressed
No. del./Total	54/293	16/47	245/481	182/256
% del.	18.4	34.0	50.9	71.1

Two observations can be made on the basis of Table 18.
First, as we might expect, we observe that stress does affect
the deletion of d, the occurrence of d in an unstressed syllable favoring deletion more than its occurrence in a stressed
syllable. But it is also noted that stress does not have the
same effect on variability that a following vowel or nonvowel
may have. When the crucial cross-products, i.e. ___##V,
Unstressed and ___##-V, Stressed, are compared, it is apparent
that the following vowel or nonvowel is the first order constraint and stress or nonstress the second order.

Up to this point, we have not separated those instances
of d that are inflectional from those that are inherent parts
of the lexical item. Previous tabulations of phonological
variability have shown that the grammatical function of a
segment tends to inhibit deletion (see, for example, the discussion of Labov et al. (1968) or Wolfram (1969) concerning
bimorphemic and monomorphemic consonant clusters) when compared with the same segment occurring as an inherent part of
the word. Ma and Herasimchuk (1968) mention this difference
but do not carry out any tabulations on the effect of grammatical versus nongrammatical functions of d.

In Table 19, the deletion of grammatical d versus nongrammatical d is tabulated. Since we have already established
the effects of a following vowel/nonvowel and a stressed/un-
stressed syllable on the deletion of d, we will consider

grammatical/nongrammatical functions of d in terms of these
previously distinguished environments. Only those cases of
grammatical d following a vowel or r are considered. This
means that all morphophonemic realizations of the -ed suffix
as -Id (phonetically [Id], [ɛd], or [ɪd]) following an alveolar stop are not included. Furthermore, instances in which
-Id forms have been assimilated to a d or a t that is part of
the stem (as in stard for started) will be considered later in
our discussion.

Table 19. Effect of grammatical marking on the frequency of Ø reali-
           zation for potential d for Puerto Rican informants.

	____##V				____##-V			
	Stressed		Unstressed		Stressed		Unstressed	
	Gram.	Nongram.	Gram.	Nongram.	Gram.	Nongram.	Gram.	Nongram.
No. del./Total	6/35	48/258	5/19	11/28	14/34	231/347	40/54	142/202
% del.	17.1	18.6	26.3	39.3	41.2	66.6	74.1	70.3

Table 19 indicates that variability is affected on the
basis of whether or not d is a grammatical marker. But it does
not appear that this is a major constraint. In fact, the comparison of the cross-products indicates that it is a third
order constraint, being ordered after the effect of the following vowel and stress. In only one case is there a slight discrepancy in cross-products (____##-V, Unstressed, Grammatical
Marker and ____##-V, Unstressed, Nongrammatical Marker); we
will have more to say about the possible reason for this slight
discrepancy below.

One final constraint on d deletion, namely, the differentiation of grammatical d on the basis of its various functions, can be examined here. Fasold (1972) suggests that the
nonpast functions of d (derived adjective or past participle)
tend to favor d deletion more than its function as a past
tense marker. In Table 20, the tabulations are given on the
basis of this breakdown. Since the only cross-products

Table 20.   Effect of grammatical function on the frequency of ∅ realization for potential d for Puerto Rican informants.

	___##V				___##-V			
	Stressed		Unstressed		Stressed		Unstressed	
	Past	Nonpast	Past	Nonpast	Past	Nonpast	Past	Nonpast
No. del./Total	6/31	0/4	3/11	2/8	9/26	5/8	6/10	32/44
% del.	19.4	0.0	27.3	25.0	34.6	62.5	60.0	72.7

Total Past Del./Total	% Del.	Total Nonpast Del./Total	% Del.
24/78	30.8	39/64	60.9

applicable to this categorization are for grammatical d, only
those figures are given for this category, broken down in terms
of the previously cited constraints.

Because of the limited numbers of examples in some categories, it is somewhat difficult to find the ordered progression
of numbers that is typical of other constraints.   Nonetheless,
when we look at the categories in which there are sufficient
examples, it appears that there is a significant difference,
particularly if we look at the total numbers of examples combining the various categories.   One word of caution, however,
should be given before concluding that it is quite clear-cut.
In the ___##-V, Unstressed, Nonpast environment, we note that
32 of 44 examples indicate d deletion.   But included in this
number are 23 examples of the derived adjective colored, all
of which indicate deletion.   The elimination of this one item,
which may be a lexical difference rather than a phonological
deletion, would make the differences between the two grammatical categories much less clear-cut.

The way in which we have set up Table 20 indicates that
we consider the constraint of grammatical category to be the
fourth order constraint, ordered after following vowel/non-
vowel, stressed/unstressed, and grammatical/nongrammatical.
Because of the limited numbers of examples in some categories
and the logical impossibility of some vital cross-products,
it is difficult to arrive at a clear-cut decision concerning

the ordering of constraints here. Fasold (1972:47) in his
analysis of constraints on d deletion in Black English, has
suggested that the grammatical function of d is ordered before
stress. However, his total number of grammatical examples of
d is actually less than the total we have analyzed here, so
that some of his important categories for determining the
ordering of constraints are only sparsely populated[2] On the
basis of our comparison of data here, we may cautiously suggest that grammatical category is to be ordered as the fourth
order constraint.

The hierarchical ordering of the four constraints that
we have isolated so far is illustrated in Figure 5, using the
figures derived in Tables 17-20.

Following the conventions we have used for incorporating
the hierarchical ordering of constraints into a grammar of PRE
phonology that formally admits variability, we can summarize
our conclusions concerning the effect of various constraints
on d deletion by the following rule:

$$(38) \quad d \rightarrow (\emptyset) \; / \; \begin{bmatrix} V \\ B \; -stress \end{bmatrix} \Gamma_{-\#} \; \underline{\hspace{2cm}} \; \#\#A \; -V$$
$$[\Delta \; -PAST]$$

This rule indicates that the first order constraint is
whether the underlying //d// is followed by vowel/nonvowel;
second order, whether the preceding vowel is stressed/un-
stressed; third order, whether it follows an internal/non-
internal word boundary; fourth order, whether it functions
as a past/nonpast marker. Implicit in the use of the capital
Greek prescripts is the fluctuation of the plus or minus values.
The value that is given in the formalization of the constraint
favors the operation of the rule, while the opposite value
inhibits it. Thus, for example, if the value of the following
vowel is -, as stated in the rule (##A-V), the deletion rule
is favored, but if it is +, then it is inhibited[3] As with the

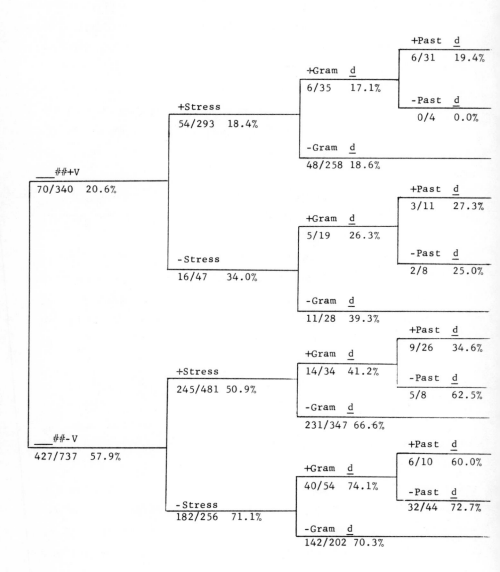

Figure 5. Hierarchical ordering of four constraints on d̲ deletion
           for Puerto Rican informants.

other variable rules states, the relation of variable constraints in terms of favoring and inhibiting deletion should
be read following the principle of geometric ordering: that
is, the relative frequency of constraints should be read as
follows:

Constraint Rank

A	B	Γ	Δ
-V	-Stress	-#	(Does not apply) >
-V	-Stress	+#	- Past >
-V	-Stress	+#	+ Past >
-V	+Stress	-#	(Does not apply) >
-V	+Stress	+#	- Past >
-V	+Stress	+#	+ Past >
+V	-Stress	-#	(Does not apply) >
+V	-Stress	+#	- Past >
+V	-Stress	+#	+ Past >
+V	+Stress	-#	(Does not apply) >
+V	+Stress	+#	- Past >
+V	+Stress	+#	+ Past

The incidence of deletion is greatest when all the values are
identical to those given in the formalization, and least when
all the opposite values obtain.

5.3   The incidence of ∅ for underlying //t//.   Up to this point,
we have only looked at ∅ realization with respect to //d//.   But
it can also be noted that there is some deletion of underlying
//t// in words such as [kæ] 'cat', [ræbI] 'rabbit', and [ra^e]
'right'.   The frequency for t deletion is given in Table 21.
The figures are broken down on the basis of whether the following environment is vocalic or nonvocalic, since we previously
observed the importance of this distinction for d deletion.

Table 21.   Frequency of $\emptyset$ realization for potential t when
followed by a vowel or a nonvowel for Puerto
Rican informants.

	___##V	___##-V
No. del./Total	49/459	219/617
% del.	10.7	35.5

The above table plainly indicates a constraint on t deletion
that is quite identical to that which we observed for d deletion, namely, that a following nonvowel favors deletion greatly
over a following vowel.

Since there are obvious similarities in terms of the output of phonological realizations for d and t, we may ask what
the relation of these two types of processes is, and how t
deletion may fit into the constraints we already established
for d. Of the four constraints we have already isolated for
d, only the following vowel/nonvowel and the stressed/un-
stressed syllable can be investigated for t since postvocalic
t cannot have any grammatical function. It is, however, possible that there is a constraint based on whether the underlying alveolar is //t// or //d//. The figures for these three
potential constraints are given in Table 22.

Several observations can be made on the basis of Table 22.
First, the way we have set up the table indicates that the
first order constraint for alveolar stop deletion is the following environment. An examination of the cross-products further indicates that the second order constraint is whether the
underlying form is //t// or //d//. A comparison of the figures
clearly indicates that d favors the operation of the deletion
rule over t. The influence of stress does not show up for t
as clearly as it does for d, but this may be due to the fact
that there are relatively few examples of t in unstressed
environments[4]. If stess is a constraint on t deletion as it is

Table 22. Frequency of ∅ realization for potential t̲ and potential d̲ in stressed and unstressed environments for Puerto Rican informants.

	___ ⧣⧣V			
	t̲		d̲	
	Stressed	Unstressed	Stressed	Unstressed
No. del./Total	46/445	3/15	54/293	16/47
% del.	10.3	20.0	18.4	34.0

	___ ⧣⧣-V			
	t̲		d̲	
	Stressed	Unstressed	Stressed	Unstressed
No. del./Total	16/44	204/573	245/481	182/256
% del.	26.4	35.6	50.9	71.1

for d̲, we would clearly expect that it is a minor one. It is obviously ordered after the following vowel/nonvowel and the voiceless/voiced constraints.

The generalization of the deletion rule to include t̲ as well as d̲ means that we will have to revise Rule (38). The effect of whether the underlying source is //t// or //d// also will have to be incorporated into the variable constraints. Our rule is now stated as:

$$(39) \quad \begin{bmatrix} -voc \\ -cont \\ +ant \\ +cor \\ -nas \end{bmatrix} \rightarrow (\emptyset) \ / \ \begin{bmatrix} V \\ \Gamma \text{-stress} \end{bmatrix} \ \triangle \ -\#\begin{bmatrix} \overline{B \ +voice} \\ E \ - \ PAST \end{bmatrix} \ \#\# \ A \ -V$$

It should be noted that because of the way we have written Rule (39) it only handles the case of alveolar deletion following a vowel (or constricted r̲). Some treatments of alveolar deletion have incorporated it as part of a more general rule, including d̲ that is part of a consonant cluster as well as d̲ that follows a vowel. This is what Labov (1969:748) has done, as indicated in the following rule:

$$t,d \rightarrow (\emptyset)/ \begin{bmatrix} \alpha cons \\ \cdot \\ \cdot \\ \cdot \end{bmatrix} \gamma(\#) \underline{\quad} \beta(\sim V)$$

Although consonant cluster reduction is an integral part
of PRE (see Wolfram 1971:356-60), we have chosen to keep the
two rules separate here. In part, this is due to the fact
that consonant cluster reduction can affect all final stops
in which the members of the cluster share the feature of
voicing (Wolfram 1969:51). This means that clusters such as
sp, ld, st, sk, etc., can be accounted for by a general consonant cluster reduction rule. The way Labov (1969) has set
up the rules, clusters involving t and d are accounted for in
the same rule as t and d following vowels; he needs another
rule to account for the reduction of clusters such as sk, sp,
etc. By setting up the t and d deletion rule following vowels
separately, the consonant cluster rule can operate more generally. Another motivating factor in setting up the rule
differently is found in the different orders of constraints.
The ordering of constraints for t and d deletion following a
vowel appears to be somewhat different from the ordering of
constraints for consonant cluster reduction. We could, of
course, set up a disjunctive rule to handle this discrepancy,
but this is not a great deal more economical when we consider
the additional rule that is still needed to handle other
types of consonant cluster reduction. Until we have additional motivation, then, we will keep these two rules apart.

It should also be noted that we have chosen to represent
the $\emptyset$ realizations for t and d as deletion processes rather
than as assimilation and subsequent degemination. Bailey
(1969b) considers standard English to assimilate t and d to
following labials and velars, e.g. righk kite, goob bye.
The fact that we get deletion before vowels and pauses as
well as consonants, however, cautions us against this

interpretation for PRE[5]. Although it might still be possible
to write the rule as involving assimilation, if we followed
Bach and Harms (1972) "crazy rules", this solution does not
seem very satisfying. In particular, deletion preceding a
pause seems to militate against interpreting it as assimilation in PRE. Furthermore, the generality of $\emptyset$ realization
before any consonant appears to be more characteristic of
deletion than of assimilation.

5.4 The comparison of d and t deletion in Puerto Rican and
Black English. In the course of our previous discussion, we
have mentioned the fact that d and t deletion has been described for Black English in several different geographical
locations, including Washington, D.C., Detroit, and New York
City. On this basis, we may conclude that a certain amount
of this deletion is an integral part of Black English. Since
the surrounding black community is the main source of non-
Puerto Rican contact, it is therefore important to compare d
and t deletion for these two populations in order to see if
we can attribute this process in PRE to linguistic assimilation to the surrounding community. In Table 23 we compare
the tabulations of d deletion for the Puerto Rican and the
black informants in our corpus. In this table, we have
broken down the figures on the basis of only three environmental categories: following vowel/nonvowel, stressed/un-
stressed syllable, and grammatical/nongrammatical function
of d.

Where there are sufficient numbers of examples to allow
comparison, it is obvious that d deletion is much more frequent in Puerto Rican English than it is in Black English.
If we collapse the distinction between grammatical and nongrammatical functions of d, because of the paucity of examples
of grammatical d in some of the above categories, we find that

Table 23. Comparison of d̲ deletion for Puerto Rican and black informants.

	___##V				___##-V			
	Stressed		Unstressed		Stressed		Unstressed	
	Gram.	Nongram.	Gram.	Nongram.	Gram.	Nongram.	Gram.	Nongram.
Puerto Rican								
No. del./Total	6/35	48/258	5/19	11/28	14/34	231/447	40/54	142/202
% del.	17.1	18.6	26.3	39.3	41.2	51.7	74.1	70.3
Black								
No. del./Total	0/14	10/93	1/2	4/22	14/33	62/183	3/10	35/69
% del.	0.0	10.8	50.0	18.2	42.4	33.9	30.0	50.7

there is a clear-cut difference in the degree of deletion for
the two groups for all environments. This combination of categories is given in Table 24.

Table 24. Comparison of d̲ deletion combining grammatical and
           nongrammatical functions of d̲ for Puerto Rican and
           black informants.

	___##V		___##-V	
	Stressed	Unstressed	Stressed	Unstressed
Puerto Rican				
No. del./Total	54/293	16/47	245/481	182/256
% del.	18.4	34.0	50.9	71.1
Black				
No. del./Total	11/107	5/24	76/216	38/79
% del.	10.3	20.8	35.2	48.1

    Table 24 leaves little doubt that d̲ deletion is consider-
ably more frequent in the speech of Puerto Ricans than of blacks.
If Puerto Ricans have the deletion rule much more frequently
than blacks, we may ask whether this rule can be attributed
simply to the influence of the surrounding linguistic community.
In the previous discussion of morpheme-final θ we observed that
the assimilation variant is found to a significantly lesser degree in the Puerto Rican community. If the realization of f̲ for

underlying //θ// is a typical case of assimilation, and it appears
to be so, then d deletion cannot be attributed simply to assimilation from the surrounding black community.

At this point we must turn to the possible influence of
Puerto Rican Spanish that is carried over in the speech of
second generation Puerto Ricans. As we have mentioned previously, one of the characteristic features of Puerto Rican
Spanish is the deletion of underlying //d// in syllable-final
position. (As in English, this is not a categorical process,
but a variable one.) There are, then, two possible sources
for d deletion: the surrounding black community and Puerto
Rican Spanish. We can hypothesize that it is the convergence
of these sources, rather than one source alone, that accounts
for the higher incidence of deletion among Puerto Ricans than
blacks.

The possible convergence of sources for d deletion can be
examined further by isolating the Puerto Rican informants who
have extensive black contacts from those who have restricted
black contacts. Table 25 gives the breakdown of deletion on
the basis of three groups: blacks (BL); Puerto Ricans with
extensive black contacts (PR/BL); and Puerto Ricans with
restricted black contacts (PR). The figures are broken down
on the basis of the following environment and the stress of the
preceding vowel, as was done in Table 24.

The figures in Table 25 indicate that, with one exception,
the incidence of deletion is greatest for the PR/BL's, next
greatest for the PR's, and least for the BL's. The one exception, ___##V in an unstressed syllable, is found in the category with the smallest number of examples, which probably accounts for the discrepancy. We may hypothesize that the figures for the PR/BL group are due to the fact that these speakers
are reinforcing the process of deletion that they may assimilate
on the basis of their close contacts with blacks with a process
that might be attributable to Spanish influence.

Table 25.   Comparison of d̲ deletion for BL, PR/BL, and
            PR informants.

	____##V		____##-V	
	Stressed	Unstressed	Stressed	Unstressed
BL				
No. del./Total	11/107	5/24	76/216	38/79
% del.	10.3	20.8	35.2	48.1
PR/BL				
No. del./Total	17/64	3/14	54/95	59/75
% del.	26.6	21.4	56.8	78.7
PR				
No. del./Total	37/229	13/33	191/386	123/181
% del.	16.2	39.4	49.5	68.0

In the preceding discussion, we have restricted ourselves
to the comparison of d̲ deletion for the Puerto Rican and the
black groups. But we can also look at these groups with respect to t̲ deletion. In Table 26 the figures for t̲ deletion
are given for the black group and the two Puerto Rican groups
delimited above. Due to the small number of examples in unstressed syllables, we will break down the environments only
on the basis of whether the following segment is vowel or nonvowel.

Several observations can be made on the basis of Table 26.
First, both Puerto Rican groups reveal a higher frequency of t̲
deletion than does the black group. Just as for d̲, there is
some explanation for this higher frequency when we look at
possible influence from Spanish. Word-final t̲ in Spanish is a
relatively rare occurrence, so that we might expect a Spanish
speaker to realize ∅ for t̲ in word-final or syllable-final
position. However, when we compare the two Puerto Rican groups,

Table 26.   Comparison of t deletion for BL, PR/BL, and
            PR informants.

	___ ‖‖V	___ ‖‖-V
BL		
No. del./Total	12/184	53/255
% del.	6.5	20.8
PR/BL		
No. del./Total	19/98	40/119
% del.	19.4	33.6
PR		
No. del./Total	30/362	180/498
% del.	8.3	36.1

we find that the PR/BL group does not exceed the PR group in
both categories. Unlike the case of d, this does not seem to
be due to the limited number of examples, since both groups
appear to have sufficient numbers of examples for a clear-cut
pattern to emerge. If the difference between the two Puerto
Rican groups in other instances is the result of the influence
of Black English on the PR/BL's, then the fact that postvocalic
t deletion is a relatively restricted phenomenon in Black English may account for the lack of differentiation in the frequencies of PR and PR/BL groups in this instance.

5.5   -Id absence. Until now, the only mention we have made of
the morphophonemic realization -Id for the -ed suffix has been
in connection with the rule that deletes the final d, so that
we have items like [rɛIdɪ] and [čitɪ] for raided and cheated
respectively. The absence of d in these instances has been
tabulated along with other examples of potential d in unstressed syllables. But it is also noted that there are instances in which the entire morphophonemic form appears to be

absent. Fasold (1972:41) has noted the same type of absence in both Black English and standard English. These instances are accounted for by several types of phonological processes.

To state it briefly, Fasold (1972) has suggested that instead of a simple phonological process that deletes the entire -ɪd form, there is a series of phonological processes that accounts for this phenomenon. Some instances of absence preceding a vowel, e.g. precede it and invade it for preceded it and invaded it respectively, can be attributed to the d deletion described previously and the subsequent assimilation of the remaining vowel ɪ to the following vowel. Fasold further suggests that for cases in which base-final t or d is preceded by a consonant, e.g. expect, bust, -ɪd absence may result from the fact that these items are interpreted as ending only in the first member of the cluster. If this is the case, the -ɪd forms are absent because of the morphophonemic restriction of -ɪd to base forms ending in t or d. Other cases, Fasold argues, are accounted for by deletion of the vowel and subsequent degemination or assimilation of the remaining d. When vowel deletion takes place, the base-final t or d is contiguous to the remaining d. If the base ends in t, an assimilation of t to d may take place (giving [hɛ^{I}d] for hated and [t^{h}rid] for treated), and if d is contiguous to a d, degemination may take place (giving [rɛ^{I}d] for raided). The particular rules through which Fasold eventually arrives at -ɪd absence in the surface realization will not concern us here; thus, we will make no attempt to summarize Fasold's specific rules and rule orderings[6]. What is of interest here is the fact that through a series of phonological rules, it is possible to account for the resultant loss of a syllable in the surface realization.

The first type of process Fasold mentions, i.e. the assimilation of a vowel after d deletion that places ɪ contiguous to another vowel, is not found in our corpus. Since Fasold

mentions that this occurs relatively infrequently, we cannot
be sure if this absence is accidental or significant. The
second reason for -ɨd absence, i.e. the interpretation of a
base-final cluster as containing only the first member, is
documented by only two examples:

    (40)   a.   Like I used to be the war counselor...
                    so it all depend on what happened in the
                    first place. (35:14)

          b.   ...they could have arres' me. (31:10)

Fasold notes that absence of this type is also to be expected
quite infrequently, and our data support this observation for
PRE.

Although there are a number of different contexts in which
deletion of the vowel and subsequent assimilation or degemination of the remaining d̲, the third type of process (or, more
correctly, processes) occurs, there is one context in which
surface syllable reduction is quite common, namely, when the
verb is followed immediately by a gerundive nominal. Specifically, this involves one verb, start, in sentences such as:

    (41)   a.   He star(d) talking to my mother.

          b.   He star(d) coming every day.

There are actually three types of realizations that can
be observed in the monosyllabic realization of this form:
star (or phonetically [sta:]), start, or stard. In Table 27,
we have separated the frequency of syllable loss for the BL,
PR/BL, and PR informants into two main categories: (1) instances in which start is monosyllabic, i.e. [sta(r)],
[sta(r)t], or [sta(r)d]; (2) instances in which it is bisyllabic, i.e. [sta(r)tɨ] or [starɨ].

There is an obvious difference in the realizations of
started as monosyllabic or bisyllabic, particularly when we
compare the informants with the BL informants. The difference
in the realizations between these groups is quite significant

Table 27. Comparison of monosyllabic and bisyllabic reali-
           zations of started in gerundive nominal con-
           structions for BL, PR/BL, and PR informants.

	Monosyllabic	Bisyllabic	% Monosyllabic
BL	20	11	64.5
PR/BL	4	4	50.0
PR	17	46	27.0

(Chi square p < .001). Although there are too few examples for
the PR/BL informants to come to clear-cut conclusions, the frequency of monosyllabic forms falls between the two groups, as
we might expect.

We may hypothesize that the relative infrequency of the
monosyllabic realizations of started is due to the difference
in the tendency to reduce syllables as observed in Spanish and
English. There is a well-known tendency in English, an accent-
timed language, to reduce the vowels in unstressed syllables
and, in some instances, to completely elide entire syllables
in unstressed environments. In Spanish, a syllable-timed
language, vowels in unstressed syllables do not reduce as they
do in English, and the tendency to elide complete syllables is
much weaker. This tendency, then, may be the reason that there
is a significant difference between the incidences of monosyllabic realizations of started when the black informants are
compared with the Puerto Rican informants. To verify this
hypothesis to our complete satisfaction, however, we would
need to compare the incidence of monosyllabic realizations for
started in standard English and in other nonstandard varieties
of English.

Before concluding our discussion of -Id here, we must
mention two types of -Id presence where it is not normally
expected in standard English. First, we observe several

instances in which -ɪd is realized as a suffix on a base ending
in t or d when the corresponding standard English construction
does not distinguish between past and present tense forms of
the verb. We thus have:

(42)   a.   ...and it hurted. (22:2)

       b.   I gotted a thirty-five. (44:3)

This type of -ed form is obviously an analogical formation on
unmarked past tense verbs ending in t or d, and is not unique
to PRE. Several instances of this analogical formation are
found for the BL informants as well, e.g. they betted on him
(1:2); it also can be observed in various nonstandard white
dialects (and, perhaps, in some standard dialects as well).

The other type of -ɪd formation has not, to my knowledge,
been observed in other nonstandard dialects of English. This
is the double or pleonastic marking of the -ed suffix, as in:

(43)   a.   ...right there it endeded. (29:3)

       b.   ...to see what they wanteded to do. (22:5)

       c.   ...he commandeded the seventy-three. (43:6)[7]

This pleonastic -ed marking appears to be a type of structural
hypercorrection that occurs as a compensation for the English
tendency to elide syllables. On the whole, this type of hypercorrection is quite infrequent, although there is one speaker
in our corpus (Informant 29) who has pleonastic -ed marking on
five out of seven potential instances of -ed, as illustrated
in the following examples:

(44)   a.   ...and so they starteded running and
            Taylor's friend got shot. (29:2)

       b.   ...and they starteded running. (29:2)

       c.   ...and they wanteded to attack them. (29:3)

       d.   ...right there it endeded. (29:3)

       e.   ...they wanteded to fight for Leemen Village
            territory. (29:5)

Although this type of hypercorrection may be expected infrequently

for some PRE speakers, the relative frequency of usage by this
informant appears to be quite unusual and may be idiosyncratic.

5.6 The incidence of t for underlying //d//. In the above discussion, we have dealt only with various aspects of underlying
//d// and //t// deletion. But we observed at the outset that it
is also possible to realize //d// as t. Phonetically, this may
be an unreleased voiceless alveolar [t⁻], a glottal stop [ʔ],
or a co-articulated glottal and unreleased alveolar stop [ʔt⁻].
This feature, sometimes referred to as devoicing, should not be
confused with the lack of voicing through the voiced stops in
standard English (sometimes represented as [d̬]). Perceptually,
these two types of devoicing appear to be quite distinct. Previous studies of devoicing, done exclusively on Black English
(Wolfram 1969 and Fasold 1972), have indicated that it is a
process that applies to many more consonants than just d; in
fact, it is true of all voiced obstruents to some extent. The
realization of t for //d// in word-final position has also been
mentioned as a possible interference variant from Spanish because of the lack of contrast between d and t in word-final
position in Spanish. As an interference variant, however, it
does not appear to occur very extensively for most speakers.

In Table 28, we have tabulated the frequencies of t, i.e.
[t⁻], [ʔ], or [ʔt⁻], realization for underlying //d//. The percentages of t realization are calculated in relation to the
total number of t and d realizations. Cases of ∅ realization
treated previously are not considered in this table. Two environments are distinguished, vocalic and nonvocalic. It
should be noted that our definition of following vocalic environment is quite rigid, so that any slight pause between
potential d and a following vowel is classified as nonvocalic.
We will see that this careful discrimination of pause following potential d is of particular importance because of the

effect of the constraint of pause on the incidence of t̲. The
category t̲ includes [t˥], [ʔ], and [ʔt˥] phonetically; d̲ includes [d], [d̆], and [d̬].

Table 28. Frequency of t̲ realization for potential d̲ in
vocalic and nonvocalic environments for Puerto
Rican informants.

	____⧣⧣V	____⧣⧣-V
No. t̲	9	134
No. d̲	261	176
% t̲	3.3	43.2

Table 28 indicates quite clearly that t̲ realization of
underlying ⫽d⫽ is a phonological process that is largely confined to nonvocalic environments. In fact, the incidence of
t̲ in vocalic environments is so limited that we may ask if the
few instances that we have are a legitimate part of the dialect
or some type of "speaker error". Typically, d̲ is realized as
a flapped alveolar [d̆] in intervocalic position. The low incidence of t̲ preceding a vowel converges with the observation
of d̲ devoicing in both Wolfram (1969:99) and Fasold (1972:55).
Although both of these studies mention the low incidence of t̲
in vocalic environments, Fasold nonetheless considers that
these rare instances should still be accounted for in the grammar of Black English. Fasold, in fact, regards it as important
evidence for ordering the constraints on variability as he does,
a matter which we will return to in more detail later.

One of the variable constraints mentioned in previous
studies of devoicing is stress. It has been suggested (Wolfram
1969:102) that unstressed syllables favor the devoicing rule.
In Table 29, we present frequencies of t̲ realization based on
the distinction between stressed and unstressed environments.
Since we have already noted that t̲ for d̲ is almost categorically

absent preceding a vowel, we will only give the incidence of t
for d in nonvocalic environments.

Table 29. Frequency of t realization for potential d in
           stressed and unstressed environments for Puerto
           Rican informants.

	Stressed	Unstressed
No. t	94	40
No. d	142	34
% t	39.8	54.1

The observation of the influence of stress reported in previous
studies of devoicing is confirmed in PRE. The realization of
t for d is favored in unstressed environments and inhibited in
stressed ones.

Another factor that has been observed to influence the
relative frequency of t in nonvocalic environments is the distinction between underlying //d// followed by a consonant and
that followed by a pause of some type. Pause is seen to favor
the incidence of t (Wolfram 1969:101). In Table 30, the effect
of this constraint is considered. Terminal pause and non-
terminal pause (any hesitation following potential d) are not
distinguished in our tabulations. Tabulations are broken down
into stressed and unstressed environments on the basis of our
previously determined constraint.

There is an obvious effect on t realization based on the
distinction between a following pause and a following consonant,
but the ordering of the constraints is somewhat unclear. The
implied order in Table 30 is that stress is hierarchically
ranked before the following pause, but the two crucial cross-
products for this decision, i.e. Stressed, ___// and Unstressed,
___##C, are so close that there is no significant difference.
The difference between Stressed, ___##C and Unstressed, ___//

is significant, but since these are not the crucial cross-
products to compare when determining the ordering of constraints,
any decision about ordering will have to be somewhat arbitrary.

Table 30.   Frequency of t realization for potential d in four
            environments for Puerto Rican informants.

	Stressed		Unstressed	
	___##C	___//	___##C	___//
No. t	37	57	10	30
No. d	50	92	14	20
% t	42.5	38.3	41.7	60.0

In Wolfram's (1969:101) study of constraints on t for d,
the possibility of following voicing has also been investigated,
but has been found to be of no consequence. A similar tabulation for these data in stressed syllables also reveals that it
is of no significance. (In fact, t realization is slightly
more frequent when followed by a voiced consonant than when
followed by a voiceless one.) This, however, is contrary to
Fasold's (1972) findings for devoicing in Washington working-
class black speech. Our impression, then, is that if voicing
is a constraint on t for d, it is a very minor one.

At this point, we can summarize the constraints that we
have established in terms of a variable rule for devoicing,
formalized as:

$$(45) \quad d \rightarrow t / \begin{bmatrix} V \\ A \text{ -stress} \end{bmatrix} \underline{\quad} \#\# \begin{bmatrix} -V \\ B \text{ -segment} \end{bmatrix}$$

Several points need to be noted in our formalization of
Rule (45). In the first place, we have written the rule so
that it operates only in nonvocalic environments. This means
that we are assuming that the phonological process is pro-
hibited from operating before a vowel, i.e. an immediately
following vowel without any intermittent pause. The rare cases

of t before vowels which we mentioned earlier are dismissed as
performance factors of some type. This decision is a statistical
one, based on the fact that t for d preceding a vowel occurs in
less than 5 percent of all cases. If we were to account for
these infrequent instances in our formal statement, the distinction between following vowel/nonvowel would obviously be the
first order constraint.

The hierarchy of constraints formalized here is quite different from the one suggested by Fasold (1972:47) for Black
English. Fasold suggests that the first order constraint is
voicing/voicelessness, the second order constraint is the
absence/presence of a vowel, and the third order constraint is
the presence/absence of a pause. He does not mention the possible constraint of stress, presumably because there are too
few examples in his data for him to make his calculations so
detailed. Although his suggested hierarchy of constraints
would, on the surface, appear to be radically different from
the one suggested here, some of this is due to his interpretation of the distinction between a following vowel/nonvowel
as a genuine constraint on variability. Once he concludes that
vowel/nonvowel is a legitimate constraint, he unites the voicing
of the following vowel (since in English all vowels are voiced)
and the voicing of the following consonants together as the
most inhibiting factor on d devoicing, whereas the lack of
voicing is the factor that favors it most. If Fasold were to
interpret the following vowel as categorically prohibiting devoicing, his constraints would be rearranged considerably and
would not conflict seriously with the ones suggested here.

So far, we have not discussed the relation of the devoicing rule (Rule (45)) to the deletion rule (Rule (39)) outlined
previously. Labov et al. (1968), in their treatment of these
relations, consider the output of the devoicing rule applied
to d to be a segment that merges with t. The t, d deletion

rule then operates on the output of the devoicing rule. This
is, of course, based on the assumption that the output of d
devoicing is identical to that of t. Fasold (1972:50-53),
however, raises the question of whether the phonetic outputs
from underlying //d// and //t// are identical. He notes that two
of the phonetic realizations of postvocalic, syllable-final
//t// and //d// are identical, namely, the unreleased stop [t˺]
and the glottal [ʔ]; the third variant, the co-articulated
glottal and unreleased stop [ʔt˺], however, appears to be
unique to the phonetic realization of underlying //d//. If we
assume that Fasold is correct in his phonetic impressions, we
can raise the question of why this devoicing is unique to
//d//: is it a phonetic vestige of the underlying voiced segment, or is it due to some phonological environment that may
characterize //d// but not //t//? It has been pointed out in
Wolfram (1970) that the lengthening of vowels that is characteristic before voiced segments in English is still retained
when underlying //d// is devoiced, giving phonetic items like:

(46) a. [mæːᵊʔt˺] 'mad'

b. [gaːʔt˺] 'God'

This phonetic realization, noted for Black English, is also
characteristic of the PRE phonetic realizations of [ʔt˺].[8]
Now, if this is the case, then it may be that the co-articulated
glottal and unreleased stop is a function of length and cannot
occur before underlying //t//. If we specify the [ʔt˺] realization as a function of preceding length, we can account for the
realization of the unique variant for underlying //d//.

Although the preceding discussion may appear to open up
the door for allowing d → t and t → ∅ as the logical relation
of the two processes, we must not forget the different frequency distributions for the deletion of t and d. If we first
change d to t, then we have difficulty accounting for the clear-
cut preference for the deletion of underlying //d// over //t// (see

Table 22). We could revise our constraints so that preceding
vowel length is an important constraint on the deletion of t
in order to justify the relations Labov et al. (1968) originally suggested, but this solution seems to be somewhat ad
hoc[9]. Despite the apparent reasonableness of the step-wise
gradation of devoicing from voicing through total deletion,
we must conclude with Fasold that "devoicing and deletion are
linguistically separate phenomena" (Fasold 1972:53)[10].

5.7 The comparison of t for underlying //d// in Puerto Rican
and Black English. We have previously mentioned that t for
underlying //d// is a characteristic of both Puerto Rican and
Black English. In fact, the variants that are initially set
forth for our analysis of t for underlying //d// in PRE are precisely the ones that both Wolfram (1969) and Fasold (1972)
have identified for Black English. It yet remains, then, to
compare the incidence of t for underlying //d// among the Puerto
Rican and black informants. This is done in Table 31 in which
figures are given for stressed and unstressed syllables and
for following consonant or pause.

As indicated in Table 31, the same general effect of environments is observed for the two groups. The major difference between the groups is found in the frequency: the black
informants generally realize t more frequently than do the
Puerto Ricans. Although we note that t is somewhat more frequent in Black English than it is in Puerto Rican English, we
may recall that ∅ realizations are more frequent in Puerto
Rican English. We may then ask how the groups contrast when
they are compared in terms of the total frequency of non-d,
i.e. t or ∅, realizations. The figures for the two non-d
realizations are given in Table 32. Figures are given only
for stressed and unstressed environments preceding a nonvocalic environment.

Table 31. Comparison of t realization for potential d in
           four environments for Puerto Rican and black
           informants.

	Stressed		Unstressed	
	___##C	___//	___##C	___//
Puerto Rican				
No. t	33	57	10	30
No. d	50	82	14	20
% t	39.8	41.0	41.7	60.0
Black				
No. t	26	41	11	16
No. d	39	34	7	7
% t	40.0	54.7	61.1	69.6

Table 32. Comparison of total non-d realizations in stressed
           and unstressed environments for Puerto Rican and
           black informants.

	Stressed				Unstressed			
	Ø	t	Total Non-d	//d//	Ø	t	Total Non-d	//d//
Puerto Rican								
No.	245	90	335	481	182	40	222	256
% of //d//	50.9	18.7	69.6		71.1	15.6	86.7	
Black								
No.	76	67	143	216	38	27	65	79
% of //d//	35.2	31.0	66.2		48.1	34.2	82.3	

Table 32 indicates that the two groups do not differ significantly in terms of the total non-d realizations. However, they
do differ in the types of realizations: Puerto Rican English
shows the Ø realization significantly more frequently (Chi

square p < .001) than does Black English, whereas Black English realizes t more frequently.

Finally, we can look at the incidence of t realization
for the BL, PR/BL, and PR informants. We hypothesize that
PR/BL informants will use t more frequently than do the PR
informants. Table 33, which compares the three groups, allows
us to test our hypothesis. The realizations are compared in
stressed and unstressed syllables and following consonant or
pause.

Table 33.   Comparison of t realization for potential d in four
             environments for BL, PR/BL, and PR informants.

	Stressed		Unstressed	
	___##C	___//	___##C	___//
BL				
No. t	26	41	11	16
No. d	39	34	7	7
% t	40.0	54.7	61.1	69.6
PR/BL				
No. t	6	15	5	6
No. d	8	9	3	2
% t	42.9	62.5	62.5	75.0
PR				
No. t	27	42	5	24
No. d	42	73	11	18
% t	39.1	36.5	31.3	57.1

Despite the few examples in some of the categories delimited in Table 33, our hypothesis is confirmed: PR/BL informants do realize t more frequently than do PR informants.
In fact, the figures for the PR/BL group exceed (but not to
any degree of statistical significance) the frequency of t
realization observed in the black group. We thus conclude

that t realization is a feature that shows assimilation to
Black English. For Puerto Ricans, one of the linguistic effects of extensive contacts with Black English speakers is the
increased frequency of t realization.

5.8 Summary. In the preceding discussion, we have seen that
alveolar stop deletion following vowels and d devoicing are an
integral part of PRE. Unlike the case of θ, which we discussed
in Chapter Four, these processes cannot be accounted for solely
on the basis of assimilation to the surrounding Black-English-
speaking community. Rather, there appears to be a convergence
of a Black English phonological process and a process that
might be attributed to the influence of Puerto Rican Spanish.
Our conclusion that it is the combination of these sources that
accounts for alveolar deletion is based on the frequency distribution. If deletion were due simply to Puerto Rican Spanish
interference phenomena, we would not expect the high frequency
level of occurrence, since straightforward interference for
these informants tends to be very low, so low that we previously
labeled it vestigial interference. On the other hand, if it
were due simply to assimilation to the black community, we
would not expect both those Puerto Ricans with extensive black
contacts and those with restricted black contacts to exceed
the frequency of occurrence found among Black English speakers.
But both groups have considerably more alveolar stop deletion
than the black group. We therefore conclude that the phonological processes in Black English and Puerto Rican Spanish
are converging to account for the incidence of deletion.

The process of d devoicing may also be due, in part, to
converging processes, but it appears to be more sensitive to
assimilation to the black community than is deletion. This
conclusion is again based on the frequency levels: the frequency levels for this feature indicate that Puerto Ricans

with extensive black contacts may have a higher incidence of devoicing than do speakers from the surrounding Black English community, but that Puerto Ricans with restricted black contacts typically have a lower incidence than is found in Black English.

There are two rules that are needed to formally account for deletion and devoicing in PRE:

$$(47) \quad \begin{bmatrix} -voc \\ -cont \\ +ant \\ +cor \\ -nas \end{bmatrix} \rightarrow (\emptyset) \ / \ \begin{bmatrix} V \\ \underset{I}{} -stress \end{bmatrix} \ \Delta \ -\# \ \begin{bmatrix} \underline{} \\ B \ +voice \\ E \ - \ PAST \end{bmatrix} \ \#\# \ A \ -V$$

$$(48) \quad \begin{bmatrix} -voc \\ -cont \\ +ant \\ +cor \\ -nas \end{bmatrix} \rightarrow ([-vd]) \ / \ \begin{bmatrix} V \\ A \ -stress \end{bmatrix} \ \underline{}^{\#\#} \ \begin{bmatrix} -V \\ B \ -segment \end{bmatrix}$$

Both of these rules have a number of variable constraints on their occurrence, demonstrating the regular patterning of variability in PRE that matches variability studies in other settings. Although it may be tempting to suggest that deletion operates on t after d has been devoiced to t, the evidence does not support this conclusion. Linguistically these two rules are quite independent, and we suggest that deletion should be ordered before devoicing.

NOTES

1. What is transcribed here as a voiced stop often fades into voicelessness [d̥]. This is to be clearly differentiated from the variants of t.

2. The way in which Fasold (1972) uses the evidence from his application of statistical tests to support his claims about the validity of his constraints on variability can be quite misleading. He applies the Chi square test of statistical significance (which is, in itself, a very weak

statistical calculation) for each major constraint he iso-
lates for d without reference to the intersection of other
constraints. For example, he applies Chi square to the
category past-tense use of d, as opposed to other grammatical functions of d, without breakdown into other constraints he has isolated, such as the distinction between
d in vocalic and nonvocalic environments. Therefore,
when he concludes that the distinction between past and
other grammatical functions of d is significant, we cannot
be sure if this is a function of intersecting constraints
that he has not isolated, e.g. the fact that one grammatical
category may represent more instances in which it is .fol-
lowed by a vowel. Curiously, his summary of the different
intersecting constraints neither gives the raw figures nor
applies any statistical test of significance (there is no
way of retrieving them from the other tables). It is in
this summary table that the breakdown of raw figures and
the application of statistical tests are most essential in
assessing the validity of the conclusions he draws from
the data.

3. By using the symbol ~ to refer to the absence of something,
    e.g. ~ V, Labov has made it possible to regularize the con-
    ventions so that plus (+) always favors and minus (-)
    always inhibits the incidence of rule application. Fasold
    (1972) has suggested that the use of ~ to indicate the ab-
    sence of something is preferable to simply + or - because
    technically it is the absence or presence of environments
    rather than the plus or minus values that affects vari-
    ability.

4. In our tabulation of stressed and unstressed environments
    for t, we counted only the incidence of t in unstressed
    syllables or polysyllabic words. It is suspected that if
    we had taken unstressed syllables in terms of the context
    of phrasal stress, our figures might be more convincing.

5. It is possible that there are some special cases in which
    an assimilation process may be operating. For example,
    with the item let me, we get [lɛmmi] in the majority of
    cases. If we do interpret this as assimilation, it ap-
    pears that this type of assimilation is quite lexically
    restricted.

6. For a comprehensive summary of the rules involved, see
    Fasold (1972:99-114).

7. Although it might be suspected that these forms are cases
    of verb + ed and the pronoun it (which could have the same

phonetic realization), the broader context of these utterances does not indicate that this is the case.

8. Although we have not done specific tabulations of the different phonetic realizations of the variant, it appears that [ʔt˥] is considerably more frequent among Black English speakers than it is among Puerto Rican English speakers.

9. Such a decision would have to be based on the assumption that this sort of phonetic detail is available at this stage in the phonological rules. In most analyses, this is information that would come in lower level rules than the ones we are discussing here, and hence would not be available as environmental conditioning.

10. The important principle that emerges from these relations is that variable frequencies may provide important evidence for "feeding" relationships and rule ordering. This will be discussed in detail in a future paper.

6 NEGATION

After looking exclusively at phonological aspects of PRE in
the previous two chapters, we turn our attention to a grammatical aspect of PRE. Our study of negation in this chapter
will allow us to compare and extend some of the general principles that have emerged in our study of phonological variables.
Like other nonstandard varieties of English, the treatment of
negation in PRE is, in many respects, identical to its treatment in standard English. It is beyond the scope of this study
to give a description of negation that would largely duplicate
or summarize other descriptions of standard English negation[1].
In this chapter, we will deal only with those aspects of PRE
that differ from standard English; standard English will be
used only as a point of reference for the discussion of negation in PRE. Two main areas will be covered: (1) the use of
certain negative particles; (2) the use of negatives with
indefinites.

6.1 Negative particles. We will here concern ourselves with
sentential negation when the negative particle stands alone
or is attached to auxiliaries or the copula. (Its attachment
to indefinites and adverbs will be discussed in Section 6.2.)
The various morphophonemic realizations of the negative particle are discussed under the alternant forms.

6.1.1 The use of no. In the overwhelming number of cases that

we have in our corpus, the particle <u>not</u> and its morphophonemic
alternates occur with auxiliaries and copulas, the same way
that they do in standard English. Thus, the following type of
construction is commonplace:

(49) a. They won't be able to win. (5:3)

b. The cats can't get in the coop. (10:2)

c. Why don't you give those pants a break. (14:5)

d. He's not nuts. (28:8)

But there are several cases that depart from the standard
English expectations in ways that are quite predictable from
the use of the Spanish particle <u>no</u>. We have:

(50) a. He no have to pay nobody money. (27:10)

b. You no smell no nasty air. (44:5)

c. It no gonna get you nowhere. (11:12)

d. I no used to it. (22:11)

The uses illustrated in (50) can, of course, be related to the
Spanish particle <u>no</u>, in Spanish sentences like:

(51) a. No va a la casa.   'He is not going to the
                             house'.

b. No está aquí.   'He is not here'.

Several aspects of this apparent influence from Spanish
must be mentioned. In the first place, the use of the particle <u>no</u> for sentential negation is quite rare in PRE. There
are only 10 examples of this type in the entire corpus, representing less than 2 percent of all potential occurrences.
Furthermore, only 5 of the 29 informants actually use the form,
and even among these informants, it is used very infrequently.
In fact, none of the speakers who uses it does so in more than
8 percent of all potential occurrences.

It is further observed that 6 of the 10 occurrences appear
where <u>don't</u> might be used in standard English. This stands to
reason when we observe that <u>don't</u> in some nonstandard dialects
can be realized as [ð̃ũn] and even [ð̃ũ] because of the operation

of phonological processes that reduce it (see Labov et al.
1968:257). This makes phonetic realizations of don't and no
very close. The difficulty we faced in determining which form
occurred for a number of cases in allegro speech is perhaps the
best testimony of how close these can be.

There are also three examples of no used in a negativized
copula, as in (50c) and (50d). In these cases, it is interesting to note that there is no surface realization of the
copula. Also conspicuous by its absence is the change of
linear order that might have been predicted from Spanish because the particle no is always preauxiliary. But there are
no cases like:

(52)   a.   *He no can do it.

       b.   *He no is here.

Sentences like (52) are quite common negative patterns in the
first stages of English acquisition by Spanish speakers, but
they are not present at all in our corpus.

Although there are no examples of no for didn't, there are
two cases in which not is used in a way that reflects this
Spanish influence, as in:

(53)   He not even missed one guy. (22:8)

The infrequent use of the particle no in a way that reveals Spanish influence indicates that it cannot be described
as a characteristic of PRE. Even speakers who have it use it
so seldom that it can hardly be considered an integral part of
the varieties of PRE that we are dealing with here. The majority of cases in which it is used reflects a relatively unobtru-
sive use of no (for don't) because of phonetic similarity. We
conclude, then, that the occasional uses of no are matters of
vestigial interference that parallel the vestigial interference
pattern we have already cited in our description of phonological
variables.

6.1.2 <u>The use of ain't</u>. <u>Ain't</u> in PRE may have several different functions, and is used in a way quite similar to its uses
in other nonstandard varieties of English, both white and
black.

6.1.2.1 <u>Ain't for</u> $\begin{Bmatrix} am \\ are \\ is \end{Bmatrix}$ + <u>not</u>. In the first place, <u>ain't</u>

may correspond to standard English $\begin{Bmatrix} am \\ are \\ is \end{Bmatrix}$ + <u>not</u>. This standard

English negative construction may be alternately realized as

(1) full copula and full negative: $\begin{Bmatrix} am \\ are \\ is \end{Bmatrix}$ + <u>not</u>; (2) contracted

copula and full negative: $\begin{Bmatrix} 'm \\ 're \\ 's \end{Bmatrix}$ + <u>not</u>; or (3) full copula and

contracted negative: $\begin{Bmatrix} aren't \\ isn't \end{Bmatrix}$. We may get:

   (54) a. I ain't a greedy guy. (9:10)

          b. You ain't gonna do nothing to that
              problem. (14:4)

          c. They know he ain't gonna beat him up. (9:4)

      Although one might have the initial impression that <u>ain't</u>
occurs almost categorically as a correspondent for the three
alternative standard English types, its actual frequency is
less than 50 percent of all potential occurrences, i.e. where
one of the three types of standard English alternates may occur.
But, as we shall see, there is considerable variety in the
realization of the nonstigmatized alternatives.

      In the first place, the full forms (<u>am not</u>, <u>are not</u>, and
<u>is not</u>) are relatively rare in standard English and are used
mostly for negative emphasis. In our corpus, the full forms
are also quite infrequent; in fact, there are only three full
negative + full copula forms that occur, and these seem to be
used emphatically, as in:

(55)   The winter is nót like here.   (23:3)

This leaves the standard forms 'm/'re/'s + not and aren't/
isn't as the candidates for alternation with nonstandard ain't[2].
The alternation among these three types is shown in the following table:

Table 34.   Frequency of ain't usage for Puerto Rican informants.

	No.	% of Total
'm/'re/'s + not	56	45.2
aren't/isn't	5	4.0
ain't	63	50.8
Total	124	

It should be obvious from the above table that the alternatives for our Puerto Rican informants are primarily 'm/'re/'s +
not and ain't. In fact, the incidence of aren't/isn't is so
small that we can hardly consider it an integral part of the
dialect of most speakers. Aren't does not occur at all in the
corpus, so the conclusion about its status is self-evident.
Although isn't accounts for all five occurrences of this type,
one speaker is responsible for three of these. Based on other
criteria, e.g. the fact that he has the second lowest frequency
of multiple negation of all the informants, we can suggest that
this speaker is not entirely representative of the nonstandard
dialect(s) present in our corpus. We cautiously conclude that
the rare occurrences of isn't are due to dialect importation
from standard English. On the other hand, however, fluctuation
between 'm/'re/'s + not and ain't is inherently variable in the
dialect(s) of our informants.

Having established the inherent variability of 'm/'re/'s +
not and ain't, we can now turn to possible constraints on the
occurrence of these forms. For example, is there any constraint
that might take the fluctuation between 'm/'re/'s + not and ain't

in the following sentence out of the realm of "random optionality", i.e. the absence of constraints on the relative frequency of occurrence?

> (56)   No, I'm not gettin' off this car; we ain't
>   doin' nothin', we just sittin' down. (26:8)

One way in which we can break the variants down is according to the copula form to which not is attached, i.e. am, are,
or is:

Table 35.   Frequency of ain't usage for contracted copula +
             not for Puerto Rican informants.

	am	are	is
No. 'm/'re/'s + not	23	24	14
No. ain't	7	28	28
% ain't	23.3	53.8	66.7

The most striking difference shown in the above table is
that between am and are/is (Chi square is $p < .01$), although
there is also a minor frequency difference between are and is.
In attempting to account for the most significant frequency
difference, we must refer to our observation that ain't is
used predominantly as a correspondent of standard English
aren't and isn't. In current standard English, am + not does
not have a parallel negative construction: that is, *amn't
does not occur. We would expect less use of ain't where
standard English has no corresponding contraction because of
its predominant correspondence for negative contractions.

Another possible constraint that has been investigated
with reference to the relative frequency of ain't is the influence of multiple negation: that is, when the negative concord rule has applied to a sentence, does this favor the occurrence of ain't? We may hypothesize that a sentence like:

> (57)   That man ain't nowhere in sight. (11:9)

in which the negative concord rule has applied, is more likely
to contain ain't than is one in which the negative concord
rule cannot apply, e.g. He's not here now. The following
table summarizes the relationship between multiple negation
and ain't in the data, dividing the structures on the basis of
the contrast of am, are, and is, as suggested above:

Table 36.   Frequency of ain't usage in multiple and nonmultiple
            negative clauses for Puerto Rican informants.

| | Multiple Negative Clauses | | Nonmultiple Negative Clauses | |
	No. ain't/Total	% ain't	No. ain't/Total	% ain't
am	3/7	42.9	4/23	17.4
are	20/24	83.3	8/18	44.4
is	16/21	76.2	12/33	36.4
Total	39/52	75.0	24/74	32.4

The effect of multiple negation is to increase the likeli-
hood of ain't occurrence. In fact, this constraint has a
stronger influence than whether or not the form to which the
negative is attached is am[3]. We thus conclude that the constraint of multiple negation is first order and that +am is
second order. We may suggest the following hierarchical ordering for the constraints given in Table 36.

Formalizing the hierarchy of constraints into a rough

approximation of the rule by which we derive ain't from$\left\{\begin{array}{c} am \\ are \\ is \end{array}\right\}$

+ not, we may get:

(58) $\left\{\begin{array}{c} am \\ Bare \\ \Gamma is \end{array}\right\} \rightarrow ey \ / \ \underline{\quad} \ not \ X \ A[+Neg]$

where +Neg and not are members of the same
clause

This rule summarizes the geometrical ordering given in Figure 6: the first order constraint is whether ain't occurs in the context of multiple negation; the second order constraint, whether it is plus or minus underlying ARE; and the third order constraint, whether it is plus or minus underlying IS.

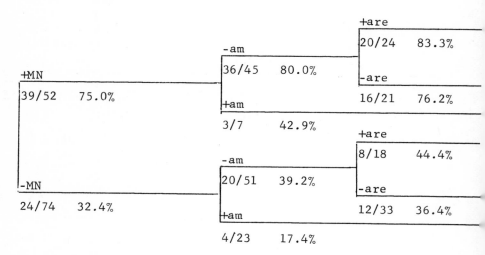

Figure 6.   Hierarchical ordering of three constraints on ain't occurrence for Puerto Rican informants.

6.1.2.2 Ain't for have + not. As in other nonstandard English dialects, ain't can also be used in PRE as a correspondent for standard English have + not.

(59) I ain't been to no fight yet. (11:11)

But there also appears to be inherent fluctuation between this fo and have + not; in fact two-thirds of all potential occurrences a realized by have + not.

(60) I haven't met their family. (18:8)

Most of our PRE speakers must be characterized as having this sor of variation inherent in their dialect.

Although we have too few potential occurrences of have + not to do an analysis of the contextual constraints on the frequency

ain't, which might parallel the analysis we did for $\left\{\begin{array}{l} am \\ are \\ is \end{array}\right\}$ + not,

might predict that the constraint of multiple negation would
have a similar effect, i.e. raising the incidence of ain't.
But, on the other hand, we would not expect person/number to
be relevant to the variability of have + not and ain't, since
there is no structural motivation of the type we presented
earlier for am on which to base such a prediction.

6.1.2.3 Ain't with got. Ain't can also occur as a negativized
auxiliary form with got as a main verb. We thus get:

    (61)   a.   He ain't got no good education. (21:15)

          b.   He ain't got no clothes, wear no
              clothes. (42:2)

     As we might suspect, this form also fluctuates with a less
stigmatized variant. But instead of alternating with have + not
or $\left\{ \begin{array}{c} am \\ is \end{array} \right\}$ + not, the predominant variation in this case is between ain't and do + not, because of the status of got as a
main verb. We get:

    (62)   a.   If you don't got nothing to do in the
              summer, you go to it. (22:11)

          b.   I don't got no time to play. (14:2)

Of the 13 examples of the Neg + got construction, 8 of them
occur with don't and 5 with ain't.

6.1.2.4 Ain't for didn't. In addition to the previously mentioned uses of ain't, it is also observed that there are occasional uses of ain't as a correspondent of standard English
didn't. We thus have:

    (63)   a.   I ain't do this, I ain't do that. (18:5)

          b.   Taylor, he ain't jump, he was
              carried down. (29:2)

This type of correspondence, when tabulated for the entire
Puerto Rican sample, accounts for only 5 percent of all potential occurrences. What is more important, however, is the

fact that only 6 informants account for all occurrences of
ain't for didn't, and for these informants, it is used in 33
percent of all potential occurrences.

Labov et al. (1968) observe that the use of ain't for
standard English didn't is one aspect of ain't usage in which
Black English differs from white nonstandard speech. It is
therefore instructive to note that of the 6 speakers who account for all occurrences of ain't for didn't, 4 have extensive black contacts. We conclude that ain't for standard English didn't is a correspondent that is largely restricted to
those speakers who have direct contacts with blacks. It is
virtually nonexistent in the speech of Puerto Ricans with restricted black contacts.

6.1.3 Pleonastic tense marking with didn't. In negative
sentences containing the auxiliary didn't, tense may be marked
pleonastically in one variety of PRE: that is, tense may be
marked both in the negativized auxiliary and in the main verb.[4]
We get:

(64) a. I didn't did it. (27:8)

      b. I didn't meant to say it that way. (11:5)

      c. We didn't never called it a game. (20:2)

This type of pleonastic tense marking is found for a significant minority of the Puerto Rican informants (8 of 27 informants who have five or more potential occurrences of past
tense negatives with didn't). Like other features which we
have discussed, pleonastic tense marking is not categorical;
it varies with the standard English forms of tense marking,
as in:

(65) a. I didn't even give him carfare to their
          home. (27:12)

      b. They didn't have what they usually have.
          (30:3)

The relative frequency of pleonastic tense marking for those speakers who use it ranges from 18 to 53 percent, but generally the standard English tense-marking convention appears to be more frequent than its nonstandard counterpart. (For those speakers who have at least one instance of pleonastic tense marking, 20 of the 56 potential occurrences (36 percent are realized with the double marking.)

In attempting to account for the occurrence of pleonastic tense marking, we apparently cannot turn to other nonstandard dialects of English, as we have done for some of our other features. In particular, there is no apparent influence from Black English to account for this phenomenon. Although Labov et al. (1968:259) and Fasold (personal communication) report that there is an occasional occurrence of this sort of form, both seem to think that it is a type of performance error rather than an integral pattern of the dialect. There are, furthermore, no instances of this type of construction by the black informants in our corpus and no correlation between its usage and the extent of black contacts on the part of the Puerto Rican informants. We can apparently, then, rule out the influence of surrounding nonstandard dialects to account for this phenomenon.

On the other hand, there is no direct influence from Spanish that might account for this pleonastic tense marking, since tense marking of this sort does not occur in Spanish. But the lack of isomorphic correspondence does not necessarily exclude indirect influence, e.g. hypercorrection, to account for these constructions. To begin with, we must note that in English, if there are no other auxiliaries, i.e. modal, have, be, in the verb phrase to which not can be attached, then do must be present. But in Spanish, there is no parallel requirement, so that we have:

(66)   a.   No hizo nada.   'He didn't do anything'.

      b.   El muchacho no vino.   'The boy didn't come'.

We see that in English, the tense is marked in the auxiliary
in negative verb phrases, whereas in Spanish, since no auxiliary is required with negatives, it is marked in the verb.

This difference leads us to account for pleonastic tense
marking by hypothesizing that there are several stages of
interference that the Spanish speaker may go through in learning English.   In the first stage, the Spanish speaker attempting to speak English might simply substitute the Spanish negative for the negativized past tense auxiliary, producing:

(67)   He no eat the food.

for standard English 'He didn't eat the food'.   It is important
to note that the use of no for didn't leaves the sentences unmarked for tense.   This seems to be a pidginized stage of
language learning with respect to tense and negation.

Thus, a second stage might be hypothesized, in which the
verb might take the tense marking in compensation for the fact
that it is not attached to a negativized auxiliary.   Realizing
that there is no tense marking, a speaker might simply place
the tense marker on the verb by analogy with the Spanish tense-
marking scheme.   This would result in:

(68)   He no ate the food.

Finally, with the acquisition of the standard English
didn't, the tense may still be retained on the verb, since the
attachment of the negative to a tense-carrying auxiliary is not
found in Spanish.   This, then, gives us:

(69)   He didn't ate the food.

In a sense, this sort of pleonastic tense marking is simply a
type of hypercorrection, in which a false analogy results in
the placement of a form where it is not required by the rules
of the language.[5]

Although the stages described above might give a reasonable explanation for the occurrence of pleonastic tense marking in PRE, the fact remains that this formation cannot simply be dismissed as language interference, and hence outside the scope of an adequate description of PRE. This feature must be described as an integral part of the tense system for one variety of PRE. Furthermore, it must also be pointed out that this is a new rule that cannot be derived simply by reference to the rules of English and Spanish. This rule, that copies the tense on the auxiliary and the verb, may be given roughly as:

(70)   X   [+ PAST]   do   NOT   [+ VERB]   Y
       1   2   3   4   5   6   →
       1        $\emptyset$ 3+2   4   5+2   6

As written above, the rule can operate only when <u>not</u> is present in the sentence. This restriction is based on the fact that we have not found any instances of pleonastic tense marking among the affirmative counterparts. We do not have:

(71)   a.   *He did came yesterday.

       b.   *Did he came yesterday?

Because there is so little potential for occurrences of the above type in our corpus, it is difficult at this point to determine whether or not the absence of sentences like (71) is meaningful. At any rate, if these sentences were found (the second one seeming more likely than the first), it would be a relatively simple matter to adjust the tense-copying rule toward greater generality. Our suspicion is that the more general rule is probably the more correct form for some speakers.

Before concluding our discussion of pleonastic tense marking, it is important to note that "irregular verbs" constitute the majority of verb forms involved in this construction. In these verbs, past tense is formed by some internal change, e.g. <u>sing</u>, <u>sang</u>; <u>come</u>, <u>came</u>, as opposed to the simple addition of the -<u>ed</u> suffix, e.g. <u>work</u>, <u>worked</u>; <u>pull</u>, <u>pulled</u>. The distribution

of pleonastic tense marking on the basis of verb form is shown
in the following table:

Table 37. Frequency of pleonastic tense marking in irregular
           and regular verbs for Puerto Rican informants.

	Irregular Verbs	Regular Verbs
Realized pleonastic tense	17	3
Potential occurrences	38	19
% pleonastic	44.7	15.8

The above distribution indicates that irregular verbs
favor pleonastic tense marking. Does this mean, then, that the
rule that accounts for pleonastic tense marking should include
a constraint based on whether the verb form is irregular or
regular, i.e. must we specify this constraint in Rule (70) by
$\begin{bmatrix} + \text{ VERB} \\ A \text{ IRREGULAR} \end{bmatrix}$? Before assuming that this is what is needed,
we may look for some possible phonological explanation for this
difference.

The past tense of regular verbs is generally formed by the
addition of some morphophonemic alternate of -ed. In the case
of words ending in a consonant other than t or d, this results
in clusters, as in verbs like [mest] messed, [kɔld] called, or
[bəmpt] bumped. When we have a resultant cluster, such as st,
ld, pt, etc., the cluster is eligible for the phonological process of consonant cluster reduction, so that the actual phonetic forms for messed, called, and bumped are [mɛs], [kɔl], and
[bəmp] respectively. This process, which has been described
in detail for Black English by Labov et al. (1968), Wolfram
(1969), and Fasold (1972), is also found in PRE, presumably as
a convergent feature that might be predicted from the influence
of Puerto Rican Spanish and Black English. There is formal
motivation for consonant cluster reduction irrespective of our

observation about verb forms[7]. On the other hand, phonological
processes such as cluster reduction do not affect strong verbs,
since they are not formed by the addition of a suffix that can
sometimes result in a consonant cluster.

We may therefore question whether the difference between
the frequencies of pleonastic tense marking for irregular and
regular verbs is a function of the cluster reduction rule
(which operates on the grammatical marker of regular verbs but
not of irregular ones), or whether it is a constraint that must
be described as inherent in the tense-copying rule. The difference of 30 percent between the two frequencies would certainly be in range that could be accounted for by this phonological rule. We thus conclude that the tense-copying rule
should be written without reference to the constraint [A
IRREGULAR]. The difference in the frequencies will be accounted
for when the lower level phonological rule operates on the output of this rule.

6.2 Negatives with indeterminates[8]. In discussing the use of
negatives with indeterminates, it is necessary to start out by
noting that there are some aspects of the rules needed for PRE
that are shared with all standard and nonstandard dialects of
English, some that are shared with other nonstandard varieties
of English, and some that may be unique to PRE.

6.2.1 Rules for negative sentences with indeterminates. The
"negative attraction" rule, first formulated by Klima (1964:
274), is applicable to PRE, as well as to standard and other
nonstandard dialects of English[9]. This rule can be summarized
roughly by saying that the negative is obligatorily attracted
to the first indefinite if it precedes the verb. This accounts for sentences of the following type:

(72) a. Nobody does his work.

      b. Nobody was hit by anybody anywhere[10]

while not permitting sentences like:

(73) a. *Anybody doesn't do his work.

      b. *Anybody was hit by nobody anywhere.

As Klima points out, the negative attraction rule operates not only with any of the morphophonemic alternates of <u>not</u> but also with adverbs that are "inherently" negative, such as <u>scarcely</u> and <u>hardly</u>.

(74) a. Hardly anybody came.

      b. Scarcely anything happened.

There are two ways of specifying this type of attraction rule, depending on where the negative is originally placed in a sentence. One may choose to place the negative at the beginning of the sentence (see Fasold and Wolfram 1970:71 and McKay 1969) and specify the conditions under which the negative must obligatorily be attached to the indefinite, i.e. the first preverbal indefinite. On the other hand, one may choose, as Labov (1970:66) has done, to attach the negative obligatorily to the preverbal indefinite by moving the negative from its preverbal position (determined by a prior rule) to the indefinite. Labov (1970:67) specifies this as:

(75) Indef - X - Neg

        1   2   3 →

      1+3   2

When the indefinite occurs following the verb, the negative attraction rule may or may not apply. The negative may be realized as the negative particle with the auxiliary (or copula) as in:

(76) He didn't buy anything.

or it may be attracted to the postverbal indefinite, as in:

(77) He bought nothing.

The latter is an example of a rule option more associated
with literary than with colloquial standard English usage.
Both Labov et al. (1968:289) and Fasold and Wolfram (1970:73)
have suggested that this rule is not a part of some nonstandard
dialects, particularly Black English: that is, there is no
rule of the type:

(78) Neg - X - Indef

    1   2   3 →

          2   1+3

where X does not contain Indef

Whether or not such a rule can be found to operate for Puerto
Rican English or, for that matter, for Black English will be
discussed in more detail later.

Whereas both of the above rules show how negatives operate
with indefinites in standard English, another rule is needed to
account for the well-known nonstandard English phenomenon of
"double" or "multiple" negation, in which one underlying negative can be realized at two or more places in the surface
structure. Thus we have:

(79) a. He didn't do nothing to nobody.

      b. He didn't have no friends.

      c. He don't never come no more.

These types of sentences are the result of a rule that
copies the preverbal negative on any indefinite following the
verb, and has been described simply as:

(80) Neg - X - Indef

    1   2   3 →

    1   2   1+3

What takes place is a copying of the negative (called
negative concord by Labov et al. 1968) on as many postverbal
indefinites as there are in a sentence. This rule can be
extended to include all indefinites within the surface sentence limits,[11] as in:

(81) We ain't had no trouble about none of us
      pullin' out no knife.

As has been stressed in other discussions of multiple
negation, it must be remembered that this type of negation is
the result of one underlying negative, and is to be distinguished from standard English sentences expressing propositions
that contain more than one negative.[12]

Thus, a standard English sentence such as:

(82) He didn't do nothing; he was always busy at
      one job or another.

is the realization of two underlying negatives, while a nonstandard sentence such as:

(83) He didn't do nothing because he was so lazy.

is the realization of only one underlying negative.

The difference between He didn't do nothing in the two
sentences can be seen in the following simplified P-markers:[13]

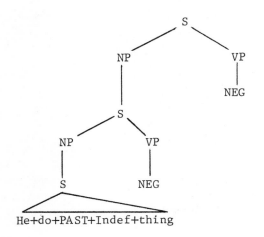

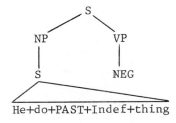

Although we do not doubt the ability of nonstandard speakers to use propositions containing more than one underlying negative,[14] when a nonstandard dialect reveals the categorical use of multiple negation with indefinites (see below), sentences like (82) may not be grammatical. Labov (1972b:816) maintains that this type of sentence is grammatical for nonstandard dialects: a Black English speaker, for example, would contrast the construction <u>He didn't do nothing</u> in sentences (82) and (83) by placing emphatic stress on <u>nothing</u>, as the standard English speaker is apt to do. However, in their comprehensive description of Black English, Labov et al. (1968) give no evidence that would support this contention.[15] Similarly, Wolfram's (1969) Detroit study and McKay's (1969:73) analysis of negation have not revealed any evidence that would support the contention that sentence (82) is grammatical in nonstandard dialects.[16] This raises the possibility, then, that multiple negation may be a constraint that blocks this semantically possible proposition from being grammatical.

It is interesting to note, in this regard, Rivero's (1970) discussion of surface constraints in Spanish that prohibit certain types of semantically logical negative propositions from being grammatical. For example, a sentence such as *<u>No siempre no canta</u> 'He doesn't always not sing', while semantically logical, is ungrammatical because of a surface structure constraint that limits the number of <u>no</u> particles to the number of S-nodes in the surface structure. In the same sense, we suggest that multiple negation may be a constraint that prohibits negative indefinites from reflecting two underlying negatives within the same clause.

6.2.2 <u>The extent of multiple negation</u>. Although multiple negation is a well-known characteristic of most, if not all, nonstandard English varieties, the extent to which the negative

concord rule applies may vary. Shuy, Wolfram, and Riley (1967
III:22) and Labov et al. (1968:267) reveal it to be quite variable for white working-class speakers. On the other hand,
Labov et al. (1968:276) conclude that it is a categorical rule
for Black-English-speaking preadolescents and teen-agers.
Wolfram (1969:157) indicates that it is categorical for some
of the preadolescent and teen-age blacks in Detroit.

In Figure 7, the distribution of the frequency of multiple
negation is indicated for PRE informants. Only informants with
five or more potential occurrences are included in the tabulation, since frequencies based on fewer examples are not useful. The tabulation includes negative sentences with a postverbal indefinite or with the adverb _ever_ when occurring with
a negativized auxiliary. Practically, this means that for the
indefinite pronouns and determiners, all negative sentences in
which _any_ might be the standard English correspondent are
counted[17]. But it excludes sentences in which _any_ is not a
potential surface structure alternative, as in:

(84) a. He's nothing like that.

      b. He was nothing.

since there is no negativized auxiliary in the surface structure. These types of structures will be discussed in detail
in Section 6.2.2.2.

For the adverb _ever/never_, it excludes sentences in which
there is no surface structure realization of negation elsewhere, e.g. on the auxiliary or in an inherent negative such
as _hardly_, eliminating sentences like:

(85) a. He never comes.

      b. He'll never do it.

And, finally, following Labov et al. (1968:278), it excludes indefinites outside the clause, where the negative may
be incorporated appositionally into _either_, _anyhow_, or _any-
thing_[18], in such sentences as:

(86) a. Your mother ain't good looking,
          either. (23:10)

      b. He don't get a second try, or
          anything. (9:1)

As we will see, these structures meet special conditions for

fluctuation that skew our view of how the negative concord rule

applies.

No. of Informants

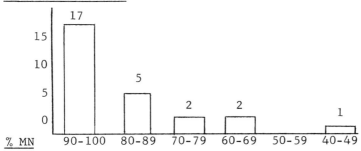

Figure 7. Frequency of multiple negation for
           Puerto Rican informants.

The above figure plainly indicates that most of the speakers

definitely tend toward the categorical or nearly categorical

usage of multiple negation. Of the 17 speakers in the 90-100

percent range, 12 use multiple negation categorically. Of the

27 speakers tabulated, 22 have more than 79 percent multiple

negation, and only one of the speakers falls below 50 percent.

    It is instructive to compare the extent of multiple ne-

gation among our PRE informants with figures from one of Labov

et al.'s (1968:276) black peer groups (the Jets, in single

interview style for comparability); from the white nonstandard

group Labov et al. (1968:276) studied (Inwood); from Shuy,

Wolfram, and Riley's study of a white group in Detroit (1967

III:22); and from Wolfram's (1969:157) black lower-working-

class informants from Detroit. This comparison is made in

Table 38.

Table 38. Comparison of multiple negation in Detroit and New
           York City for Puerto Rican, black, and white
           informants.

	% MN	No. of Cat. MN Users/Total No. of Informants
Puerto Rican		
East Harlem (NYC)	87.4	12/27
Black		
Jets (NYC)	97.9	11/13
Detroit	77.8	4/12
East Harlem (NYC)	97.8	7/10
White		
Inwood (NYC)	81.0	2/8
Detroit	56.3	No data

In terms of both the relative frequency of multiple negation and the number of speakers who use multiple negation
categorically, the PRE speakers fall between the white nonstandard groups and the black groups. The frequency of multiple negation for the Puerto Ricans is actually higher than
for the black lower-class group in the Detroit study, but this
group includes adults and both males and females. In terms of
the most comparable group, the black informants in this study,
multiple negation for the Puerto Ricans does not reveal the
same extent of application.

In discussing multiple negation, we have considered our
Puerto Rican informants only as a group. We can, however,
hypothesize that Puerto Ricans with extensive black contacts
will use multiple negation more frequently than will those with
restricted black contacts, because of its categorical usage in
Black English. The breakdown according to these groups is indicated in Table 39. In addition to the relative frequency of

multiple negation, the number of informants who use it categorically is given for each of the groups. Only informants
who have at least five potential examples of multiple negatives
are included in our consideration of categoricality.

Table 39.   Comparison of multiple negation for BL, PR/BL,
             and PR informants.

	No. MN/Total	% MN	No. of Cat. MN Users/Total No. of Informants
BL	131/134	97.8	7/10
PR/BL	63/65	96.9	5/6
PR	213/256	83.2	7/21

     Table 39 confirms our hypothesis concerning Puerto Ricans
with extensive black contacts. Five of the six informants in
this classification reveal multiple negation categorically, and
there is no significant difference between the frequencies of
multiple negation for this group and for the black group. On
the other hand, only 7 of the 21 Puerto Ricans with limited
black contacts use multiple negation categorically. Furthermore, the relative frequency for this group tends to match the
frequency with which multiple negation is found in Labov et
al.'s (1968) nonstandard white group. We conclude, then, that
Puerto Ricans with extensive black contacts will use multiple
negation to approximately the same extent as it is used in
Black English, i.e. categorically, while Puerto Ricans with
restricted black contacts will realize multiple negation to
approximately the same extent as it is realized in white nonstandard dialects in New York City.

6.2.2.1 Sentence-modifying indefinites. At this point, let
us return to the categories that we have eliminated from our
tabulation of multiple negation because they meet special

conditions for variability. Previous studies by Labov et al.
(1968:177) and Wolfram (1969:157) for Black English indicate
that indefinites that are appositional to the negativized
clause, as in (86) above, show less multiple negation than do
indefinites within the negativized clause. When this distinction is made, we find the following distribution:

Table 40. Frequency of multiple negation in main clause and
           modifying clause for Puerto Rican informants.

	No. MN/Total	% MN
Main clause	266/298	89.3
Modifying clause	14/23	60.9

The difference in frequencies confirms the constraint on
multiple negation affected by the structural distinction of
"clause integral" versus "clause modifying" for PRE as a nonstandard English variety. For categorical users of multiple
negation, this is a variable subcategory of the negative concord rule, as Labov et al. (1968:278) have suggested for Black
English; for variable users of multiple negation, this is a
constraint on variability.

6.2.2.2 _Multiple negation with copula_. The second type of
structure that we have eliminated from our tabulation is sentences in which the negative element is attached to a postverbal indefinite but not to the auxiliary. We suggested
earlier that there may be no rule in some nonstandard dialects
(particularly Black English) that allows for sentences like:

　　　(87) a. *He bought nothing.
　　　　　　 b. *He picked up nothing from school.

For our PRE informants, there are only three such occurrences
(less than 2 percent) with the main verb, and two of these are
by the one speaker who has less than 50 percent multiple negation.

Does this mean, then, that there is no rule like Rule (88),
in which the negative can optionally be transported to a postverbal indefinite from its position on an auxiliary or a copula,
i.e. the tense carrier?

Before concluding that there is no optionality of this
type for the PRE speaker, we must look at what happens to the
negative in certain types of constructions. First, we must
note what happens with indefinites in negative sentences with
a copula that could potentially be multiply negativized. We
observe:

    (88)   a.   There's no Italians. (32:10)

            b.   They're no good. (19:2)

This type of occurrence fluctuates with multiple negatives
like:

    (89)   a.   There ain't no leader. (31:7)

            b.   You ain't nothing. (28:10)

This sort of fluctuation is quite frequent, as can be seen
in the following table. Because the absence of multiple negation is observed so frequently with existential _there_ (or, for
some speakers, _it_), the table is broken down on the basis of
existential _there_, e.g. _There's no Italians_ or _It's no Italians_,
versus other subjects, e.g. _They're no good_.

Table 41. Frequency of multiple negatives with copula and
           indefinite for Puerto Rican informants.

	No. MN/Total	% MN
Existential _there/it_	19/36	52.8
Other subjects	7/12	58.3
Total	26/48	54.2

The sort of variation indicated in (88) and (89) is obviously inherent within PRE, as it is within other nonstandard
dialects of English. Speakers who show categorical multiple

negation elsewhere consistently reveal fluctuation in sentences
like (88) and (89). In this respect, this fluctuation may differ from sentences like (87), which might be considered importations from standard English because of their very limited
occurrence.

Several options may be suggested in an attempt to account
for this variation. As a first alternative, we may suggest
that Rule (80) is peculiar to verb phrases containing a copula.
But if we choose this option, it would mean that a sentence
like (90) would be grammatical:

(90)   *It's like that no more.

Our inclination, however, is to suggest that if (87) is ungrammatical for nonstandard speakers, then (90) is also ungrammatical.
The limited evidence that we have in our corpus would seem to
confirm this, for we get sentences like (91), but not like (90).

(91)   It ain't like that no more.   (5:7)

Another possible alternative may be related to copula contraction. We may hypothesize that if copula contraction (or,
for some speakers, deletion) has taken place preceding an indefinite, then multiple negation may become variable: that is,
a speaker may inherently alternate between sentences like (92)
and (93):

(92)   a.   He's not no good at all.

       b.   He's not nothing.

(93)   a.   He's no good at all.

       b.   He's nothing.

If this were the case, then the phonological process of contraction (or deletion) would be a surface constraint that allows
multiple negation to be variable for speakers who may use it
categorically in other types of environments. The contraction
of the copula may inhibit the categorical operation of multiple
negation because it eliminates the possibility of the negative
particle's attaching itself to the copula, e.g. *It'sn't here;

instead, the particle must stand alone, e.g. <u>It's not here</u>.
This phonological process may then allow the negative particle
to optionally be deleted. It is really copula contraction as
it affects negative contraction that results in the variability.

If this is the correct analysis, we would expect that in
the past tense, where copula does not normally contract (and is
therefor eligible for negative contraction), multiple negation
would be categorical for speakers who use it variably in nonpast forms. Thus, (94) would be ungrammatical, but (95) grammatical.

    (94)   *There was nothing we could do.

    (95)   There wasn't nothing we could do.

There are only six past tense occurrences of copula with
negative indefinites in our corpus, and three of them are multiply negated, so that the evidence at this point does not confirm
this solution. If this were confirmed by further evidence, it
would be an attractive alternative, however, since we would
expect the same principle to hold for contractable modals
occurring with the postauxiliary adverb <u>never</u>, making both (96)
and (97) grammatical for categorical users of multiple negation.

    (96)   He'll never make it.

    (97)   He won't never make it.

McKay (1969) indicates that only 97 is grammatical for
Black English, but says nothing about present tense copula, so
it is difficult to determine if she admits the fluctuation we
have observed for both Puerto Rican and Black English in the
much more frequently occurring nonpast copula forms. A third
alternative may be related to what we can call the "contiguity
condition". Through the application of the negative concord
rule and the placement of the negative on the copula, it is
observed that two negatives are immediately contiguous. When
this is the case, we may suggest that there is an optional rule
that may delete the first negative, specified roughly as:

(98)   X   Cop   NEG   NEG + Indef   Y
        1   2   3   4   5   →
        1   2   ∅   4   5

If the fluctuation is specified through an optional rule such
as (98), it accounts for the ungrammaticality of (90) for some
speakers, while allowing fluctuation between (88) and (89) and
between (92) and (93), which our data indicate to be variable.
Of course, this rule operates on the output of the negative
concord rule and the rule that places the negative to the right
of the copula. Although at first glance, this may not appear
to be the most attractive alternative, when we investigate
multiple negatives with the preverb never/ever, we find that
the contiguity condition may have greater applicability than
just to the copula.

6.2.2.3 <u>Multiple negation with hardly and never</u>. In addition
to the fluctuation we observe with copulas, we note that there
is considerable fluctuation of multiple negatives with the
negative adverbs <u>hardly</u> and <u>never</u>. Most characteristically
there is variation between do+NEG+[NEG] adverb and just [+NEG]
adverb. For example, we get:

     (99)   a.   We don't never go in front of them. (21:4)

           b.   I don't hardly go with them. (22:10)

   (100)   a.   I never go with them no more.

           b.   We hardly play with that. (35:1)

     The following frequency distribution is observed for two
negative adverbs:

Table 42.   Frequency of do+NEG with negative preverbs
               for Puerto Rican informants.

	do+NEG+NEG Prev./Total	% MN
<u>hardly</u>	10/19	52.6
<u>never</u>	13/52	25.0

This sort of variation, like that noted above, is an integral part of PRE, as it is of other nonstandard dialects of English. How, then, do we account for such variation?

To begin with, we must note that when the adverb occurs in the postauxiliary position, multiple negation may not take place. Thus sentences like (101) are grammatical but those like (102) would not be:[19]

(101) a. He never did come.

      b. He never would come.

(102) a. *He never didn't come.

      b. *He never won't come.[20]

Thus, one alternative for specifying this restriction may be related to movement of the adverb to a postauxiliary position. If a permutation such as (103) takes place, the negative may be attached to the auxiliary.[21]

$$(103) \quad X \quad Adv \quad TENSE \left\{ \begin{array}{c} have \\ M \\ be \end{array} \right\} \quad [+VERB] \quad Y$$

$$\begin{array}{cccccc} 1 & 2 & 3 & 4 & 5 & \rightarrow \\ 1 & 3 & 2 & 4 & 5 & \end{array}$$

Does multiple negation obligatorily take place when Rule (103) has been applied? If this were the case, then there would be no variation between (104) and (105).

(104) a. Words won't never harm me. (22:10)

      b. You couldn't hardly compare. (32:8)

(105) a. He thought he would never make it. (10:4)

      b. I could hardly breathe, pain me so hard, boy. (20:7)

For speakers who use multiple negation categorically in other than the variable context described here, four out of eight examples are realized as multiple negatives. Although this is only a limited number of examples as the basis for our conclusion, the evidence we do have does not confirm the

categorical operation of multiple negation for adverbs that
have been moved to a postauxiliary position. And when modals
that contract with the preceding noun phrase are considered,
it is quite clear (for both Puerto Rican and Black English)
that multiple negation does not appear categorically, for
there is clear evidence that sentences like (106) are grammatical in both Puerto Rican and Black English:[22]

    (106) a. He'll never do it.

            b. He'd never if he could.

    Contractability with the preceding noun phrase definitely
tends to impede multiple negation, and may have to be built
into the description as a constraint on multiple negation.
But as we suggested in our discussion of copula and postverbal
indefinites in negative sentences, it does not appear to be
the sole reason for specifying the optionality of multiple
negation for speakers who otherwise have categorical application of the negative concord rule. When the type of optionality that we have here is compared with that discussed for
copula sentences with postverbal indefinites, we again note
that the negatives here meet the contiguity condition that we
discussed for copula. The presence of adverbs to which the
negative has been attached or in which the negative is inherent and the placement of the negative on the auxiliary result in immediately contiguous negatives. Thus, we can suggest that the contiguity condition has more general application
than was specified in Rule (98). Excluding irrelevant details,
this can be given as:

$$(107) \quad X \quad \text{Tense} \left\{ \begin{array}{c} \text{have} \\ M \\ \text{be} \end{array} \right\} \quad \text{NEG} \quad [+\text{NEG}] \ [+\text{Indeterminate}] \quad Y \rightarrow$$

$$
\begin{array}{ccccc}
1 & 2 & 3 & 4 & 5 \\
1 & 2 & \emptyset & 4 & 5 \\
\end{array}
$$

This rule must, of course, operate on the output of the negative concord rule. Since this rule operates after the negative concord rule has applied and cannot remove the negative that has been attached to or is inherent in the indeterminate, it rightly disallows sentences like (108) for speakers who use multiple negation categorically in other contexts:

(108) a. *You don't ever do it.

b. *He wouldn't ever do it.

Furthermore, the rule must be ordered so as to apply only after the adverb has been moved to a postauxiliary position, since the negatives cannot be contiguous otherwise. The contiguity condition accounts for the grammaticality of sentences like (88) and (100), while prohibiting sentences like (87).

The grammars of speakers who have multiple negation, but for whom (87) may be grammatical, might be characterized by inserting X between the two negatives: if X is null, we may expect the frequency of negative deletion to be increased. One will note that such a formulation for nonstandard speakers differs from its formulation for standard English speakers, i.e. a "negative transportation" rule. But since we need the negative concord rule and the rule for the contiguity condition anyhow, it is more economical to expand the latter rule than to introduce a negative transportation rule like (78).

6.2.3 Preverbal indefinites. Although the frequency of multiple negation for some Puerto Rican English speakers may more closely match its frequency in Black English than in other nonstandard dialects, there are other aspects of multiple negation in Puerto Rican English that differ from those of Black English. One characteristic of Black English is multiple negation involving an auxiliary and a preverbal indefinite. Thus, we may get:

(109)   a.   Nobody didn't do it.

        b.   Nobody couldn't come.

which are equivalent to standard English:

(110)   a.   Nobody did it.

        b.   Nobody could come.

This type of multiple negation is found in studies of
Black English as reported by Labov et al. (1968), Wolfram
(1969), and McKay (1969). Its occurrence in Black English is
quite variable, the frequency among pre-adolescents being in
the 25 to 50 percent range. It is also reported that this
sort of multiple negation is found in one variety of white
nonstandard speech (Labov et al. 1968:273), but it is apparently not found in the speech of the white nonstandard groups
that Labov et al. (1968:277) studied in New York and is not
characteristic of most northern white nonstandard speech.[23]

In the entire corpus, there are only two occurrences of
multiple negation involving a preverbal indefinite and a
negativized auxiliary (representing less than 7 percent of the
total occurrences), and both of these are used by the same
speaker:

(111)   a.   Nothing couldn't hurt him, nothing.   (19:14)

        b.   Nothing couldn't hurt him.   (19:16)

Surprisingly, this speaker does not have extensive contacts with blacks, judging on the basis of both our objective
data and our subjective impressions. His speech on the whole
tends to show more Spanish traits than most of the other
Puerto Ricans in the corpus, but this particular construction
does not appear to be attributable to Spanish influence, since
sentences like:

(112)   a.   *Nadie no lo hace. 'Nobody doesn't do it'.

        b.   *Nadie no puede venir. 'Nobody can't come'.

are generally also ungrammatical in Spanish. Whatever the
explanation may be for the uses by this one speaker (see

Kiparsky 1968:192 ff. for a possible explanation in terms of
rule simplification related to acquisition), it is clear that
this type of structure cannot be described as an integral part
of multiple negation in PRE for most speakers.

Related to the negation of a preverbal indefinite and a
negativized auxiliary is what Labov et al. (1968:283) have
called "negative inversion", in which the auxiliary and the
negativized indefinite are reversed in declarative sentences,
producing:

(113)   a.   Didn't nobody do it.

         b.   Couldn't nobody come.

This feature, quite typical of Black English and of some
southern white varieties, is totally absent in our corpus.
Although more potential examples than the 37 that we have
might produce the occasional use of such a structure among
some of our informants with extensive black contacts, it is
clear that it is not a feature that has become an integral
part of PRE.

In part, the conclusion that there are no instances of
negative inversion in our corpus is due to the interpretation
of copula with indefinites as the result of a process other
than negative inversion for PRE speakers. We do have some
examples of ain't or isn't preceding the indefinite, as in:

(114)   a.   Ain't no leaders, ain't nobodies gonna
               take after us. (31:7)

         b.   Isn't none of 'em where I live. (26:3)

         c.   When you die, you die, ain't no way
               to come back. (18:10)

Labov et al. (1968:285 ff.) suggest that for Black English, there are two alternative analyses for (114): one can
interpret it either as a matter of deletion of existential
there or it, or as a case of negative inversion, as in sentences like (113). Labov et al.'s choice of the latter option

is largely due to the fact that other structures are not limited
to copula, but occur with modals and <u>do</u> auxiliary (Labov et al.
(1968:285-86). Without this evidence, there is weak motivation
for considering it a matter of negative inversion. Furthermore, speakers who have this structure show its variation with
<u>it</u> or <u>there</u>. For example, quite close to sentence (114a),
Informant 31 produced:

> (115) There ain't no leader. (31:7)

Similarly, Informant 18 produced the following sentence:

> (116) He kept saying, ain't no gold, ain't no gold,
>   everytime he said there ain't no gold, the
>   guy used to smack him. (18:4)

We thus conclude that there is a simple rule, like (117), that
operates to delete <u>it/there</u> after prior rules have combined
clauses and inserted a dummy subject.[24]

> (117) It/There   Cop NEG   Indef   X
>
>   1   2   3   4   →
>
> $\emptyset$ 2   3   4

Finally, it has been observed that Black English may trans-
fer a negativized preverbal auxiliary across clauses, so that
sentences like:

> (118) a. It wasn't no girls couldn't go with us.
>
>   b. It ain't no cat can't get in no coop.

are equivalent to standard English:

> (119) a. There weren't any girls who could go
>   with us.
>
>   b. There are no cats that can get in any coop.

As might be expected from our previous observations about
auxiliaries and preverbal indefinites in negative sentences,
this form is not found among our PRE speakers.

6.3 <u>A special use of hardly in PRE</u>. Although most instances
of <u>hardly</u> and <u>never</u> follow the patterns observed in other

nonstandard dialects, both white and black, there are several
instances of <u>hardly</u> in PRE that depart rather radically from
these patterns. Observe the following examples:

    (120) a. Hardly everything's Puerto Rican.... (22:10)

             b. Hardly everyone was in prison.... (20:4)

             c. I only came in when it was hardly
                 ending. (31:4)

             d. ...and his leg hardly broke. (22:7)

In attempting to account for these examples, we must first
look at more context, particularly for the first two examples.
Just on the basis of the above sentences we do not know whether
<u>hardly everything</u> means that the majority or that only a few
of the speaker's acquaintances are Puerto Rican. If the latter
is the case, it might mean that the negative attraction rule
with preverbal indefinites might have to be modified in order
to accommodate this construction. But more context plainly
indicates that the former meaning is intended:

    (121) FW: Are there mostly Puerto Ricans where
                 you live?

           IN: Yep. Hardly everything's Puerto Rican,
                 only a couple Italian people, that's
                 all. (22:10)

When wider context is examined for the second example, we find
that 'many' rather than 'few' is the intended meaning:

    (122) Hardly everybody was in prison and Coop ran
            almost freed us; everybody was caught. (20:4)

In attempting to account for the uses of <u>hardly</u> we have
encountered above, it is informative to look at several Spanish
sentences:

    (123) a. Casi ninguno vino.   'Hardly anyone came'.

             b. Casi nada está terminado. 'Hardly anything
                 is finished'.

             c. Casi todo el mundo vino. 'Almost everyone
                 came'.

             d. Casi todo está terminado. 'Almost every-
                 thing is finished'.

It is important to observe that casi can occur in both
affirmative and negative sentences in Spanish; in negative
sentences it is translated as hardly and in affirmative sentences as almost. Casi is inherently neither affirmative nor
negative in Spanish. What we may predict from this pattern
is a use of hardly that might be semantically analogous to its
use in Spanish. This means that the inherent negativity of
hardly may not necessarily characterize some speakers' use of
it. If [+NEG] is removed from the lexical characterization of
hardly, it functions much like the adverb almost, which is
inherently unmarked either affirmatively or negatively. By
the simple removal of [+NEG] in the lexical representation of
one variety of PRE (spoken by a minority of informants) we can
account for what appear to be some rather radical departures
from other nonstandard English varieties.

6.4 Summary. In our preceding discussion of negation in PRE,
we have seen that there is a great deal of overlap between the
treatment of negation in PRE and its treatment in other nonstandard dialects. Multiple negation is a phenomenon that is
widespread in PRE, as it is in other nonstandard dialects, and
for some speakers (particularly those with extensive black
contacts), negative concord is a categorical rule. The categoricality of this rule, of course, is specific to certain
types of environments, excluding sentence-modifying negatives
and certain negative constructions meeting what we have called
the contiguity condition. Negative particles also tend to
parallel their usage in other nonstandard dialects, particularly
the uses of ain't.

Although there may be influence from Black English with
respect to the extent of multiple negation, some features of
negation unique in a northern setting to Black English do not
seem to be assimilated to the extent that we have seen for

phonological features of Black English. This suggests a difference between the assimilation processes of grammatical and
phonological features, a matter which we shall take up in more
detail in the next chapter.

Finally, we have seen that there are several aspects of
negation in PRE that may be unique to this dialect. In part,
this is due to aspects of vestigial interference in grammar
that parallel similar phenomena in phonology. But we have
also seen, at least in one case (viz. pleonastic tense marking), that some independent development may have taken place
in PRE.

NOTES

1. For such studies, one can refer to Klima's (1964) compre-
    hensive study of standard English negation and to the
    report of Stockwell, Schachter, and Partee (1968), which
    includes negation as one of the major areas covered in the
    UCLA syntax project.

2. For those speakers who have the copula deletion rule, we
    can also get ∅ for these contracted forms, so that we have
    We not gonna do it.

3. One might argue that the difference between am and are/is
    is simply a function of the fact that there are fewer
    potential occurrences of ain't in the context of multiple
    negation. Two facts militate against this, however. In
    the first place, the discrepancy still obtains for non-
    multiple negation contexts, where there is a more repre-
    sentative number of potential occurrences. Secondly, the
    frequencies in the multiple negation context are in the
    direction we would predict, despite the fact that there
    are only seven potential occurrences. Other studies
    (Labov et al. 1968, Fasold 1972) have revealed that con-
    straints on frequency can be established from a surpris-
    ingly small number of occurrences.

4. For those Puerto Rican English speakers who use ain't for
    didn't, an ambiguity arises that is not encountered by
    Black English speakers who use ain't for didn't, namely,

whether ain't in a sentence such as He ain't called a cab
is equivalent to 'He hasn't called a cab' or 'He didn't
call a cab'. Only the former interpretation is possible
for Black English speakers.

5. It is essential here to note that the term hypercorrection
has been used by sociolinguists in two senses, which we
refer to here as "structural hypercorrection" and "frequency hypercorrection". Structural hypercorrection has
been used to refer to the extension of the use of forms,
based on an unfamiliarity with the structural restrictions
that cover their usage. Thus, when Black English speakers
use -Z on nonthird person forms because of their unfamiliarity with the standard English rule governing -Z third
person singular usage, we have an instance of structural
hypercorrection. In the case of frequency hypercorrection,
the structural placement may be correct, but the relative
frequency exceeds the expected norms due to stylistic constraints on formality. This is the type of hypercorrection
Labov (1966) referred to when he described the higher frequency of r usage by lower-middle-class speakers in New
York City when compared with middle-class speakers in the
more formal styles of speech.

6. The reason that this total does not match the total potential occurrences given previously, i.e. 56, is that
some verb forms involve both the addition of a suffix and
an internal change, e.g. leave, left, causing them to be
classified in both categories the way we have tabulated
them here.

7. For a description of this phenomenon in PRE, see Wolfram
(1971:356-60).

8. Indeterminate is used here to cover indefinite determiners,
nouns, and certain adverbs such as never.

9. A more technically accurate account of the rules for negative sentences with indeterminates has recently appeared
in Labov (1972b). The summary here is intended to be only
approximative.

10. This rule must, of course, apply after the passive transformation has taken place.

11. Although there is no actual grammatical limit to the instances of multiple negation within a surface sentence,
in my study of Black English in Detroit (Wolfram 1969) and

in this corpus, I have found no instances of more than four surface negatives for one underlying negative. McKay (1969) also finds a stylistic limitation to four negatives in her corpus. For qualifications to this statement, see Labov (1972b).

12. For a recent discussion of standard English sentences that contain more than one negative in their underlying structure, see Baker (1970).

13. One can introduce the negative presententially or in the verb phrase, and various arguments have been advanced for choosing each alternative. I have chosen the latter here, but will not go into detail about this since it is not essential to our discussion.

14. For example, a sentence such as I couldn't not go; I hadda go, recently heard from a Black English speaker at a basketball game, reveals two underlying negatives.

15. In Labov's (1972b:816) more recent report of negation, he does include an example to demonstrate the grammaticality of two or more underlying negatives with indefinites.

16. McKay goes somewhat further in her generalization, stating that "there is no evidence that the meaning of a sentence can be changed by negating more than one constituent, nor is there any expectation of finding such evidence" (McKay 1969:73). This observation, however, does not seem supportable in light of data of the sort mentioned in Note 14 above. The observation appears to be restricted to the negation of indefinites.

17. In the tabulation of multiple negation reported in Wolfram (1969:159-61), the generic use of the article a in negative sentences is counted as a potential multiple negative. Although the distinction between specific and generic articles may be technically correct, there are too many ambiguous examples to make this dichotomy meaningful for a tabulation of this sort. We have therefore counted no examples of determiner a as instances of potential multiple negation.

18. Labov et al. (1968:278) include anymore in this list but give no examples, so it is unclear how they define its sentence-modifying use. If their definition refers to sentence-final uses such as He doesn't come to our house anymore, our data here reveal that 31 out of 37 cases of

sentence-final <u>any/nomore</u> are realized by multiple negation. This frequency (84 percent multiple negation) is much more like the indefinites discussed below.

19. Sentences in which the auxiliary is realized in the surface structure following the adverb appear to have an emphatic meaning. McKay attributes this to the addition of EMPHATIC to the auxiliary. If the EMPHATIC has been added to the auxiliary, then Rule (103) is blocked (see McKay 1969:80).

20. We are, of course, referring to the sentences on (102) as the realizations of one underlying negative. Sentences such as 102 can be grammatical if they are the realizations of more than one underlying negative.

21. For more details concerning the conditions for such a rule, see McKay (1969:79 ff.).

22. The contracted modal '<u>d</u> or '<u>ll</u> can, of course, be deleted by a low-level phonological rule.

23. The only instances of this type of multiple negation found among the white community in Detroit (Shuy, Wolfram, and Riley 1967) come from Appalachian in-migrants.

24. Both <u>it</u> and <u>there</u> are listed here as dummy subjects since the informants fluctuate between their usage, as in <u>It ain't no games around here</u> (31:1) and <u>There ain't no leader</u> (31:7).

7 SOCIOLINGUISTIC PRINCIPLES

From the descriptive analysis of the preceding chapters, a
number of apparent sociolinguistic principles have emerged.
Some of these relate specifically to the study of language
contact and assimilation, while others relate to more general
sociolinguistic considerations. In reality, of course, these
two aspects are inseparable as the study of speech in the context of the community provides a base for evaluating current
issues in sociolinguistics. In this chapter, we will consider
some of these issues and look at their implications for the
study of language in its social context. For the most part,
we will depend on the descriptive data discussed in the previous chapters as our empirical base, but in some cases we
will introduce supportive data from our more complete description of Puerto Rican English in East Harlem (Wolfram
1971). Although the specific point of reference is the Puerto
Rican community in East Harlem, the sociolinguistic issues we
discuss here are more broadly based in their application. It
is this more general framework that is the focus of this
chapter.

7.1 <u>Vestigial interference</u>. At various points in our discussion of the features of PRE, we have referred to the concept of vestigial interference. We use the term to refer to
the infrequent occurrence of straightforward interference
variants from Puerto Rican Spanish. It has been demonstrated

that when there are two different variants that may correspond
to a standard English form, one from Spanish-influenced English
and one from Black English, the occurrence of the interference
variant is usually quite rare.

In phonology, we have seen that the interference variant
[s] for standard English morpheme-final θ is limited to occasional realizations by a minority of informants. In grammar, the use of no for negativized auxiliary constructions,
e.g. don't, didn't, is classified as a matter of vestigial
interference. These two examples are only tokens of a number
of other cases that might be classified as vestigial interference. For example, first generation Spanish immigrants
learning English will often have difficulty producing and dis-
criminating between vowel sounds such as æ and ɛ. Given the
word pair bet and bat and asked to produce them and determine
if there is any difference in their pronunciations, only 1 of
our 29 Puerto Rican informants pronounced them identically
(although he did perceive a difference between them). Only 2
of the informants were unable to perceive any difference between the two words (although they did pronounce them differently). It is quite clear that the second generation informants, despite the fact that their first language is Puerto
Rican Spanish, reveal neither the types nor the extent of interference variants that their first generation parents do.

In our characterization of vestigial interference, two
basic criteria have been used. First, we have applied the
criterion of limited usage with reference to the "proportion
of informants" who realize a particular interference variant.
For example, in the preceding paragraph, we have referred to
the fact that only 3 of the 29 informants gave responses to the
ɛ/æ contrast that might be influenced from the phonological
system of Puerto Rican Spanish. But we have also used the
criterion of frequency in terms of the "proportion of

occurrences" of an interference form. This frequency level is
based on our calculations of actual occurrences of a form in
relation to its potential occurrences. Theoretically, of
course, the two criteria need not go hand in hand. The theoretically possible combinations of informant and occurrence
proportions can be illustrated as:

Informant Proportion	Occurrence Proportion
Majority	Significant
Majority	Nonsignificant
Minority	Significant
Minority	Nonsignificant

It is the last category, minority informant proportion and
nonsignificant occurrence proportion, that usually characterizes
vestigial interference, although we have several instances of
minority informant proportion but significant occurrence proportion. For straightforward interference, we do not typically
have examples of majority informant proportion and either significant or nonsignificant occurrence proportion.

In our definition of vestigial interference on the basis
quantitative measurement, it should be noted that we have used
an arbitrary cutoff point. For example, if a particular interference item is actualized in less than 5 percent of all the
cases in which it could legitimately be realized, then we consider it to be a matter of vestigial interference. And if less
than one-fourth of all informants realize a particular interference variant, then we classify it as vestigial interference.
Despite the arbitrary nature of our cutoff point, we have maintained that it may have important implications for our formal
representation of PRE. When there is a minority of informants
who evidence a significant proportion of interference forms,
it seems quite evident that we have to formally represent these
forms in terms of a variety of PRE. But in the case of nonsignificant occurrence proportion for a minority of informants,

we have questioned whether we need to describe the form as an
integral part of PRE.

At this point, we would caution that the notion of quantitative significance, as we have used it in the preceding paragraphs, should not be confused with social significance. It may
well be the case that very infrequent occurrences of a particular form are sufficient to socially mark an individual. In
fact, there seems to be some indication that vestigial interference phenomena may be sufficient for identifying the Spanish
background of our Puerto Rican informants to outside listeners.

In terms of language change, vestigial interference is
apparently the last stage in the process of linguistic assimilation. The next stage is the categorical absence of the
interference variant, fully completing the process of assimilation. When we look at the process of change from our viewpoint of language variability, we may hypothesize that linguistic assimilation in second language acquisition recapitulates
the processes found in other types of language change. For example, if we adopt a model of language change that includes
variability in an integral way (Bailey 1973b), we may hypothesize
that there are several different stages through which the change
will go. The beginning point is the categorical usage of an
interference variant and the end point is the categorical adoption of the corresponding variant in the second language. In
between these two points there is variability in the use of
the interference and correspondence variants. The variable
stages, we may hypothesize, will show some of the same environmental constraints that have been isolated in studies of
"inherently variable" speech behavior.

The first stage, as we have mentioned above, is the categorical occurrence of the interference variant. In the next
stage, we may have categorical interference in some environments but variable behavior in others. For example, standard

English θ and the s interference variant for standard English
θ may be variable in word-initial position, e.g. sink ~ think,
while s may be categorical in word-final position[1].

In the next stage, we have variability in a number of
(if not all) environments. If we follow the reasoning of
Bailey (1973b) and Bickerton (1971), we may expect that higher
frequencies will occur in those environments in which variability first occurred. Thus, if θ and s fluctuate in both
word-initial and -final positions, we may expect that θ will
be more frequent in word-initial than in word-final position,
since variation first took place in word-initial position.

Following a stage of "maximum variability", some environments will categorically adopt the new variant, while
other environments will continue to indicate variability.
Again, those environments in which variability is first initi-
ated will lead the way and become the first to categorically
adopt the new variant. In our example, we would expect this
to be θ in word-initial position.

Finally, there is categorical adoption of the new variant
in all environments as the process of assimilation is completed. Before the process is completed, however, we may
expect occasional lapses. If our hypothesis of how the change
takes place is correct, we would expect these lapses to be
environmentally restricted. This is, in fact, what we observe
when we look at the behavior of θ and s. It is only in word-
final position that we observe this vestigial interference.
It is this observation, in fact, that leads us to reconstruct
the various stages of θ acquisition the way we do.

In this section, we have talked about vestigial interference only as it relates to one particular language style.
Presumably, we would expect that there may be considerable
variation in the extent of interference. For example, we may
find that interference levels shift, depending on the formality

of the style; the more informal the style, the higher the incidence of interference. Or we may find that the level of
interference on the part of another interlocutor may effect
interference. If we were to extend our investigation of interference over a complete range of topics, styles, and inter-
locutors, we may find that our classification of vestigial
interference is stylistically confined: that is, it may be
that vestigial interference is found in one style but that
other styles may show a significant level of interference.
If empirical data indicate that this, in fact, is the case,
it would be apparent that our grammar of these speakers would
have to be revised to formally incorporate some of the features
that we have questioned on the basis of our current data revealing vestigial interference.

7.2 __Convergent processes__. Our discussion of vestigial interference in the above section refers only to variants found in
Spanish-influenced English that have no parallel processes in
the surrounding Black-English-speaking community. But there
are also variants in Spanish-influenced English that may parallel the variants that would be predicted from the surrounding
black community (but not standard English), as we have illustrated in our discussion of syllable-final $/\!/d/\!/$.

There are actually two kinds of Puerto Rican Spanish influence that may result in parallel processes between Black
English and Puerto Rican English. In the first type, there is
a correspondence in the morpheme structure sequence rules, but
Spanish and Black English both have identical processes operating on underlying forms. This is the case for $/\!/d/\!/$ deletion,
which we have discussed in Chapter Five. Both Black English
and Puerto Rican Spanish have words ending in $/\!/d/\!/$ as part of
their morpheme structure sequence rules, but there is a deletion rule operating in both language varieties.

The second type of convergence involves differences in morpheme structure sequences. A different morpheme structure sequence for Puerto Rican Spanish may result in interference that parallels the output of a Black English rule. For example, the absence of word-final consonant clusters in Spanish results in the absence of final members of consonant clusters in the English of many Puerto Ricans -- the result of interference. Words like test, ground, and wild may be produced as tes', groun', and wil' respectively. In Black English, there is clear evidence for underlying word-final clusters (see Wolfram 1970), but there is a phonological operation that deletes the final member of the cluster. This results in an output for Black English speakers analogous to that caused by interference in Spanish-influenced English, though for different reasons.

In our original consideration of convergent processes in Chapter Five, we discussed only the first type. For a convergent process of this sort, we observe that PRE speakers as a group reveal a greater incidence of the $\emptyset$ variant for //d// than is found in Black English. With straightforward assimilation variants, as we will see in Section 7.3, the group shows a reduced frequency when compared with the surrounding Black-English-speaking community. Although the Puerto Rican group as a whole may show a greater frequency of a convergent variant than does the Black-English-speaking group, it is observed that Puerto Ricans with extensive black contacts show a greater frequency of convergent processes than do Puerto Ricans with restricted black contacts. We have hypothesized previously that the higher figures for the PR/BL group may be due to the fact that these speakers are reinforcing the process of //d// deletion, that may have assimilated on the basis of their close contacts with blacks, with the more general convergence of these processes predictable from Spanish influence.

The frequency distributions for the convergent processes described in the preceding paragraph appear to be much more typical when similar surface realizations result from identical processes operating on similar types of morpheme structure sequence than when similar realizations result from different morpheme structure sequence rules. This can be illustrated by looking at examples of the two types of processes. In Table 43, the Ø for syllable-final underlying //d// represents the first type, and the reduction of word-final consonant clusters represents the second type. For //d//, we can simply adapt one of our previous tabulations, and for the consonant cluster reduction, we can adapt Shiels' (1972:217) tabulations. Only two main environments are looked at for both tabulations.

Table 43. Comparison of two types of convergent processes in vocalic and nonvocalic environments for BL, PR/BL, and PR informants.

	Ø for //d//		Word-Final Cluster Reduction	
	___##V	___##-V	___##V	___##-V
BL				
No./Total	16/131	114/295	120/222	296/329
% del.	12.3	38.6	54.1	90.0
PR/BL				
No./Total	20/78	113/170	65/133	160/181
% del.	25.6	66.5	48.9	88.4
PR				
No./Total	50/262	314/567	253/561	631/739
% del.	19.1	55.4	45.1	85.4

Although the actual environmental effects on variability are much more detailed than those given above, Table 43 is sufficient to demonstrate the difference we are talking about.

For the realization of //d// as Ø, Puerto Ricans with both

extensive and restricted black contacts exceed the frequency
levels of the black group. But in the case of consonant
cluster reduction, neither group of Puerto Rican informants
exceeds the frequency levels of the black group. We should
mention, however, that there is no significant difference between the frequency levels of the black group and the Puerto
Rican group with extensive black contacts for consonant cluster
reduction. If these two phonological features are truly indicative of the two basic types of processes resulting in convergence, then it is essential to distinguish between them in
order to account for the observed differences in the frequency
distribution. It is apparent that surface realizations resulting from similar underlying forms and derivations are more
supportive of convergence than are similar surface realizations
arrived at through different processes. Convergent processes
of the second type show frequency levels more aligned with
assimilation variants than with those involving the first type
of convergence. We may hypothesize that differences involving
morpheme structure sequence rules are more obtrusive cases of
interference and, therefore, would tend to be avoided by a
group of speakers desiring to restrict their interference.

Before concluding our discussion of convergent processes,
it should be noted that the various groups of speakers indicate parallelism in the types of environmental constraints on
variability. The types of linguistic environments and the
ordering of constraints appear to be identical for the Black-
English-speaking group, the Puerto Ricans with restricted black
contacts.

In attempting to account for this similarity, several
alternative explanations can be offered. First, we may suggest
that the parallelism is observed because of the universality
of constraint effect and ordering. We may anticipate our discussion of variability in Section 7.6 by noting that this

explanation may account for the identity in effect predictability, but it is not certain if it can account for the similarity in the hierarchical ordering. If hierarchical order is
unmarked, then it is possible that our general theory can
account for it, but if it is a marked order, then it is improbable that it can be accounted for on this basis alone.

Another explanation may be that there is convergence between the two language sources, not only in terms of the processes but also in terms of the hierarchical ordering of constraints. This means, for example, that the ordering of constraints for syllable-final //d// deletion in Puerto Rican
Spanish matches that in Black English. Even though we have
not calculated the constraint orders for Puerto Rican Spanish
//d// deletion, this explanation is improbable because of the
difference in potential environments observed for the two
language sources. For example, it is impossible to replicate
for Puerto Rican Spanish the grammatical-marking function of
syllable-final //d// found in English.

The third explanation is that there is a general assimilation of Black English constraint orders by the Puerto Rican
groups. The processes are convergent, but the constraint
orders on variability are different. The ordering may assimilate while the processes converge. If assimilation of constraint orders is taking place in accordance with the Black
English model, it would appear that Black English is a dominant
source for the particular process and that the Puerto Rican
Spanish process plays a supportive role.

One may question, at this point, whether the order of
constraints adopted in an emerging language variety must always directly reflect the order found in one of the source
languages: that is, if environment X is a first order constraint, environment Y second order, and environment Z third
order in L_1, and environment Z is a first order constraint,

environment $\underline{Y}$ second order, and environment $\underline{X}$ third order in L_2, must the order of the variety that results when L_1 and L_2 come into contact directly reflect either L_1 or L_2? Although we would expect this direct reflection in most instances, it does not appear that we can theoretically so limit our expectation. We can anticipate our discussion of new rule emergence in Section 7.5 here by suggesting that there may be an analog with variable constraints. Constraint orders that emerge from L_1 and L_2 contact may result in an order different from either source. For example, a compromise between L_1, in which $\underline{X}$ is a first order constraint, and L_2, in which $\underline{X}$ is a third order constraint, may be reached by making it a second order constraint when the two languages come into contact. While we have no empirical data to support this type of restructuing at present, we would not want to theoretically exclude the emergence of new constraints when languages come into contact (but see the discussion of marking on p. 220).

7.3 <u>Assimilation variants</u>. In addition to the interference variants that are predictable on the basis of Spanish influence and the convergent processes of Spanish-influenced English and Black English (vis-a-vis standard English), there are also variants that can be reasonably accounted for only in terms of assimilation to Black English[2]. Our description of [f] as a surface realization of $/\!/\theta/\!/$ is an example of such a case. The variant <u>f</u> is not predicted on the basis of Spanish influence; nor is it predicted on the basis of standard English. In accounting for this variant, we must turn to the surrounding black community, the main source of English outside the context of the Spanish neighborhood. Other examples of this type of straightforward assimilation might be found in the monophthongization of certain vowel glides, e.g. <u>ay</u> in <u>time</u>, <u>try</u>, and <u>ride</u>; in certain types of negatives, e.g. <u>Didn't nobody do it</u>

as a declarative sentence; and in certain verb uses, e.g. the
use of habitual be as in Sometime he be busy and sometime he
don't (see Wolfram 1971:252-376). It is noted that, at least
with phonological features, the assimilation variants can be
found among Puerto Ricans with both extended and restricted
black contacts. The differences between the two groups are
essentially quantitative: that is, we observe a certain
amount of black influence in the phonology of both groups, but
one group simply shows a higher frequency of the assimilated
variants.

The black influence on both groups of Puerto Rican teen-
agers may be due to the fact that it is virtually impossible
for a Puerto Rican teen-ager in Harlem to avoid some contact
with blacks, despite the fact that he may not include them
in his peer group. It may be that this restricted contact is
insufficient for the assimilation of Black English features to
a limited extent. But even if the Puerto Ricans with restricted
black contacts do not assimilate phonological features from the
sporadic contact they have with blacks, it is quite reasonable
to suggest that some assimilation may be acquired indirectly:
that is, Puerto Rican adolescents with restricted black contacts may be assimilating phonological features of Black English from Puerto Ricans with more extensive black contacts than
themselves.

The frequency levels of assimilation variants show both
similarities to and differences from other types of variants.
The PRE group as a whole shows a frequency level considerably
greater than straightforward interference. Type I convergence,
i.e. identical surface realizations resulting from similar
underlying units and derivations, appears to reveal somewhat
greater relative frequency levels, but Type II convergence,
i.e. identical surface realizations resulting from different
underlying units and derivations, shows a somewhat parallel

type of frequency distribution. The comparison of the two types
of convergent processes with straightforward assimilation can be
observed by comparing Table 43 with the frequency levels of an
assimilation variant. In Table 44, two assimilation variants,
the monophthongization of ay glides in certain types of environments and the [f] realization for //θ// in morpheme-final
position, are compared with the convergence variants from
Table 43. Although we have not specifically discussed the
former assimilation variant in this study, our earlier investigation (Wolfram 1971) includes a fairly extensive analysis of
this variable. In Black English, there are a number of environments in which the upgliding offset of diphthongs can be
reduced or deleted, so that we have a centralized glide or a
monophthong. Words like time, try, and ride may be realized
as [ta:m], [tra:], and [ra:d] respectively. Although this
realization is quite common in some southern varieties of white
English, it is not typically used in white dialects spoken in
northern contexts such as New York City. There are a number of
different environments in which the nonupgliding variant may be
realized, but our table only includes the incidence of the
variants in word-final position, the environment in which the
a variant is most likely to occur. The tabulations for the
convergent features are taken from Table 43. For //d// deletion,
we have included only the tabulations for a following nonvowel,
and for word-final cluster, we have included only the tabulations for a following vowel. These environments are chosen
since they are the most socially diagnostic.

The two examples of assimilation in Table 44 indicate
similar frequency distributions. In both cases, there is a
nonsignificant difference between the frequency levels of the
blacks and the Puerto Ricans with extensive black contacts,
but the Puerto Ricans with restricted black contacts reveal a
reduced frequency by comparison. This is quite unlike Type I

Table 44. Comparison of convergent and assimilation variants
for BL, PR/BL, and PR informants.

	BL	PR/BL	PR
CONVERGENCE			
Type I - Ø for //d//			
No./Total	114/295	113/170	314/567
% del.	38.6	66.5	55.4
Type II - Word-final cluster reduction			
No./Total	120/222	65/133	253/561
% del.	54.1	48.9	45.1
ASSIMILATION			
f for //θ//			
No./Total	36/44	20/23	53/97
% f	81.8	87.0	54.6
a for //ay//			
No./Total	190/247	104/148	261/657
% a	76.9	70.3	39.7

convergence, where both Puerto Rican groups significantly exceed
the frequency level of the black group. In all cases, however,
a higher frequency level is realized by the Puerto Ricans with
extensive black contacts. This general tendency is indicative
of the persistent differences that arise between the two groups
of Puerto Rican speakers.

Although our comparison of assimilation and convergent
features here is quite specific to PRE, it is quite likely that
similar language contact situations would reveal analogous patterns. This demonstrates the necessity of looking at the interaction of quantitative and qualitative dimensions of languages
in contact. The different frequency distributions can be

accounted for only by looking at the structural relations that
can exist between the languages.

7.4 <u>Grammatical and phonological assimilation</u>. In the preceding section, we have limited our discussion of assimilation
phenomena primarily to phonological assimilation. It should
not, however, be assumed that grammatical and phonological
variants will necessarily assimilate in exactly the same ways.
In fact, there is some evidence that there is quite a basic
difference in assimilation when separated on the basis of
phonology and grammar. We have seen that, to some extent, the
influence of Black English phonological features is common to
Puerto Ricans with both extended and restricted black contacts,
the differences between groups being quantitative. We thus see
that a feature like the [f] realization of morpheme-final $/\!/\theta/\!/$
is an integral part of most varieties of PRE. On the other
hand, our examination of negative constructions in Chapter Six
seems to indicate that the same is not true for grammatical
features. Those aspects of negation unique in New York City
to Black English appear to be much more restricted to Puerto
Ricans with extensive black contacts, if they are to be found
at all.

The basic difference between the two types of features
can be illustrated by contrasting a Black English grammatical
feature with one of the phonological features we have previously discussed. One grammatical feature that is considered
unique to Black English is the use of "distributive be". This
particular grammatical feature has been described by a number
of linguists who vary slightly in their analysis, but who
generally agree that it refers to a repeated occurrence of
some type (see Fasold 1969a:746). The distributive function
of <u>be</u> is illustrated in sentences such as:

(124) a. He don't usually be home.

b. Sometimes he be at home; I know he do.

In Table 45, the distribution of distributive be is given for nine informants: three informants each representing Black English speakers, Puerto Ricans with extensive black contacts, and Puerto Ricans with restricted black contacts. These informants, chosen on the basis of nonlinguistic criteria (see Wolfram 1971:252-376 for the criteria used to select them), represent typical informants in each of the cultural categories. For these same informants, we have tabulated the incidence of a for ay as a representation of a phonological assimilation.

Table 45. Comparison of grammatical and phonological assimilation for selected BL, PR/BL, and PR informants.

	BL	PR/BL	PR
GRAMMATICAL ASSIMILATION			
Distributive be			
No./Total	20/53	7/46	0/33
% be	37.7	15.2	0.0
PHONOLOGICAL ASSIMILATION			
a for //ay//			
No./Total	191/277	122/262	59/318
% a	69.0	46.6	18.6

If these two features are typical of how grammatical and phonological features assimilate, then we see quite an apparent difference. Phonological features appear to be much more susceptible to assimilation than are grammatical ones. The main differences in phonological assimilation, as indicated by the Puerto Rican groups, is one of quantity, but there appears to be a qualitative difference in grammatical assimilation.

Distributive be is categorically absent in the speech of Puerto
Rican informants with restricted black contacts. Apparently,
it is only through direct peer contact that extensive grammatical assimilation takes place.

Another essential aspect of grammatical and phonological
assimilation relates to the way in which these features are
assimilated. Where both grammatical and phonological processes
are assimilated in the speech of Puerto Ricans (mainly of
Puerto Ricans with extensive black contacts), the grammatical
processes are assimilated as grammatical processes and the
phonological processes as phonological ones. At first glance,
this might appear to be a trivial observation, but a closer
examination of some of the features that might be interpreted
to result from either a grammatical or a phonological process
indicates that this is a significant discovery. For example,
suffixal Z absence in Z_1, e.g. cent for cents; in Z_2, e.g.
boy hat for boy's hat; and in Z_3, e.g. He run for He runs,
may be the result of either a phonological or a grammatical
process (see Wolfram 1971 for a description of suffixal Z).
Likewise, certain types of suffixal D absence in D_1, e.g.
The man walk out yesterday; in D_2, e.g. He was mess up; and
in D_3, e.g. The mess-up man, may be the result of either a
phonological or a grammatical process. Fasold (1971) clearly
demonstrates the potential ambiguity of various surface realizations and the criteria for determining whether these realizations are the result of phonological or grammatical processes.
He specifically mentions characteristics that help determine
whether the absence of a particular surface form is the result
of phonological or grammatical rules; these characteristics
can be summarized as follows:

    1. If the absence is accounted for syntactically, it
    is expected that the operations in the phonological
    component will have no influence on the output, but if

it is the result of phonological deletion rules, the
deletion should be heavily influenced by phonological
characteristics.

2. Irregular forms will be affected in grammatical
deletion.

3. Hypercorrection will be evident if the absence
of a surface form is due to the lack of underlying units
in the syntactic component. If, however, surface absence
is due to the deletion of a low-level phonological rule,
hypercorrection will not be expected.

4. Grammatical sensitivity will be more evident in
cases in which surface absence is due to grammatical
rules, whereas surface absence that is the result of
phonological rules will evidence phonological sensitivity: that is, grammatical variability will likely
reveal sensitivity to grammatical environment and
phonological variability to phonological environment.

5. Phonological deletion of segments that function
as grammatical markers will reveal analogous deletion
of segments that are not grammatical markers, whereas
grammatical deletion will not.

Applying Fasold's principles to suffixal $\underline{Z}$ and $\underline{D}$ absence
in Black English, it has been concluded that $\underline{Z}$ absence in
Black English is the result of a grammatical process and $\underline{D}$
absence the result of a phonological process. Suffixal $\underline{Z}$
absence affects all morphophonemic realizations of underlying
$\underline{Z}$, e.g. /z/, /s/, /ɨz/, whereas $\underline{D}$ absence is primarily restricted to certain phonological shapes of $\underline{D}$. Furthermore,
irregular past tense verbs are not affected by the phonological process effecting $\underline{D}$, e.g. go - went; regular past
tense formation that results in clusters subsequently reduced
by a word-final consonant cluster reduction rule is affected.
Postulating that there is no underlying Z_3 morpheme, it is

found that Z_3 hypercorrection, e.g. I goes, you goes, etc.,
is observed to a considerable extent in formal situations by
some speakers of Black English. It is further noted that suffixal D is very sensitive to a number of phonological constraints, e.g. following vowel or nonvowel, stop + stop cluster
as opposed to stop + continuant cluster, etc., whereas suffixal Z is sensitive to grammatical constraints, e.g. whether
it is Z_1, Z_2, or Z_3. And, finally, suffixal D deletion shows
a clear analog to phonological processes that operate on
identical segments not functioning as grammatical markers,
e.g. mist reveals deletion of the final t as in missed, whereas suffixal Z does not reveal the same close parallelism.

   Although some of Fasold's criteria for determining phonological and grammatical processes are not completely relevant
to the study of D and Z morphemes in PRE, we come to the same
conclusion concerning suffixal D and Z deletion: D deletion
is primarily the result of a phonological process, whereas Z
deletion is the result of a grammatical process. For example,
as observed in PRE, D deletion shows the sensitivity to phonological constraints on variability that we expect of phonological processes, whereas Z deletion does not. And there is a
clear parallelism in the deletion of grammatical- and nongram-
matical-marking d and t, whereas Z does not show nearly the
same tendency. The observation that suffixal Z absence is the
result of a grammatical process is particularly significant
when we realize that Z deletion in Puerto Rican Spanish may be
the result of a phonological process in which syllable-final
s may be deleted (see Ma and Herasimchuk 1968). At some stages
in the acquisition of English by Spanish speakers, it is possible that suffixal D deletion may be due to grammatical rules,
but it is quite clear that it is the result of a phonological
process in the PRE we are studying here.

   To say that grammatical and phonological processes in

Black English will be assimilated as grammatical and phonological processes respectively in PRE does not, however,
necessarily imply that the same general grammatical and phonological processes will be involved, although we would suspect
that this would be the case in most instances. We are simply
claiming that the same general level of the language component
is responsible for the derivation of surface forms. For example, some speakers of PRE with restricted black contacts
show ARE copula absence, e.g. You nice, They nice, as an integral part of their dialect, while showing little or no incidence of IS deletion, e.g. He nice (see Wolfram 1971:314-26).
For these spakers, it seems reasonable to hypothesize that
ARE deletion may be related to the r-lessness that is quite
typical of both black and white speech in New York City. In
the first stage, r is reduced to a schwa-like quality, and in
the second stage, the phonetic vestige of r is eliminated.
This phonological process is somewhat different from the general rules for copula deletion including IS and ARE that Labov
(1969) has postulated, but like his account of copula deletion
for Black English, it originates in the phonological component
of PRE.

At this point, we can only hypothesize as to why phonological features are more subject to widespread assimilation
by Puerto Ricans than are grammatical ones. One possible
reason may relate to the nature of the linguistic levels involved. For one, the units of phonology are a relatively small,
closed set of items that occur, for the most part, with quite
high frequency. The restrictions of the inventory and the
relatively high frequency with which the units occur may make
phonological items more susceptible to assimilation through
indirect means or restricted contact. Or we may suggest that
the more superficial the level of language involved, the more
susceptible it is to borrowing. Since phonological rules

operate on a much more superficial level of language than do
grammatical rules, they are more susceptible to borrowing.

One might also hypothesize that the difference in the
assimilation of phonological and grammatical phenomena is due
to sociocultural reasons. Previous studies of socially diagnostic linguistic variables (Wolfram 1969) indicate that grammatical variables differentiate social groups more sharply
than do phonological ones: that is, various social groups are
more definitively marked on the basis of grammatical features.
Given the fact that Puerto Ricans with restricted black contacts often negatively view linguistic assimilation from
blacks (see Section 2.5.5), it may be suggested that the
relative obtrusiveness of grammatical features makes them
less susceptible to borrowing than the less obtrusive phonological ones. Linguistic and sociocultural explanations for
the difference in assimilation phenomena are, of course, not
mutually exclusive. It is quite possible that they reinforce
each other.

7.5 <u>The emergence of new rules</u>. Thus far in our discussion,
we have allowed only for rules in PRE that are the direct result of either some aspect of Spanish influence or assimilation
to the English of the surrounding community. Theoretically,
then, only those realizations that are predictable on the basis
of Puerto Rican Spanish or the surrounding dialects of English,
e.g. Black English of the immediately contiguous community,
standard English of the classroom, etc., are recognized. This
assumes that there is an isomorphic correspondence in the rules
of PRE and the rules of the source languages or dialects. This
assumption appears to be an integral part of many models of
bilingualism, whether one essentially views the bilingual as
having one merged system, coexistent systems, or a combination
of the two in which parts of the system are merged and other

parts coexistent. For example, Fasold, in summarizing the
viewpoint of coexistent systems in bilingualism, observes:

> This model, assuming completely disjoint coexistent
> systems, accounts for the speaker's syntactic com-
> petence as long as he produces no ungrammatical
> sentences in either language which are traceable
> to rules in the other (Fasold 1972:138-39).

According to this viewpoint, languages in contact will
not step outside the bounds of either of the languages. What
these traditional views disallow is the operation of rules
that might not be related isomorphically to one of the source
languages or dialects. This is, in fact, true in the vast
majority of cases. Thus, the instances of $//\theta//$, $//d//$, and
multiple negation could, for the most part, be related directly to either surrounding dialects of English or Puerto
Rican Spanish. It therefore might be compelling to conclude
that the traditional assumption is, in fact, quite correct.

Before doing so, however, we must recall our description
of pleonastic tense marking (Section 6.1.3). In negative
sentences containing the auxiliary do, we have observed that
tense may be marked pleonastically in the auxiliary and in the
main verb, giving us sentences like I didn't did it and I didn't
meant to say it that way. We further see that this construction
cannot be directly related to Puerto Rican Spanish, Black English, or standard English. As we have mentioned earlier, there
is a plausible explanation as to how this construction arises
in the process of language acquisition through indirect influence that results in rule generalization. However we wish
to explain it, we are still confronted with a rule that does
not have a direct parallel in any of the source languages.
Thus, a view of languages in contact that accounts only for
direct rule correspondence is inadequate.

For example, consider Fasold's (1972:138-39) model of
interference from disjoint systems. He suggests a model in

which a speaker may follow only the rules from one language or
the other. In terms of Spanish-English bilingualism, we can
illustrate this by a sentence such as <u>He no likes the city</u>.
In this sentence, English rules are followed until the realization of the auxiliary is required for the negative. At this
point, there is a shift to the Spanish rule. If we adopt
Fasold's schematic representation, this can be illustrated as
follows:

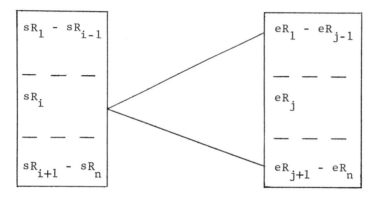

Figure 8. Traditional bilingual interference
model: Spanish-English.

English rules are followed until the placement of the
negative on the auxiliary is required, at which point there
is a transference to Spanish. This is represented by sR_i in
the above diagram. After that point, there is once again a
return to the English rule system. Such a model, however,
does not provide for the innovation we are talking about.
In this case, we have a new rule, which may be represented in
Figure 9.

In the following diagram, we can account for the innovative aspects of interference found in the new rule. In addition to the more usual types of interference diagrammed in
Figure 8, possibilities for innovation must be accounted for

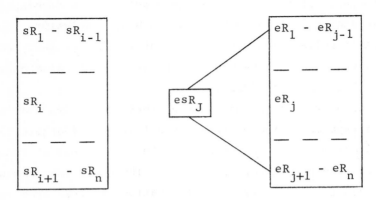

Figure 9. Bilingual interference model accounting
for rule innovation: Spanish-English.

in a realistic model of bilingual interference[3] It seems
reasonable to expect that the majority of these innovations
will be the result of rule generalization. Since structural
hypercorrection may be a manifestation of rule generalization
(see DeCamp 1972), it stands to reason that hypercorrection
is one of the main sources for this type of innovation[4] In
our diagram, the relationship between the regular English rule
and the new rule is indicated in the subscripts. The same
subscript letter is used, but the new rule is now assigned a
capital subscript, while the alternative rule remains lower
case.

When new rules result from rule generalization, it is
quite possible that interference phenomena may show certain
parallels with first language acquisition because of a universal disposition for certain types of generalization. It is
therefore interesting to note that the pleonastic tense marking
that we have described for PRE is also found in monolingual
children acquiring English[5] Although we have only cited the
example of rule generalization, it is not at all certain that
rule innovations should be theoretically limited to this

phenomenon. It is possible for new rules to be developed by
"false analogy" or as compromise linguistic solutions to quite
divergent rules. The essential point is that we must recognize
this sort of innovative process in our theoretical construct of
second language interference.

Since it appears that some of these new rules that arise
may be representative of transitional stages of acquisition,
we may ask what eventually happens to these types of innovations
in a developing language community. There are two options. One
is to stabilize such types of innovations so that they remain an
integral part of the speech community. This can take place, of
course, only if this community resists complete assimilation to
the language of the surrounding community. This would appear to
be the case for a community of speakers that has developed a
unique dialect, such as the Pennsylvania Dutch in southeastern
Pennsylvania. On the other hand, innovative features may be
lost as a variety moves toward complete assimilation. At this
stage in the development of PRE, it is impossible to determine
exactly what is happening with regard to pleonastic tense.
There are, however, several factors that seem to indicate that
it will eventually be eliminated. For one, it is presently
used by a minority of informants (though at significant levels
of occurrence). Thus, it only characterizes one variety of
PRE. And when we look at the informants who use it, we find
that it is those informants for whom the incidence of vestigial
interference is most typically found. These informants seem
to be the followers rather than the leaders with respect to
language change. The minority proportion of informants who
use the construction and the lingering incidence of vestigial
interference in these informants' speech would therefore seem
to indicate that it will be eliminated rather than stablized
in the development of PRE. This is consonant with the tendency
toward assimilation to the surrounding English dialects by
second generation Puerto Ricans in New York City.

7.6 <u>Linguistic variability and variable rules</u>. Fundamental
to our entire sociolinguistic description of PRE is the study
of linguistic variability. As we have discussed in Chapter
Three, the study of linguistic variability adds an entirely
new dimension to the study of language in its social context.
On a formal level, we have observed that systematic variability
can be incorporated into our description of PRE. Following our
description of PRE from this perspective, it is appropriate to
look again at the suppositions on which the theory of variable
rules is based. Are such rules justified, and, if so, in what
form?

As we have discussed in Chapter Three, a primitive supposition for variable rules is the notion of inherent variability. We have operated on the assumption that patterned
fluctuation cannot be dismissed arbitrarily either as code
switching across different linguistic systems or as syste-
matically irrelevant dialect borrowing. Historically, of
course, much of what we now call inherent variability may have
originated as dialect borrowing, but this fact does not miti-
gate our responsibility to account for fluctuation as an intrinsic part of a language system. It has sometimes been
claimed that theoretically all fluctuating items can deter-
ministically be accounted for through the provision of more
detail on linguistic and/or sociopsychological conditioning.
Although this claim cannot be disproved logically, none of the
existing data appears to support such a position (see Sankoff
1972). The observed fluctuation in the most constant of styles
and environments cannot be ignored if we are to give an adequate
account of language system. We are further confronted with
structured sensitivity of fluctuating forms to linguistic constraints on variability. The integral role of variation in PRE
simply confirms what has been observed in other studies of real
language behavior.

In the preceding paragraph, we have mentioned that intrinsically variable items often show a great deal of structured sensitivity to independent linguistic constraints. This raises the question of whether this sensitivity is a unique characteristic of inherent variability: that is, can dialect mixture or borrowing be distinguished from intrinsic variation on this basis? Although it may be tempting to set this up as a criterion for distinguishing these two concepts on a formal linguistic basis, it should be cautioned that this position may not be justified when looked at in closer detail. If we assume that certain aspects of constraining effects are universal (see p. 221), then it might be quite possible for certain types of dialect mixture to show considerable sensitivity to linguistic constraints in the borrowing language. For example, suppose that L_1 does not have any word-final consonant clusters but that L_2 does. A speaker of L_1 borrows a word from L_2 that ends in a consonant cluster. In some instances, it is observed that the cluster is intact, and in other instances, it is reduced in order to conform to the morpheme structure sequence rules of L_1. One would predict that the cluster would have a tendency to be reduced more frequently when followed by a vowel than when followed by a consonant for natural phonetic reasons, i.e. the more consonants in a sequence, the more difficult it is to produce the sequence. It seems apparent that such items will reveal ordered constraints on variability. If one maintains that any item that reveals this type of sensitivity must be considered as an integral part of language variety, then it would appear that the concept of dialect mixture is completely unjustified. Although we may wish to retain the concept of dialect mixture on other bases, the systematic linguistic constraints on variability apparently cannot be useful criteria[6].

Another premise on which variable rules are based is what we have labeled "replicable regularity" (see Section 3.2.2).

The regularity of constraining factors on variability supports
our contention that structured variation must be accounted for
in our representation of a speaker's language competence. The
actual frequency levels appear to be part of a speaker's performance and, as such, only have heuristic value for the
establishment of constraint orders of more or less. Recently,
Cedergren and Sankoff (1972) have attempted to extend the
notion of competence to include some of the probablistic
aspects of variable rule occurrence. They distinguish rule
probabilities from rule frequencies, assigning the former to
competence and the latter to performance (Cedergren and Sankoff
1972:38). Although the distinction between rule probabilities
and frequencies may extend a theory of performance, at this time
it is difficult to see why probabilities should be included as
an aspect of abstract competence. This appears to be making a
claim that is too strong in terms of a speaker's capability
in his language. The crucial aspect of the speaker's competence in variable rules is, in our interpretation, the
hierarchy of constraining effects, and all other aspects appear to be part of performance. Future studies of psycho-
linguistic abilities, however, may show that this claim will
have to be modified as we ultimately attempt to account for
the capabilities of the human mind.

        In the preceding chapter, the actual description of vari-
ation was based on groups of speakers, but a comparison of the
tabulations for individual speakers would typically reveal
parallel constraint effects: that is, if we take the constraints we have formalized for PRE and compare them for individual PRE speakers (as we did for consonant clusters in
Table 4), we would find the constraints to be quite regular
from speaker to speaker. There are, however, two exceptions
to this regularity that may make the characterization of the
speech represented for the social group as a whole appear to

be more systematic than does the speech of the individual.
In some cases, there are not sufficient examples in some of
the subcategories of the constraints to reproduce the clear-
cut effect of the constraint orders as it is represented for
the group as a whole. This type of inconsistency arises simply
from the limited number of examples available for a given informant and would be remedied by a more adequate population of
examples. There are, however, also instances when there appear
to be sufficient examples for discovering the regularity for
individual speakers that we have represented for the group;
yet, we do not obtain the expected regularity. These cases
are somewhat more difficult to dismiss. It is important to
note that these instances are restricted to cases in which the
ratio of effect on the various constraints is relatively close.
For example, suppose we have a case in which the ratio of the
geometrically ordered constraints on variability is as follows:[7]

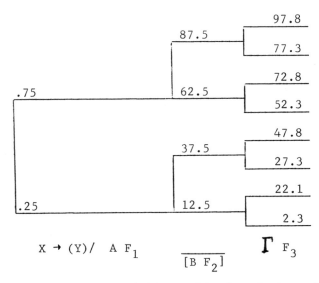

Figure 10.   Theoretical hierarchical ordering of three
              constraints showing different effect ratios.

In the above ordering, we would certainly not expect individual deviation in terms of the first and second order constraints. But the second and third order constraints might
reveal less regularity because their relative effect is somewhat closer. It would appear that the closer two constraints
are in terms of the ratio of their effect, the more likely it
is that we can find some individual discrepancy in the ordering
of constraints. For example, if the effect of one constraint
is 4 to 1, i.e. the rule will be effected 4 times in a given
environment to every 1 time that it is not, and the effect of
another constraint is 5 to 4, we would certainly not expect
differences in the ordering of constraints among individual
members of a relatively homogeneous community. But if the
effect of one constraint is 4 to 3 and the effect of another
constraint is 5 to 4, then we might expect some individual reordering of constraints, even within a relatively homogeneous
group of speakers.

For the most part, of course, we are impressed with the
amazing consistency with which constraints are ordered identically from speaker to speaker and, in this study, from social
group to social group. The main differences between groups
are only matters of relative frequency. The actual comparative
ratios that might make two constraints susceptible to individual differences in ordering are, of course, arbitrary at
this point. We would certainly expect two constraints with
effect ratios of 9 to 8 and 8 to 7 to be more susceptible to
a certain amount of individual variation. But the actual cutoff point for constraint reordering (and, in fact, the cutoff
point for representing constraints formally in the grammar) is
quite arbitrary and can be determined only through investigation.
In a sense, the difficulty in determining the cutoff point is a
reflection of the hazy interface that exists between competence
and performance. Eventually, it may be possible, however, to

specify the cutoff point at which individual reordering can be
expected by relying on a mathematical base for our formulation.

From a purely practical standpoint, there are difficulties
in dealing with a great number of constraints, since the number
of subdivisions in the geometric ordering is doubled every time
another constraint is introduced. This means that if we isolate 7 constraints, it is possible to get 256 branchings in the
hierarchy, i.e. 2, 2x2, 2x4, 2x16, 2x32, 2x64, 2x128 = 256.
The expectation of getting sufficient examples to adequately
determine the ordering of constraints naturally diminishes as
the number of branchings proliferates. In most instances, we
find that the clear-cut effect on variability is quite high
in the first several orders of constraints, but that it tends
to diminish after that.

A problem of more theoretical consequence arises when all
the branchings necessary to establish hierarchical orderings
are not logically possible, either because of the features of
a specific language variety or because of metatheoretical
constraints on human language. The logical impossibility of
some categories may disallow observing cross-products crucial
for establishing the rank orders. This problem, which has
arisen at various stages in this study, has also been confronted by Fasold (1972). Although we might calculate expected frequencies for hypothetical categories in order to
establish our geometric ordering, the theoretical implication
of this observation is that strict geometrical ordering may be
too strong a requirement.

In the above paragraphs, we have tried to account for
certain apparent irregularities that may arise in the ordering
of constraints for a relatively homogeneous group. It is, of
course, also necessary to recognize that structural reordering
of constraints may take place in social or temporal space. It
is quite possible, as demonstrated by Labov et al. (1968), that

constraint reordering may be a function of regular language
change. In the case of regular reordering, however, it seems
quite possible to expect that susceptibility to imminent change
may follow the same sort of distribution we found for individual variation. For example, we would expect two constraints
with effect ratios of 5 to 4 and 6 to 5 to be susceptible to
imminent change, while constraints having ratios of 5 to 1 and
6 to 5 would not be nearly as susceptible.

One must caution, at this point, that the mathematics of
constraint reordering must not be considered apart from, although it can be considered complementary to, the notion of
marking in constraint orders. If it is true, as Bailey (1973b)
suggests, that constraints are typically reordered from marked
to unmarked orders, then it is possible for constraint reordering to counteract reordering changes we might predict
from a purely mathematical base.[8] Suppose, for example, that
we have three environmental constraints in a given variable
rule: $\underline{X}$, the first order constraint, effects a 50 percent
frequency level for the occurrence of a given form; $\underline{Y}$, the
second order constraint, a 45 percent frequency level; and $\underline{Z}$,
the third order constraint, a 40 percent frequency level.
If they are already in their unmarked order, the order would
not be expected to change, despite the closeness of the effect
ratios. (They may, of course, merge and reduce the number of
constraint orders.) On the other hand, if both $\underline{X}$ and $\underline{Y}$ are
in an unmarked order with reference to each other, but both
$\underline{X}$ and $\underline{Y}$ are in a marked order with reference to $\underline{Z}$, then $\underline{Z}$ may
be reordered before both of them, while the order of $\underline{X}$ and $\underline{Y}$
with respect to each other remains intact.

In the previous discussion, we have attempted to justify
a general theory of variable rules. But the justification of
a general theory of optionality does not warrant the actual
incorporation of variable rules into PRE. Our rationale for

this must come from the supposition that variable constraints
are language specific. In Chapter Three, we have noted that
there are two issues involved in the question of constraint
universality: "effect predictability", the particular type
of environment and the effect it will have on variation; and
"order predictability", the hierarchical arrangement of constraints.

   In our study of PRE, we have seen that the effect of
linguistic constraints on variability tends to confirm the
effects found in other studies, such as Labov et al. (1968),
Wolfram (1969), Legum, et al. (1971), and Fasold (1972). For
example, we observe that a following consonant consistently
favors the deletion of a preceding consonant when the latter
is part of a consonant cluster. We also find that nongrammatical markers favor deletion when compared with grammatical
markers. Similarly, we observe that elements occurring in
unstressed syllables are more likely to be deleted or modified
than are elements found in stressed syllables. In these cases,
we may suggest that the effects of linguistic constraints on
variability are universal. Although we can hypothesize the
effect that a given environment will have on variability, it
is obvious that there are certain conditions that must be met
for the operation of these predicted effects. For example,
we stated above that we would typically expect the absence of
grammatical marking. But Cedergren (personal communication)
suggests that this should be qualified so that it applies only
to grammatical markers that are not transformationally introduced[9]. Without clear counterevidence, it is most reasonable
to claim that effect predictability is part of a general metatheory of optional rules.

   If constraining effects are universal, then it is unnecessary to indicate what the favoring effect is for a specific language. In our description, we have indicated whether

the + or - value favors the operation of a rule, but this information is apparently redundant since it can be predicted
on the basis of our metatheory. For example, it is unnecessary
to specify that [-stress] favors the application of the
syllable-final //d// rule; it is sufficient to state [stress]
without any explicit plus or minus value as favoring the rule
application. The metatheory of optional rule application will
imply the value that will favor or inhibit rule application.

Whereas it is quite reasonable to suggest that constraint
effect is not language specific, the same claim cannot be made
with reference to the hierarchical ordering of various constraints. The comparison of heterogeneous language communities
indicates different orders of constraints. If we cannot predict hierarchical orders on the basis of our general theory,
then such information must be incorporated into our particular
grammar of a language. There may, however, be some conditions
under which we need not specify particular hierarchical orders
based on the notion of marked and unmarked orders. If we can
formulate what the unmarked orders are, then it would be sufficient to allow our general theory of marking to account for
the specification of a hierarchical order, if it is unmarked.
For a specific language, we need formally state only those
constraints that follow a marked rather than an unmarked order.
At this point, there are practical problems involved in formally
following this principle since we do not have a comprehensive
catalog of unmarked hierarchical orders as a part of our metatheory, but this is an empirical deficiency that does not affect the theoretical validity of this position.[10]

7.7 Conclusion. Although the study of PRE in Harlem has sufficient value in itself to warrant descriptive study, this discussion has been concerned more with general sociolinguistic
principles that emerge from the study of this language contact

situation. This language situation has allowed us to apply
some of the recent insights of sociolinguistic variability
to a unique contact situation in which several different
sources may account for a resultant dialect. In particular,
we have seen that the application of a quantitative dimension
to the study of fluctuating speech behavior results in the
emergence of important observations concerning the relative
effect of linguistic assimilation. No doubt some of the principles that we have focused on will have to be revised or
abandoned on the basis of further empirical data, but we are
impressed with the convergence of our study with variable
studies conducted on other populations. Linguists who strive
for the goals of descriptive and explanatory adequacy in current linguistic theory can no longer afford the luxury of
cavalierly dismissing the systematic nature of language
variation.

NOTES

1. Since we are dealing here with a limited example, we will
    eliminate the t variant in our discussion of interference,
    despite the fact that it is quite a legitimate interference
    variant.

2. This is not to say that the features discussed previously
    are necessarily unique to Black English, since many of
    them can also be found in southern white speech. However,
    in a northern context such as New York City, they are
    found only in black speech due to the transformation of
    many southern features into class and ethnic patterns in
    a northern context.

3. This does not mean that scholars of bilingualism have not
    observed the occurrence of certain types of innovations.
    There is occasional reference to it in the literature
    (Weinreich 1953:40-41), but its implications for models
    of bilingual interference seem to be ignored.

4. DeCamp (1972:87) points out that hypercorrection implies

rule generalization but that the converse is not true: that is, rule generalization does not necessarily imply hypercorrection. For a rejection of this position, see Bailey (1973b).

5. My four-year-old son went through a stage of approximately six months during which pleonastic tense marking was a very common phenomenon. In his case, he had a more general version of Rule (70) described in Section 6.1.3.

6. There does not appear to be any formal linguistic basis for distinguishing these two notions. Both Fasold and I have maintained that certain types of hypercorrection may help identify dialect mixture, but hypercorrection itself is a concept that cannot be justified on a purely linguistic basis; hypercorrection necessarily involves certain linguistic processes and certain social phenomena (see DeCamp 1972:90).

7. We have assumed throughout this description that hierarchical effect of constraints is geometrically ordered. This is based on our supposition that the variable constraints operate independently. If we found that there were certain significant synergistic effects in the combination of constraints, a geometrically ordered hierarchy would have to be abandoned. In the absence of conflicting data, our assumption of geometric ordering appears to be most reasonable.

8. There are several apparent exceptions to the principle that change in marking always involves going from marked to unmarked members. For example, a lower level change may go from an unmarked to a marked member in order to accommodate a higher level change from a marked to an unmarked member. This exception, however, is only apparent in that it follows the principle on a higher level. A more real exception is found in the case of language creolization, in which maximal unmarking eventually acquires a representation of marking.

9. Cedergren's (personal communication) qualification is supported by data on Panamanian Spanish that show that $/\!/r/\!/$ is more often deleted when it is [+ infinitive] than when it carries no grammatical marking. The grammatical marking of $/\!/r/\!/$ in this case is transformationally introduced.

10. Evidence for marking comes from the order of acquisition by children, linguistic change, neutralizations, and statistical universals, according to Bailey (1973b).

APPENDIX A : QUESTIONNAIRE

Tape No. _____

INFORMANT DATA SHEET

(To be completed after the interview)

Name _____ Age _____

Address _____ Race _____

Grade _____ School _____

Parents' Birthplace:

    Father _____ GF _____

                              GM _____

    Mother _____ GF _____

                              GM _____

Occupation of head of household _____

Highest grade level of head of household _____

How long lived in New York _____

Other places lived _____

Race of peer contacts _____

Section I: Free Conversation

A.   Games and Leisure

What kinds of games do you play around the neighborhood
(stickball, games with bottle caps, marbles, handball,
flying pigeons, etc.)?

How do you play these games (rules for the games, deciding
who's IT, etc.)?

Do you follow any of the New York sports teams?   What do
you think of the Mets this year?   How about the Knicks for
next year (or Joe Namath and the Jets)?

What are your favorite TV programs?   Describe a recent
program.

What is your favorite movie of all time?   What happens?
(If you can elicit movies without trouble, ask about West
Side Story and an opinion of how life in Harlem is por-
trayed in this movie.)

Tell me about your experience here at camp.   Describe a
typical day.   Contrast this with the city day.

B.   Peer Group

How about the guys you hang around with?   In this group is
there one guy that everybody listens to?   How come?

What makes for a leader in the group (tough, hip with girls,
good sounder, etc.)?

Do the guys in the group sound on each other?   How does this
work?   What do you sound on?   Can it be true, etc.?   (If
rapport is right, get some sounds.)

What makes a good sounder?

Say a new kid moves into the tenement.   Is there any way he
can get into your group?

Who are some of the guys you're tight with?   Name some.

Of the guys you named, are there any Negroes?   Puerto Ricans
in the group?   How about whites?

Any of these guys speak Spanish? How about their parents?

C. <u>Aspirations</u>

How about when you're through with school? Any idea of
what you might do? What does a _____ do?

If someone came up to you and said, "Here's all the money
in the world", what would you do with it?

What is a successful man? (If informant responds, have
him define unsuccessful, good, bad, smart man.)

D. <u>Fighting and Accidents</u>

What kinds of things do fights usually start about on the
street?

Any rules for a fair fight? (How about if someone was
kicking somebody or hitting them with a chain or lead pipe,
what would you do?)

Ever see anybody get beat up real bad? What happened?

Do the kids around here still fight in gangs? How do these
start? (If answer negatively, pursue why gang fights have
stopped.)

Ever been in a hospital, or automobile accident? Describe.

How about a situation where you thought, "Man, this is it,
I'm gonna die for sure now"? What happened?

Section II: Cultural Values

I would like you to define some things for me as you look at
them. I'll give a sentence and you complete the sentence.
For example, if I say, "A good sounder is somebody that....",
you might say "...always has something to come back with".

1. The leader of a group of guys is somebody that _____.

2. A smart person is somebody that _____.

3. A person with common sense is somebody that _____.

4. If a guy gets a girl into trouble, he should _____.

5. If you're going to get into a fight, the best weapon to
    have with you is a _____ because _____ .

6. A tough dude is somebody that _____ .

7. The thing I like the best about Harlem is the fact that
    _____ .

8. The thing I like the least about Harlem is the fact that
    _____ .

9. If you want to be hip with girls, you gotta _____ .

10. The best way to make it in this world is to _____ .

Section III: Auxiliary Probe

Sample Stimulus	Sample Response
1. My cousin should do his work. Should what?	I know he should. Do his work.
2. Daryl hit his brother. Did what?	I know he did. Hit his brother.
3. He will be five next month. Will what?	I know he will. Be five next month.

Stimulus

1. José can drive a motorcycle.

2. María put it down.

3. The lady a teacher.

4. If he got a walkie talkie, he be
    happy.

5. He ain't see the boy.

6. John wants you to leave.

7. The people over at my house now.

8. You walked home.

9. Sometime Joseph be up there.

10. He should work harder.

11. He be here in a few minutes.

12. Daryl got a brother.

13. He will explain that to you.

14. Dwight been met that girl at the pool.

15. He could be at the country club now.

16. Every day last year he be at the pool.

Section IV: Possessive

Now, we're going to ask you to fill in the blanks in a different kind of question. If I said, "This man has a hat", you might say, "It's not the woman hat, it's the _____ ".

(Note: It is very important that you say "woman hat", not "woman's hat". The same is true for all questions in this test. If an informant corrects you, you may begin saying "woman's hat", etc.)

1. This girl has a bike. It's not the boy bike, it's the _____.

2. This dog has a bone. It's not the cat bone, it's the _____.

3. This mouse has some cheese. It's not the rat cheese, it's the _____.

4. Jack Johnson has a car. It's not Paul Brown car, it's _____.

5. Derrick Black has a toy. It's not Paul Brown toy, it's _____.

Section V: Word-Final Consonant Clusters with -ing

Now, I'll give you a different exercise, and you see if you can make the sentences the same way I do in these examples.

Sample Stimulus	Sample Response
1. They eat.	They eat. They are eating.
2. They play.	They play. They are playing.
3. They buy things.	They buy things. They are buying things.

Stimulus

1. They rest.

2. They ask.

3. They paste it.

4. They bust it.

5. They lift it.

6. They test it.

7. They risk a chance.

Section VI: Plurals

Now, I'll show you a picture of something. It may be something
you've seen before, or it may be something you've never seen.
Then I'll show you a whole bunch of the same thing and ask you
what they are. (Use No. 1 as an example.)

1. This is a tree. Now here's a bunch of them. What are
    they?

2. This is a lun. I bet you never saw one of them before.
    But if you did, these would be a bunch of _____.

3. This is a desk. And these are _____.

4. This is a biz. And if you had a whole bunch of them, they
    would be _____.

5. This is a fust. And these would be a bunch of _____.

6. This is a foot. And here are two _____.

7. This is a <u>box</u>. And these are _____.

8. This is a <u>cent</u>. And now there are three _____.

9. This is a <u>dollar</u>. And now there are three _____.

Section VII: Passive Test

<u>Sample Stimulus</u>   <u>Sample Response</u>

1. Yesterday somebody kicked   1. Yesterday he was kicked.
   him.

2. Yesterday somebody followed   2. Yesterday he was followed.
   him.

3. Yesterday somebody killed   3. Yesterday he was killed.
   him.

4. Yesterday somebody found him. 4. Yesterday he was found.

<u>Stimulus</u>

1. Yesterday somebody punched him.

2. Every day somebody rob him.

3. Every day somebody grab him.

4. Right now somebody like him.

5. Every day somebody cheat him.

6. Right now somebody hear him.

7. Right now somebody's shooting him.

8. Yesterday somebody was chasing him.

9. Right now somebody's scaring him.

10. Yesterday somebody was holding him.

Section VIII: Reading Lists

(Use cards for informant.)

WORD LIST

hut	sin	chew	pin
wolf	west	deaf	pen
hot	sing	jello	desks
woof	Wes	mother	watch
month	pass	right	find
sold	bet	kite	wash
boat	past	school	fine
soul	bat	Tom	clothe
vote	caught	Sam	tooth
so	side	sod	arithmetic
code	coat	sad	Catholic
feel	shoe	boil	yellow
coal	mass		death

MINIMAL WORD PAIR LIST

rows	rose	side	sod
run	rum	shoe	chew
hut	hot	mass	mask
sold	soul	deaf	death
boat	vote	yellow	jello
sin	sing	time	Tom
rain	reign	pin	pen
west	Wes	watch	wash
bet	bat	boil	ball

APPENDIX B : FOLLOW-UP INTERVIEW

1. How long have you lived in Harlem or the Bronx? _____

2. Where else have you lived in your life? _____

3. Where do most of your friends live, e.g. in the immediate neighborhood? If not, why not? _____

4. Where do you spend most of your time outside of school, i.e. what streets, etc.? _____

5. Are most of the teachers at your school black, Puerto Rican, other? _____

6. Are most of the students at your school black, Puerto Rican, other? Try to estimate: 3/4, 1/2. _____

7. Are the people in your neighborhood mostly black, Puerto Rican, other? _____

8. If you were in trouble and needed help, who would you talk to?_____

9. Is he/she black, Puerto Rican, other? _____

10. At your church, are most of the people black, Puerto Rican, other? _____

11. Is the minister black, Puerto Rican, other? _____

12. How often do you use Spanish? _____

13. How good is your Spanish, i.e. can you talk about any-thing you want in Spanish? _____

14. How old were you when you learned Spanish, English? Which did you learn first? _____

15. Do you ever spend much time with people who just came to New York from Puerto Rico? _____

16. What language do you use with your parents? _____

       with your brothers/sisters? _____

       with your grandparents and relatives? _____

       with your girlfriend? _____

       with your friends? _____

       in the street with people you
         don't know well? _____

       with neighbors who are older? _____

       with neighbors who are younger? _____

       in neighborhood stores? _____

       with your teachers? _____

       with your minister? _____

       when you make jokes? _____

       at a dance? _____

       when you are angry? _____

       on the subway/bus? _____

17. Is there anyone you speak only Spanish to? _____

18. Do you ever help people out by speaking English
for them because they can't? _____

19. When you're not in school, which do you spend most of
your time doing?
       ____ just hanging out and rapping with friends

       ____ at home with your parents

       ____ at home watching TV

       ____ at home reading

       ____ at a club or center

       ____ at the movies

       ____ at your girlfriend's house

       ____ playing sports

       ____ alone at home

       ____ alone on the street

20. Is there any difference between the way Puerto Ricans and
blacks talk? If so, what?

BIBLIOGRAPHY

Bach, Emmon. 1966. Two proposals concerning the simplicity
metric in phonology. Paper delivered at the 41st Annual
Meeting of the Linguistic Society of America, New York,
New York.

----- and Robert T. Harms. 1972. How do languages get crazy
rules?, in Robert P. Stockwell and Ronald S. Macaulay (eds.),
Linguistic change and generative theory, 1-21. Bloomington,
Ind.: Indiana University Press.

Bailey, Charles-James N. 1969a. A possible explanation for
an assimilation curiosity, in Working papers in linguistics (Vol. 1, No. 5), 187-89. Honolulu: Department of
Linguistics, University of Hawaii.

-----. 1969b. Syllable boundaries, in Charles-James N.
Bailey (comp.), Working papers in linguistics (Vol. 1,
No. 9), 205-08. Honolulu: Department of Linguistics,
University of Hawaii.

-----. 1973a. Variation resulting from different rule order-
ings in English phonology, in Charles-James N. Bailey and
Roger W. Shuy (eds.), New ways of analyzing variation in
English, 211-252. Washington, D.C.: Georgetown University
Press.

-----. 1973b. Variation and Linguistic Theory. Arlington,
Va.: Center for Applied Linguistics.

-----. 1973c. The patterning of language variation, in R.W.
Bailey and J.L. Robinson (eds.), Varieties of present-day
American English. New York: Macmillan Co.

Baker, C.L. 1970. Double negatives. Linguistic Inquiry
1:169-86.

Bickerton, Derek. 1971. Inherent variability and variable
rules. Foundations of Language 7:457-92.

Broom, Leonard and Norval D. Glenn. 1965. Transformation of
the Negro American. New York: Harper and Row.

Burma, John H.   1954.   Spanish-speaking groups in the United
    States. Durham, N.C.: Duke University Press.

Cedergren, Henrietta. 1972. The social dialects of Panama.
    Ph.D. diss., Cornell University.

----- and David Sankoff. 1972. Variable rules: performance
    as a statistical reflection of competence. Unpub. MS.

Chomsky, Noam. 1965. Aspects of the theory of syntax.
    Cambridge, Mass.: M.I.T. Press.

----- and Morris Halle. 1968. The sound pattern of English.
    New York: Harper and Row.

Cooper, Robert L. and Lawrence Greenfield. 1968. Language
    use in a bilingual community, in Joshua A. Fishman et al.,
    Bilingualism in the barrio, 485-504.

DeCamp, David. 1972. Hypercorrection and rule generalization.
    Language in Society 1:87-90.

Doob, Christopher Bates. 1970. Family background and peer
    group development in a Puerto Rican district. Sociological
    Quarterly 11:523-32.

Fasold, Ralph W. 1967. Two fricatives in Black English:
    a generative phonology approach. Washington, D.C.:
    Center for Applied Linguistics. Mimeographed.

-----. 1969a. Tense and the form be in Black English.
    Language 45:763-76.

-----. 1969b. Orthography in reading materials for Black
    English speaking children, in Joan C. Baratz and Roger W.
    Shuy (eds.), Teaching black children to read (Urban Lan-
    guage Series, 4), 68-91. Washington, D.C.: Center for
    Applied Linguistics.

-----. 1970. Two models of socially significant linguistic
    variation. Language 46:551-63.

-----. 1971. Minding your Z's and D's: distinguishing syn-
    tactic and phonological variable rules, in Papers from the
    seventh regional meeting of the Chicago Linguistic Society,
    360-67. Chicago: Chicago Linguistic Society.

-----. 1972. Tense marking in Black English: a linguistic
    and social analysis (Urban Language Series, 8). Arlington,
    Va.: Center for Applied Linguistics.

-----. 1973. The concept of 'earlier-later': more or less
    correct, in Charles-James N. Bailey and Roger W. Shuy
    (eds.), New ways of analyzing variation in English,
    183-97. Washington, D.C.: Georgetown University Press.

----- and Walt Wolfram. 1970. Some linguistic features of
    Negro dialect, in Ralph W. Fasold and Roger W. Shuy (eds.),
    Teaching standard English in the inner city (Urban Language
    Series, 6), 41-86. Washington, D.C.: Center for Applied
    Linguistics.

Fickett, Joan G. 1971. Aspects of morphemics, syntax, and
    semology of an inner-city dialect, 'Merican'. Ph.D. diss.,
    University of Buffalo.

Fischer, John L. 1958. Social influences on the choice of a
    linguistic variant. Word 14:47-56.

Fishman, Joshua A. 1968a. Sociolinguistic perspective on the
    study of bilingualism. Linguistics 39:21-49.

-----. 1968b. A sociolinguistic census of a bilingual neigh-
    borhood, in Joshua A. Fishman et al., Bilingualism in the
    barrio, 260-99.

-----. 1971. Attitudes and beliefs about Spanish and English
    among Puerto Ricans. Viewpoints 47: No. 2.

-----, Robert L. Cooper, and Roxana Ma et al. 1968. Bi-
    lingualism in the barrio. Final Report, U.S. Office of
    Education Contract No. OEC-1-7-062817-0297. New York:
    Yeshiva University.

Glazer, Nathan and Daniel Patrick Moynihan. 1963. Beyond
    the melting pot. Cambridge, Mass.: M.I.T. Press.

Greenfield, Lawrence and Joshua A. Fishman. 1968. Situational
    measures of language use in relation to person, place and
    topic among Puerto Rican bilinguals, in Joshua A. Fishman
    et al., Bilingualism in the barrio, 430-58.

Handlin, Oscar. 1965. The newcomers: Negroes and Puerto
    Ricans in a changing metropolis. Cambridge, Mass.:
    Harvard University Press.

Herman, Simon N. 1961. Explorations in the social psychology
    of language choice. Human Relations 14:149-64.

Hoffman, Gerard. 1968. Puerto Ricans in New York. a lan-
    guage-related ethnographic survey, in Joshua A. Fishman
    et al., Bilingualism in the barrio, 20-76.

Kantrowitz, N. and D.M. Pappenfort. 1966. Social statistics
    for metropolitan New York. New York. New York University.

Kiparsky, Paul. 1968. Linguistic universals and linguistic
    change, in Emmon Bach and Robert T. Harms (eds.), Uni-
    versals in linguistic theory, 171-202. New York: Holt,
    Rinehart and Winston.

-----. 1971. Historical linguistics, in William Orr Dingwall
    (ed.), A survey of linguistic science, 576-649. College
    Park, Md.: Linguistics Program, University of Maryland.

Klima, Edward S. 1964. Negation in English, in Jerry A.
    Fodor and Jerrold J. Katz (eds.), The structure of lan-
    guage: readings in the philosophy of language, 246-323.
    Englewood Cliffs, N.J.: Prentice-Hall.

Kochman, Thomas. 1969. Rapping in the black ghetto. Trans-
    Action (February): 26-34.

Labov, William. 1966a. The social stratification of English
    in New York City (Urban Language Series, 1). Washington,
    D.C.: Center for Applied Linguistics.

-----. 1966b. The linguistic variable as a structural unit.
    Washington Linguistics Review 3:4-22.

-----. 1969. Contraction, deletion and inherent variability
    of the English copula. Language 45:715-62.

-----. 1970. The study of language in its social context.
    Studium generale 23:30-87.

-----. 1971. Methodology, in William Orr Dingwall (ed.),
    A survey of linguistic science, 412-97. College Park, Md.:
    Linguistics Program, University of Maryland.

-----. 1972a. Some principles of linguistic methodology.
    Language in Society 1:97-120.

-----. 1972b. Negative attraction and negative concord in
    English grammar. Language 48:773-818.

-----, Paul Cohen, and Clarence Robins. 1965. A preliminary
    study of the structure of English used by Negro and Puerto

speakers in New York City. Final Report, U.S. Office of
Education Cooperative Research Project No. 3091.

-----, Paul Cohen, Clarence Robins, and John Lewis. 1968.
A study of the non-standard English of Negro and Puerto
Rican speakers in New York City. Final Report, U.S. Office
of Education Cooperative Research Project No. 3288.

Legum, Stanley E., Carol Pfaff, Gene Tinnie, and Michael
Nicholas. 1971. The speech of young black children in
Los Angeles. Technical Report No. 33. Los Angeles:
Southwest Regional Laboratory.

Levine, Lewis and Harry J. Crockett, Jr. 1967. Friends'
influence on speech. Sociological Inquiry 37:109-28.

Lewis, Oscar 1968. A study of slum culture. New York:
Random House.

Loflin, Marvin D. 1970. On the structure of the verb in a
dialect of American Negro English. Linguistics 59:14-28.

Ma, Roxana and Eleanor Herasimchuk. 1968. The linguistic
dimensions of a bilingual neighborhood, in Joshua A.
Fishman et al., Bilingualism in the barrio, 638-835.

McKay, June R. 1969. A partial analysis of a variety of
nonstandard Negro English. Ph.D. diss., University of
California at Berkeley.

Mills, C. Wright, Clarence Senior, and Rose Kahn Goldsen.
1950. The Puerto Rican journey. New York: Russell and
Russell.

Mitchell-Kernan, Claudia I. 1969. Language behavior in a
black urban community. Unpub. Ph.D. diss., University of
California at Berkeley.

Motley, Dena. 1967. The culture of poverty in Puerto Rico
and New York. Social Security Bulletin 30:18-23.

Nahirny, Vladimir C. and Joshua A. Fishman. 1965. American
immigrant groups: ethnic identification and the problem
of generations. Sociological Review 13:311-26.

Navarro-Tomás, T. 1948. El español en Puerto Rico. Rio
Piedras, P.R.: University of Puerto Rico.

Padilla, Elena. 1958. Up from Puerto Rico. New York:
Columbia University Press.

Rand, Christopher. 1958. The Puerto Ricans. New York:
    Oxford University Press.

Rivero, María-Luisa. 1970. A surface structure constraint
    on negation in Spanish. Language 46:640-66.

Sankoff, Gillian. 1972. A quantitative paradigm for studying
    communicative competence. Paper delivered at the Conference
    on the Ethnography of Speaking, Austin, Texas.

Seda-Bonilla, E. 1961. Social structure and race relations.
    Social Forces 40:141-48.

Sexton, Patricia Cayo. 1965. Spanish Harlem. New York:
    Harper and Row.

Shiels, Marie E. 1972. Dialects in contact: a sociolinguis-
    tic analysis of four phonological variables of Puerto Rican
    English and Black English in Harlem. Unpub. Ph.D. diss.,
    Georgetown University School of Languages and Linguistics.

Shuy, Roger W., Walter A. Wolfram, and William K. Riley.
    1967. Linguistic correlates of social stratification in
    Detroit speech. Final Report, U.S. Office of Education
    Cooperative Research Project No. 6-1347.

-----. 1968. Field techniques in an urban language study
    (Urban Language Series, 3). Washington, D.C.: Center for
    Applied Linguistics.

Silverman, Stuart H. The effects of peer group membership on
    Puerto Rican English. Unpub. Ph.D. diss., Yeshiva University.

Stanley, Richard. 1967. Redundancy rules in phonology.
    Language 43:393-436.

Stewart, William A. 1966. Social dialect, in Research plan-
    ning conference on language development in disadvantaged
    children, 53-62. New York: Yeshiva University.

Stockwell, Robert P., Paul Schachter, and Barbara Hall Partee.
    1968. Integration of transformational theories on English
    syntax. Los Angeles: University of California.

Thomas, Piri. 1967. Down these mean streets. New York:
    Alfred A. Knopf.

Weinreich, Uriel. 1953. Languages in contact: findings and
    problems (Publications of the Linguistic Circle of New
    York, 1). New York: Linguistic Circle of New York.

Wheeler, Max W. 1972. Distinctive features and natural
    classes in phonological theory. Journal of Linguistics
    8:87-102.

Wolfram, Walter A. 1969. A sociolinguistic description of
    Detroit Negro speech (Urban Language Series, 5). Washington,
    D.C.: Center for Applied Linguistics.

-----. 1970. Underlying representations in Black English
    phonology. Language Sciences 10:7-12.

-----, in collaboration with Marie Shiels and Ralph W. Fasold.
    1971. Overlapping influence in the English of second
    generation Puerto Rican teenagers in Harlem. Final Report,
    U.S. Office of Education Grant No. 3-70-0033(508). Wash-
    ington, D.C.: Center for Applied Linguistics. Mimeographed.

-----. 1972. Overlapping influence and linguistic assimila-
    tion in second generation Puerto Rican English, in David M.
    Smith and Roger W. Shuy (eds.), Sociolinguistics in cross-
    cultural analysis, 15-46. Washington, D.C.: Georgetown
    University Press.

Woodward, James C. and Robert Zambrano. A sociolinguistic
    pilot study of selected variables in the English of Spanish
    Americans in Washington, D.C. Unpub. term paper, George-
    town University School of Languages and Linguistics.